International Dimensions of
ORGANIZATIONAL BEHAVIOR

THE WADSWORTH INTERNATIONAL DIMENSIONS OF BUSINESS SERIES

International Dimensions of Organizational Behavior, Second Edition
Adler

International Dimensions of Accounting, Second Edition
AlHashim/Arpan

International Dimensions of Human Resource Management
Dowling/Schuler

International Dimensions of Financial Management
Folks/Aggarwal

International Dimensions of Business Policy and Strategy, Second Edition
Garland/Farmer/Taylor

International Dimensions of the Legal Environment of Business
Litka

International Dimensions of Management, Second Edition
Phatak

International Dimensions of Marketing, Second Edition
Terpstra

International Dimensions of
ORGANIZATIONAL BEHAVIOR
Second Edition

Nancy J. Adler
McGill University

**THE WADSWORTH INTERNATIONAL DIMENSIONS
OF BUSINESS SERIES**
David A. Ricks
Series Consulting Editor

Wadsworth Publishing Company
Belmont, California
A Division of Wadsworth, Inc.

Library of Congress Cataloging-in-Publication Data

Adler, Nancy J.
    International dimensions of organizational behavior / Nancy J.
Adler.
      p. cm. —
    Includes bibliographical references.
    Includes index.
    ISBN 0-534-92274-0
    1. Organizational behavior—Cross-cultural studies. I. Title.
II. Series.
HD58.7.A33   1991   90-8589
658—dc20   CIP

Editor: Rolf A. Janke
Assistant Editor: Kathleen M. Tibbetts
Production Editor: Robine Andrau
Text Designer: Elise Kaiser
Cover Designer: Julia Gecha
Manufacturing Coordinator: Peter D. Leatherwood

Printed in the United States of America

93 94 95 — 10 9 8 7 6

▼

To my mother, Liselotte Adler, who brought together
two worlds and two very different cultures in creating
the home in which I grew up.

▲

Series Foreword

Prior to World War II, the number of firms involved in foreign direct investment was relatively small. Although several U.S. companies were obtaining raw materials from other countries, most firms were only interested in the U.S. market. This changed, however, during the 1950s—especially after the creation of the European Economic Community. Since that time, there has been a rapid expansion in international business activity.

The majority of the world's large corporations now perform an increasing proportion of their business activities outside of their home countries. For many of these companies, international business returns over one-half of their profits, and it is becoming more and more common for a typical corporation to earn at least one-fourth of its profits through international business involvement. In fact, it is now rather rare for any large firm not to be a participant in the world of international business.

International business is of great importance in most countries and that importance continues to grow. To meet the demand for increased knowledge in this area, business schools are attempting to add international dimensions to their curricula. Faculty members are becoming more interested in teaching a greater variety of international business courses and are striving to add international dimensions to other courses. Students, aware of the increasing probability that they will be employed by firms engaged in international business activities, are seeking knowledge of the problem-solving techniques unique to international business. As the American Assembly of Collegiate Schools of Business has observed, however, there is a shortage of information available. Most business textbooks do not adequately consider the international dimensions of business and much of the supplemental material is disjointed, overly narrow, or otherwise inadequate in the classroom.

This series has been developed to overcome such problems. The books are written by some of the most respected authors in the various areas of international business. Each author is extremely well known in the Academy of International Business and in his or her other professional academies. They possess an outstanding knowledge of their own subject matter and a talent for explaining it.

These books, in which the authors have identified the most important international aspects of their fields, have been written in a format that facilitates their use as supplemental material in business courses.

The Wadsworth International Dimensions of Business Series offers a unique and much needed opportunity to bring international dimensions of business into the classroom. The series has been developed by leaders in the field after years of discussion and careful consideration and the timely encouragement and support provided by the PWS-KENT staff on this project. I am proud to be associated with this series and highly recommend it to you.

David A. Ricks

Consulting Editor to the
Kent International Dimensions of Business Series
Professor of International Business,
University of South Carolina

Preface

The world of organizations is no longer limited by national boundaries. *International Dimensions of Organizational Behavior* breaks down the conceptual, theoretical, and practical boundaries limiting our ability to understand and manage people in countries worldwide. Until recently, much of our understanding of management came from the American experience: Americans and American-trained researchers observed the behavior of people in United States–based organizations. From their observations and research, they developed models and theories to explain organizational and managerial behavior. The problem was in their assumption: they implicitly assumed that what was "true" for Americans working in the United States was also true for people from other countries. Both researchers and managers assumed that American work behavior was universal. They were wrong. *International Dimensions of Organizational Behavior* challenges us to go beyond our parochialism and to see the world in global terms.

Today we no longer have the luxury of reducing international complexity to the simplicity of assumed universality; we no longer have the luxury of assuming that there is one best way to manage. Luckily, we also know that international complexity is not random. Variations across cultures and their impact on organizations follow systematic, predictable patterns. Starting with a core of traditional, primarily United States–based understanding of organizational behavior, international dimensions can be used as a guide to modify our attitudes, thinking patterns, and behavior. Far from ignoring the common body of knowledge, international dimensions expand our understanding of people's behavior at work to include the diversity and complexity of today's global economic environment.

International Dimensions of Organizational Behavior is divided into three parts. The first part, "The Impact of Culture on Organizations," describes the ways in which cultures vary, how that variance systematically affects organizations, and how people can recognize cultural variance within their own work environments. In the second part, "Managing Cultural Diversity," Chapter 4 investigates cross-cultural problem solving and organizational development; Chapter 5 describes the dynamics of multicultural teams; Chapter 6 looks at leadership, motivation, and decision making from an international perspective; and Chapter 7 summarizes international approaches to conflict management and negotiating. Based on our understanding of domestic management, the second section presents an integrated approach to cross-cultural management.

The third part, "Managing Global Managers," presents a series of issues that are unique to international and global management. This section addresses the human resource management questions involved in managing one's life and career while moving across international borders. Chapter 8 presents the entry and reentry transitions from the employee's perspective and addresses these questions: What is culture shock? How does one adjust to a foreign culture? How does one manage reentry back into one's home country and organization? Chapter 9 also presents transition issues, but from the spouse's perspective. Chapter 10 presents international career issues. How do the routes to the top of major companies vary from country to country? What are the most important benefits and drawbacks in pursuing an international career? Due to its focus on global managers and expatriates, this section goes beyond the scope of most domestically based organizational behavior books.

International Dimensions of Organizational Behavior can be used in three ways. First, it can be used as the basis of an independent cross-cultural management seminar in which each chapter of the book forms the core of a course module. If used in this way, the book can be supplemented with current readings and a more in-depth look at specific areas of the world. For example, while introducing each module of the seminar with a chapter from the book, participants might expand the material in the book by looking at how it applies to Eastern Europe or Pacific Rim countries.

Alternatively, the book can be used as a supplement to a standard organizational behavior course. In this case, professors first use their standard introduction to the study of people's behavior in organizations. Using Chapters 1 and 2, they would then introduce a module on international dimensions. Following this introduction, they would "pair" a chapter from *International Dimensions of Organizational Behavior* to each of the modules of their standard course. For example, Chapter 3 would be paired with the perception and/or communications module; Chapter 4, with the problem solving and/or organizational development and change module; Chapter 5, with the module on group dynamics and team building; Chapter 6, with the discussion of leadership, motivation, and decision making; and Chapter 7, with material on conflict management and negotiations. Finally, either in combination with a module on career management or as an independent module, the professor would present Part 3 of the book on managing global managers. The participant would then complete the course with an in-depth understanding of organizational behavior issues from both a domestic and an international perspective.

As a third alternative, *International Dimensions of Organizational Behavior* can be used as a self-contained section of a traditional organizational behavior course. In this case, professors would present their traditional, domestically based material and then add on a section on international dimensions. All chapters would be assigned for reading, but the professor would select those international aspects of the material that appear most important to present during class time.

Because the vast majority of the traditional organizational behavior literature and practice is based on the behavior of Americans, the book has used the United States as a reference point and as a point of comparison. American readers will recognize the familiar ways in which organizational behavior is usually described and be able to add international perspectives to that knowledge. Readers from countries outside of the United States will gain a better understanding of their own culture's practices and ways of doing business, both relative to traditional (United States–based) descriptions and to countries worldwide. It is not that any country's system or perspective is better or worse—more or less effective— than any other country's, it is that each is, to a large extent, distinct and therefore must not be understood as a replica of any other nation.

Notwithstanding the presentation format, it is important to remember that cross-cultural management (i.e., studying the international dimensions of people's behavior in organizations) is a new field relative to the traditional study of organizational behavior. On many issues only initial international research has been conducted. *International Dimensions of Organizational Behavior* presents an integrated selection of what is known in the field as of 1990. There is no doubt that by the year 2000, our knowledge will have grown far beyond today's understanding. Whereas the limits of our understanding are at times restrictive, they also define the boundaries and excitement of an important, rapidly expanding field of knowledge. Far from leaving with a sense of knowing all there is to know, it is hoped that readers will finish the book with a sophisticated awareness of the world beyond their own national boundaries, an understanding of the limits of their own knowledge, and a set of questions to guide their management decisions and future inquiry.

ACKNOWLEDGMENTS

The process of understanding the human dynamics in international management has brought together some of the best thinking and insights from consultants, managers, academics, and researchers worldwide. The process is evolving. What we know today is so much more than what we understood yesterday, and yet so much less than what we will need for tomorrow. The excitement and passion in the search is predicated on our need to understand ourselves in a world where no part of humanity is very far away, a world in which our success as well as our very survival depends on our respect and understanding for each other.

I would like to thank the many, many people who have contributed to this book, each from his or her unique perspective and expertise. The quality of the book is shared by all, the errors and limitations are mine alone. My thanks to: Liselotte Adler (USA), Arshad Ahmad (Pakistan), Nakiye Boyacigiller (Turkey), Jill deVillafranca (Canada), Angela Dowson (Canada), Paul Evans (England), John Graham (USA), Jon Hartwick (Canada), Mary Hess (USA), André Laurent (France), Phyllis Lefohn (USA), Eileen Newmark (USA), Pri Notowidigdo (Indonesia), France Pepper (Canada), Roger Putzel (USA), Vijit Ramchandani (India), Indrei Ratiu (Britain/Romania), George Renwick (USA), Stephen Rhinesmith (USA), David Ricks (USA), Anita Salustro (USA), Suzanne Sellitto (Canada), Richard Vilas (USA), and Frances Westley (Canada).

My thanks to the reviewers of the manuscripts of both editions of this book: Dan Brenenstuhl, Arizona State University; Wilma Hoffman,

University of Texas at El Paso; Mariann Jelinek, Case Western Reserve University; Douglas M. McCabe, Georgetown University; Robert T. Moran, American Graduate School of International Management; Karlene Roberts, University of California at Berkeley; Joseph W. Weiss, Bentley College. And a very special thanks to Robine Andrau for her excellent editing of the second edition and to Louise Dubreuil, without whose help, encouragement, and insight this book would never have become a reality.

About the Author

NANCY J. ADLER is a Professor of Organizational Behavior and Cross-Cultural Management at the Faculty of Management, McGill University in Montreal, Canada. She received her B.A. in economics, M.B.A. and Ph.D. in management from the University of California at Los Angeles (UCLA).

Dr. Adler's fields of interest include strategic international human resources management, expatriation, women in international management, international negotiating, developing culturally synergistic approaches to problem solving, and international organization development. She has authored numerous articles, produced the film *A Portable Life*, and published the books *International Dimensions of Organizational Behavior* (1986) and *Women in Management Worldwide* (1988).

Dr. Adler has been a consultant to government organizations and private corporations on projects in Europe, North and South America, the Middle East, and Asia. She has taught Chinese executives in the People's Republic of China, held the Citicorp Visiting Professorship at the University of Hong Kong, and teaches executive and management seminars at INSEAD in France and at Bocconi University in Italy. She received McGill University's first Distinguished Teaching Award in Management.

Dr. Adler serves on the Board of Governors for the American Society for Training and Development, the Canadian Social Science Advisory Committee to UNESCO, the Strategic Grants Committee of the Social

Sciences and Humanities Research Council, the Executive Committee of the Pacific Asian Consortium for International Business, Education, and Research as well as having held leadership positions in the Academy of International Business, the Society for Intercultural Education, Training, and Research, and the Academy of Management. Dr. Adler was the 1990 recipient of ASTD's International Leadership Award.

Contents

PART I THE IMPACT OF CULTURE
ON ORGANIZATIONS ▸ **1**

CHAPTER 1 Culture and Management ▸ **3**

Global Strategy and Culture **6**

Cross-Cultural Management **10**

What Is Culture? **14**

How Do Cultures Vary? **19**

Summary **33**

Questions for Reflection **33**

References **35**

CHAPTER 2 Do Cultural Differences Affect
the Organization? ▸ **39**

Work Behavior Varies across Cultures **39**

Are Organizations Becoming More
Similar? **57**

Organization Culture and National Culture **58**

Summary **60**

Questions for Reflection **60**

References **61**

CHAPTER 3 Communicating Across Cultural Barriers ▸ **63**

Cross-Cultural Communication **64**

Cross-Cultural Misperception **67**

Cross-Cultural Misinterpretation **69**

Cross-Cultural Misevaluation **82**

Communication: Getting Their Meaning, Not Just Their Words **83**

Summary **88**

Questions for Reflection **88**

References **89**

PART II MANAGING CULTURAL DIVERSITY ▸ **93**

CHAPTER 4 Cultural Synergy ▸ **95**

Invisible Culture: Strategies for Recognizing Culture **96**

Cultural Synergy **105**

Summary **115**

Questions for Reflection **117**

References **117**

CHAPTER 5 Multicultural Teams ▸ **120**

Managing a Multicultural Workforce **121**

Domestic Multiculturalism **124**

Task Groups: The Organization in Microcosm **125**

Types of Diversity in Groups **126**

Cultural Diversity's Impact on Groups **128**

Conditions for Team Effectiveness **134**

Managing Culturally Diverse Groups **139**

Summary **141**

Questions for Reflection **142**

References **142**

CHAPTER 6 Cross-Cultural Leadership, Motivation, and Decision Making ▸ **146**

Leadership **147**

Motivation **152**

Decision Making **160**

Summary **171**

Questions for Reflection **172**

References **173**

CHAPTER 7 Negotiating with Foreigners ▸ **179**

Negotiating Internationally **181**

Successful Negotiations: People, Situation, and Process **185**

Negotiation Process **192**

Negotiation Tactics **203**

Summary **215**

Questions for Reflection **217**

References **217**

PART III MANAGING GLOBAL
MANAGERS ▸ **223**

CHAPTER 8 Cross-Cultural Transitions: Expatriate
Employee Entry and Reentry ▸ **225**

Cross-Cultural Entry **226**

Home Country Reentry **232**

Professional Reentry **235**

Underutilized International Employee **245**

Summary **248**

Questions for Reflection **248**

References **249**

Selected Readings on Selection
and Training **251**

Selected Readings on Corporate Reentry **255**

CHAPTER 9 A Portable Life: The Expatriate
Spouse ▸ **257**

Moving Abroad: Premade Decisions **258**

Cross-Cultural Transitions **265**

Creating a Meaningful Portable Life **272**

Returning Home **273**

Recommendations **274**

CONTENTS

Summary **275**

Questions for Reflection **275**

References **276**

CHAPTER 10 International Careers ▸ **279**

What It Takes to Reach the Top **280**

Who Were the Expatriate Managers? **282**

Today's International Careers **283**

Women in International Management **296**

Summary **297**

Questions for Reflection **298**

References **299**

EPILOGUE ▸ **302**

INDEX ▸ **303**

PART I

▼

Impact of Culture
on Organizations

▲

CHAPTER 1

▼

Culture and Management

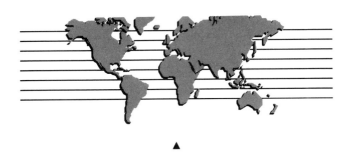

▲

Vérité en-deçà des Pyrénées, erreur au-delà.
("There are truths on this side of the Pyrenees which are false-
hoods on the other.")[1]

Blaise Pascal

Capital raised in London in the Eurodollar market by a Belgium-based
corporation may finance the acquisition of machinery by a subsidiary
located in Australia. A management team from French Renault may
take over an American-built automotive complex in the Argentine.
Clothing for dolls, sewn in Korea on Japanese-supplied sewing machines according to U.S. specifications, may be shipped to Northern
Mexico for assembly with other components into dolls being manufactured by a U.S. firm for sale in New York and London during the
Christmas season. A California manufactured air bus . . . is powered
by British . . . engines, while a competing air bus . . . flies on Canadian wing assemblies. A Frenchman is appointed president of the
U.S. domiciled IBM World Trade Corporation, while an American
establishes . . . a Swiss-based international mutual fund (16:1–2).

Managing the global enterprise and modern business management
are becoming synonymous. The term *international* can no longer be

3

relegated to a subset of organizations or to a division within the organization. Definitions of success now transcend national boundaries. In fact the very concept of domestic business may have become anachronistic. Today "the modern business enterprise has no place to hide. It has no place to go but everywhere" (32:xiii).

The post–World War II years saw a major expansion of world trade. From 1948 through 1972, world exports grew from $51.4 billion to $415.2 billion,[2] representing a sevenfold increase in monetary terms and a fourfold increase in volume (14:23). In just five years, from 1975 to 1979, world trade increased by about 32 percent in real terms (25). By 1980 international trade volume exceeded $1 trillion as compared with $800 billion in 1975 (25). In one decade the aggregate value of the goods and services exported by free world countries grew from $281.8 billion in 1970 to over $1.5 trillion by 1979 (15:1). By 1982 world exports amounted to $1,845 billion (26). Today's world trade dwarfs all prior statistics.

Moreover, the U.S. Commerce Department estimated in 1984 that some 70 percent of all firms faced "significant foreign competition" in U.S. domestic markets, up from only 25 percent a decade previously (39:11). By 1987 the chairman of the Foreign Trade Council estimated the figure to be 80 percent. Global competition is serious, it is pervasive, and it is here to stay (27).

Although international businesses have existed for centuries, the world has clearly entered an era of unprecedented global economic activity, including worldwide production, distribution, and, in increasingly large numbers, global strategic alliances. Examples of new global operations and alliances abound, with many firms earning more from international than from domestic operations. Multinational companies such as IBM, General Electric, British Petroleum, Siemans, and Eastman Kodak each do business with more than 50 countries (28:3). The 1992 economic integration of the European Economic Community has focused the world's attention on transborder business activity and the importance of trading blocks. Although the United States and Canadian economies have been inextricably linked to the world economy for years, the signing of the Canada–United States Free Trade Agreement has refocused North American attention on international business. As the Free Trade Agreement became effective in January 1989, that attention reached a crescendo.

As Professor Ian Mitroff observes, "For all practical purposes, all business today is global. Those individual businesses, firms, industries,

North America: The Dimensions of Globalization

United States exports and imports have increased more than ten times in the last two decades (28:3). Of the 1000 largest industrial companies in the United States, 700 expect their growth abroad to exceed their domestic growth in the next five years (12). With foreign production currently accounting for more than 25 percent of their domestic production, United States multinationals have a great stake in production abroad (23). United States companies own over $350 billion in assets abroad, whereas foreign investors own about $275 billion in the United States (23). From 1950 to 1976 total direct investment abroad increased almost twelvefold, from $11.8 billion to $137.2 billion (18:12). In the decade from 1966 to 1975, sales by majority-owned foreign affiliates of United States companies increased from $100 billion to over $450 billion (18:29). In the last decade overseas sales increased at a rate of 10 percent per year (14:16). After adjustments for inflation, these increases remain substantial.

More than two decades ago, many North American industries began establishing significant operations overseas. By 1974, 25 of the top 500 United States industrial corporations made more than 50 percent of their profits abroad, including International Harvester (75%), Gillette (61%), Otis Elevator (60%), Pfizer (60%), Coca-Cola (59%), and Dow Chemical (57%) (9). Since then, overseas sales have increased at an average of 10 percent, and the future has remained very promising. Today the total sales of some multinationals exceed the gross national products (GNPs) of many nations. For example, with 1980 sales exceeding $100 billion, Exxon, the largest multinational enterprise (MNE), surpassed the sum of the GNP of approximately 45 African countries (4:5). If nations and industrial firms are ranked together by GNP and total sales respectively, 37 of the first 100 on the list are industrial corporations (13).

In some ways the Canadian economy provides an even more dramatic example of the growing importance of international business activity. Already in 1986 Canada sold $94 billion in goods to the United States, $6 billion to Japan, and $8 billion to the European Community. Today over 500 Canadian-based companies have foreign subsidiaries, 43 percent more than in 1974 (17). Nearly a quarter of all goods consumed by Canadians are imported from other countries, and a slightly larger percentage of Canada's GNP is exported abroad. Foreigners own more than half of Canada's manufacturing capacity (15:1).

5

and whole societies that clearly understand the new rules of doing business in a world economy will prosper; those that do not will perish." (36:ix) Mitroff challenges us to realize that "It is no longer business as usual. Global competition has forced . . . [executives] to recognize that if they and their organizations are to survive, let alone prosper, they will have to learn to manage and to think very differently." (36:x)

GLOBAL STRATEGY AND CULTURE[3]

To succeed, corporations must develop global strategies. The 1980s have made the importance of such recognition commonplace, at least among leading firms and management scholars. New approaches to managing research and development, production, marketing, and finance, incorporating today's global realities, have evolved rapidly. Yet, only now is an equivalent evolution in understanding international organizational behavior and managing international human resource systems beginning to emerge. Although the other functional areas increasingly use strategies that were largely unheard of or would have been inappropriate only one or two decades ago, many firms still conduct the worldwide management of people as if neither the external economic and technological environment nor the internal structure and organization of the firm had changed.

Focusing on global strategies and management approaches from the perspective of people and culture allows us to examine the influence of national culture on organizational functioning. Rather than becoming trapped within the most commonly asked, and unfortunately misleading, question of *whether* organizational dynamics are universal or culturally specific, this book focuses on the crucially important questions of *when* and *how* to be sensitive to national culture.

As we investigate the influence of cultural diversity on multinational firms, it becomes clear that national cultural differences are important but that their relative impact depends on the stage of development of the firm, industry, and world economy. Using the model shown in Table 1–1, which documents the post–World War II development of the multinational enterprise (51:3;3), we can trace distinct variations in the relative importance of cultural diversity and, consequently, equally distinct variations in the most appropriate approaches to managing people worldwide.

As shown in Tables 1–1 and 1–2, immediately after World War II,

TABLE 1-1 International Corporate Evolution

	Phase I Domestic	Phase II International	Phase III Multinational	Phase IV Global
Primary orientation	Product/Service	Market	Price	Strategy
Competitive strategy	Domestic	Multidomestic	Multinational	Global
Importance of world business	Marginal	Important	Extremely important	Dominant
Product/service	New, unique	More standardized	Completely standard-ized (commodity)	Mass-customized
Technology	Product engineering emphasized Proprietary	Process engineering emphasized Shared	Engineering not emphasized Widely shared	Product and process engineering Instantly and extensively shared
R&D/sales	High	Decreasing	Very low	Very high
Profit margin	High	Decreasing	Very low	High, yet immediately decreasing
Competitors	None	Few	Many	Significant (few or many)
Market	Small, domestic	Large, multidomestic	Larger, multinational	Largest, global
Production location	Domestic	Domestic and primary markets	Multinational, least cost	Global, least cost
Exports	None	Growing, high potential	Large, saturated	Imports and exports
Structure	Functional divisions	Functional with international division	Multinational lines of business	Global alliances, heterarchy
	Centralized	Decentralized	Centralized	Coordinated, decentralized

SOURCE: © 1989 by Nancy J. Adler. See Adler and Ghadar (3) Phases I, II, and III are based on Vernon (51).

7

TABLE 1-2 Corporate Cross-Cultural Evolution

	PHASE I Domestic	PHASE II International	PHASE III Multinational	PHASE IV Global
Primary orientation	Product/service	Market	Price	Strategy
Strategy	Domestic	Multidomestic	Multinational	Global
Perspective	Ethnocentric	Polycentric/regiocentric	Multinational	Global/multicentric
Cultural sensitivity	Marginally important	Very important	Somewhat important	Critically important
With whom	No one	Clients	Employees	Employees and Clients
Level	No one	Workers and Clients	Managers	Executives
Strategic assumption	"One way"/ "one best way"	"Many good ways," equifinality	"One least-cost way"	"Many good ways" simultaneously

SOURCE: © 1989 by Nancy J. Adler. See Adler & Ghadar (3).

8

firms operated primarily from a domestic, ethnocentric perspective. Firms produced unique products that they offered almost exclusively to the domestic market. The uniqueness of the product and the lack of international competition negated the organization's need to show sensitivity to cultural differences. When organizations exported products, they did so without altering them for foreign consumption. Foreign buyers, rather than the home country product design, manufacturing, or marketing teams, absorbed any cultural differences. In some ways the implicit message sent to foreigners was "We will *allow* you to buy our product"; and, of course, the assumption was that foreigners would want to buy. During this initial phase, home country nationals and philosophies dominated management: Phase 1 MNEs regarded culture and multinational human resource management as largely irrelevant.

Competition ushered in the second phase and with it the beginning of a need to market and produce abroad. Totally unlike during Phase 1, sensitivity to cultural differences became critical to implementing effective corporate strategy in Phase 2. Phase 1's product orientation shifted to a market orientation, with companies needing to address each foreign domestic market differently. Whereas the unique technology of Phase 1 products fit well with an ethnocentric "one-best-way" approach, during Phase 2 firms began to assume that there were "many good ways" to manage, with each dependent on the nation involved. Successful companies no longer expected foreigners to absorb cultural mismatches between buyers and sellers. Rather, home country representatives had to modify their style to fit with that of their clients and colleagues in foreign markets. Moreover, although cultural differences became important in the design and marketing of culturally appropriate products, these differences became *critical* in their production in factories worldwide. Managers had to learn the culturally appropriate ways to manage people in each of the countries in which they operated.

Today many industries have entered Phase 3. The environment for these industries has changed again and with it the demands for cultural sensitivity. Within Phase 3 industries a number of companies produce an almost indifferentiable product (practically a commodity), with the only significant competition being on price. From this global price-sensitive perspective, cultural awareness falls again in importance. Price competition among almost identical products produced by numerous international competitors negates the importance of most cultural differences and almost any advantage gained by cultural sensitivity. As shown in Table 1–2, the primary product design and marketing assumption is no longer "one best way" or even "many good ways" but rather "one least-cost way." The primary market goal has become global, with no significant market segmentation. Firms can only gain competitive advantage through process engineering, sourcing critical factors on a worldwide basis, and benefiting from economies of scale. Price competition reduces culture's influence significantly.

Some observers believe that Phase 3 is the ultimate phase for all industries. This author does not. While a number of industries today are deeply involved in Phase 3 dynamics, a fourth phase is emerging. In it, top quality, least-possible-cost products become the baseline, the minimally acceptable standard. Competitive advantage comes from strategic thinking and mass customization. Product ideas are drawn from worldwide sources, as are the factors and locations of production. However, companies tailor the final product and its marketing to very discrete market niches. One of the critical components of this market segmentation, again, becomes culture.

Successful Phase 4 firms need to know how to understand their potential clients' needs, quickly translate them into products and services, produce those products and services on a least-cost basis, and deliver them back to the client in an acceptable fashion. By this phase, the exclusive product, sales, or price orientation of the past phases almost completely disappears. Companies replace them with a responsive design orientation accompanied by a quick, least-cost production function. Needless to say, culture is critically important to this most advanced stage. Similarly, the ability to manage cross-cultural interaction, multinational teams, and global alliances becomes fundamental. Whereas effective international human resource management strategies varied in past phases from being irrelevant to helpful, by Phase 4 they become essential, a minimum requirement for organizational survival and success.

CROSS-CULTURAL MANAGEMENT

The growing importance of world business creates a demand for managers sophisticated in international management and skilled at working with people from other countries. Cross-cultural management studies the behavior of people in organizations around the world and trains people to work in organizations with employee and client populations from several cultures. It *describes* organizational behavior within countries and cultures; *compares* organizational behavior across countries and cultures; and, perhaps most importantly, seeks to understand and improve the *interaction* of co-workers, clients, suppliers, and alliance partners from different countries and cultures. Cross-cultural management thus expands the scope of domestic management to encompass the international and multicultural spheres.

Parochialism

Parochialism means viewing the world solely through one's own eyes and perspective. A person with a parochial perspective does not recognize other people's different ways of living and working nor that such differences have serious consequences. People in all cultures are, to a certain extent, parochial. Recently, journalists, politicians, and managers alike have decried Americans' parochialism.[4] Americans speak fewer foreign languages, demonstrate less interest in foreign cultures, and are more naive in international business situations than the majority of their trading partners. In *The Tongue-Tied American* (46), United States Congressman Paul Simon deplored the shocking state of foreign language illiteracy in the United States and emphasized the heavy price Americans pay for it diplomatically, commercially, economically, and culturally. His message was a "shocking indictment of the complacent, potentially catastrophic monolingual arrogance of . . . [Americans], from top government leaders to the man in the street." (49) Echoing Simon's sentiments in reference to South America, former United States Congressman James W. Symington said that the problem is Americans'

> fundamental, dogged, appalling ignorance of the Latin mind and culture. Foreign students and statesmen refresh their perceptions of the United States by reading our poets, essayists, novelists and humorists. But our approach is like that of the man who, when asked which hurts most, ignorance or apathy, replied, "I don't know and I don't care." Such indifference cannot be justified by our otherwise commendable concern for what people do rather than what they think. . . . Preoccupied with acting, we seldom miss opportunities to ignore thought. [Perhaps, in the future] . . . diplomats — possibly even presidents — might know something of the cultural lessons that stir our neighbors' hearts. (47)

11

Fortune magazine reports that "A 'Copernican revolution' must take place in the attitudes of American CEOs as the international economy no longer revolves around the U.S., and the world market is shared by many strong players" (30:157). Lester Thurow, dean of MIT's Sloan School of Management, asserts that future CEOs "must have an understanding of how to manage in an international environment. . . . To be trained as an *American* manager is to be trained for a world that is no longer there" (20:50). Many business leaders predict that the next generation of top executives will have to have an international assignment to reach the top (7:B18;11). Yet this has not been true in the past, nor unfortunately is it true today.

A 1975 *Dun's* survey found that only a handful of the 87 chairmen and presidents of the 50 largest American multinational corporations could be considered career internationalists. Of the 87 top executives, 69 had had no overseas experience at all, except for inspection tours (17). Whereas almost two-thirds (62%) of U.S. executives today see "emphasizing an international outlook" as very important for the CEO of tomorrow, only a third (35%) consider experience outside of the United States as very important, and fewer than one in five (19%) consider foreign language training as very important (30:158). By comparison, 82 percent of non–United States executives consider an international outlook as very important for future CEOs; twice as many (70% versus 35%) consider experience outside of their home country as very important, and more than three times as many (64% vs. 19%) consider foreign language training as very important (30:158).

Why have many Americans ignored the need to think and act globally? Americans' parochialism is understandable and at the same time unfortunate. Because the United States has such a large domestic market (over 225 million people) and English has become the international business language, many Americans assume that they neither need to speak other languages nor go to other countries to succeed in the corporate world. This parochial assumption is certainly not true for young Swedes, Israelis, or Thais.

The United States's former political and technological dominance has also led many Americans to believe that they can conduct business strictly from an American perspective. In many fields in which American technology has been the only advanced technology available, potential foreign clients and trading partners have had no opinion but to "buy American." International business expertise was unnecessary because the product sold itself (Phase 1). In the public sector, technology transfer projects from the United States to Third World countries further encouraged viewing the world from an American perspective (Phase 2). An Indonesian's comments about Americans' views of Third World people capture this technologically based parochialism:

> The questions Americans ask me are sometimes very embarrassing, like whether I have ever seen a camera. Most of them consider themselves the most highly civilized people. Why? Because they are accustomed to technical inventions? Consequently, they think that people living in bamboo houses or having customs different from their own are primitive and backward (45).

The academic community has reinforced management's tendency toward American parochialism. The vast majority of management schools are in the United States; the majority of management professors and researchers are American trained; and the majority of management research focuses on U.S. companies. Out of over 11,000 articles published in 24 management journals between 1971 and 1980, approximately 80 percent were found to be studies of the United States conducted by Americans (1). Fewer than 5 percent of the articles describing the behavior of people in organizations included the concept of culture (1). Fewer than 1 percent focused on people from two or more cultures working together, a crucial area for international business (1). The publishing of cross-cultural management articles has increased only slightly during the 1980s (21;38). The manager about to negotiate a major contract with a foreign national (a citizen of another country), the executive about to become a director of operations in another country, and the newly promoted vice president for international sales, all receive little guidance from the available management literature.

The United States will continue to have a large domestic market, English will continue to be the language of international business, and technological excellence will continue to typify many American industries. Nonetheless, the domain of business is rapidly moving beyond national boundaries; the limitations of monolingualism are becoming more apparent; and technological superiority in many industries has become a cherished memory. Global competition in the 1990s makes parochialism self-defeating. No nation can afford to act as if it is alone in the world (parochialism) or better than other nations (ethnocentrism). The United States's economy is inextricably linked to the health of other economies. Like businesspeople the world over, Americans must now compete and contribute on an international scale.

Global versus Domestic Organizations

The two fundamental differences between global and domestic organizations are geographic dispersion and multiculturalism. The term *geographic dispersion* refers to the operation of international organizations over vast global distances. Whether organizations produce in foreign countries or only export to them, whether employees work as expatriates or only travel abroad, whether legal ownership involves joint ventures or wholly owned subsidiaries, global firms must manage despite the added complexity of working in more than one country. Geographic dispersion confronts organizations with foreign currency exchange, transportation costs, customs regulations, and many other issues involving distance and national boundaries.

Multiculturalism, the second fundamental dimension of a global firm, means that people from more than one culture (and frequently more than one country) interact regularly. Domestic firms can be multicultural if their employee or client populations include more than one culture. For example, many organizations in Quebec have Anglophones (English speakers) and Francophones (French speakers) working within the same organization, and many companies in California have Hispanic and Asian as well as Anglo-Saxon employees. Multiculturalism adds to the complexity of global firms by increasing the number of perspectives, approaches, and business methods. Whereas most international business books have focused on understanding and managing geographical dispersion, this book focuses primarily on multiculturalism, and raises such questions as: Do people vary across cultures? Do cultural differences affect organizations? Do international managers recognize cultural differences? What are the best strategies for managing corporate multiculturalism?

WHAT IS CULTURE?

To understand the differences between domestic and global management, it is necessary to understand the primary ways in which cultures vary. Anthropology has produced a literature rich in descriptions of alternative cultural systems, containing profound implications for managers working outside of their native countries.

Anthropologists have defined culture in many ways. *Culture* is "that complex whole which includes knowledge, belief, art, law, morals, customs, and any capabilities and habits acquired by a man as a member of society" (47:1). It is "a way of life of a group of people, the configuration of all the more or less stereotyped patterns of learned behavior, which are handed down from one generation to the next through the means of language and imitation" (5:4). After cataloging more than one hundred different definitions of culture, Kroeber and Kluckhohn (31:181) offered one of the most comprehensive and generally accepted definitions:

> Culture consists of patterns, explicit and implicit of and for behavior acquired and transmitted by symbols, constituting the distinctive achievement of human groups, including their embodiment in artifacts; the essential core of culture consists of traditional (i.e., historically derived and selected) ideas and especially their attached values; culture systems may, on the one hand, be considered as products of action, on the other, as conditioning elements of future action.

Culture is therefore (10:19)

    a. Something that is shared by all or almost all members of some social group,

    b. Something that the older members of the group try to pass on to the younger members, and

    c. Something (as in the case of morals, laws and customs) that shapes behavior, or . . . structures one's perception of the world.

Managers frequently see culture as "the collective programming of the mind which distinguishes the members of one human group from another . . . the interactive aggregate of common characteristics that influences a human group's response to its environment" (24:25). In general, we see people as being from different cultures if their ways of life as a group differ significantly, one from the other.

Cultural Orientations

The cultural orientation of a society reflects the complex interaction of the values, attitudes, and behaviors displayed by its members. As shown in Figure 1–1, individuals express culture and its normative qualities through the values that they hold about life and the world around them. These values in turn affect their attitudes about the form of behavior considered more appropriate and effective in any given situation. The

15

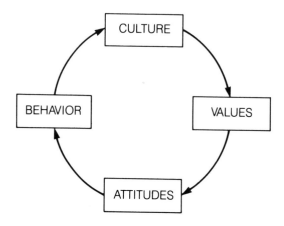

FIGURE 1-1   Influence of Culture on Behavior

continually changing patterns of individual and group behavior eventually influence the society's culture, and the cycle begins again. What are the differences among values, attitudes, and behavior?

Values

A value is that which is explicitly or implicitly desirable to an individual or a group and which influences the selection from available modes, means, and ends of action. Values can be both consciously and unconsciously held (29). Values are therefore relatively general beliefs that either define what is right and wrong or specify general preferences (8:23). Research has shown that personal values affect corporate strategy (22) and that managerial values affect all forms of organizational behavior (19;40), including selection and reward systems (8); superior/ subordinate relationships (34); and group behavior, communication, leadership, and conflict levels. For example, Latin American managers consider one's family to be very important — a value that leads them to hire members of their own family whenever possible. American managers strongly believe in individual achievement — a value that emphasizes a candidate's performance on qualifying exams rather than family membership. Both of these examples illustrate behavior influenced by a value.

Attitudes

An attitude is a construct that expresses values and disposes a person to act or react in a certain way toward something. Attitudes are present in the relationship between a person and some kind of object. For example, market research has shown that French Canadians have a positive attitude toward pleasant or sweet smells, whereas English Canadians prefer smells with efficient or clean connotations. Advertisements for Irish Spring soap directed at French Canadians therefore stressed the pleasant smell, whereas the ads for English Canadians stressed the inclusion of effective deodorants.[5]

Behavior

Behavior is any form of human action. For example, based on their culture, Middle Easterners stand closer together (a behavior) than North Americans, while Japanese stand farther apart than either North Americans or Middle Easterners. Latin Americans touch each other more frequently during business negotiations than North Americans, and both touch more frequently than do Japanese. People's behavior is defined by their culture.

Cultural Diversity

Diversity exists both within and among cultures; but within a single culture, certain behaviors are favored and others repressed. The norm for a society is the most common and generally most acceptable pattern of values, attitudes, and behavior. For example, in international business a man wearing a dark gray business suit reflects the norm through a favored behavior, whereas a man wearing a green business suit does not. A cultural orientation describes the attitudes of most of the people most of the time, not of all of the people all of the time. Accurate stereotypes refer to societal or cultural norms.

Societies enforce norms by communicating disapproval toward transgressors — people who engage in prohibited behavior. Some norms, such as laws, are very important; whereas others, such as customs and habits, are less important. A norm's importance is measured by how severely society condemns those who violate it. In the United States, for example, an important norm proscribes bribery. Companies caught using bribery to increase business are publicly prosecuted and fined through a severe sanction. A less important norm in the United States has people say "Good morning" when greeting colleagues at the beginning of the day, but if I fail to say "Good morning" one day, it is unlikely that I will be severely punished. At worst, my colleagues may assume that I am preoccupied or perhaps tired.

Anthropologists Kluckhohn and Strodtbeck (29) discuss a set of assumptions that allows us to understand the cultural orientation of a society without doing injustice to the diversity within the society.[6] The six assumptions, as adapted by Rhinesmith (42), are that

1. "There are a limited number of common human problems for which all peoples at all times must find some solutions." For example, each society must decide how to clothe, feed, and house its people. It must decide on systems of communication, education, transportation, health, commerce, and government.

2. "There are a limited number of alternatives which exist for dealing with these problems." For example, people may house themselves in tents, caves, igloos, single-family dwellings, or apartment buildings, but they cannot survive the winter without some form of housing.

3. "All alternatives are present in all societies at all times, but some are preferred over others."

4. "Each society has a dominant profile or values orientation and, in addition, has numerous variations or alternative profiles." For example, people may cure disease with chemotherapy, surgery, acupuncture, acupressure, prayer, or nutrition. The Chinese tend to prefer acupressure and acupuncture; the British chemotherapy and surgery; and the Christian Scientists prefer prayer.

5. "In both the dominant profile and the variations, there is a rank-ordering of preference for alternatives."

6. "In societies undergoing change, the ordering of preferences will not be clear cut." For example, as the computer revolution changes society, organizations' preferences to communicate using fax, telex, telephone, electronic mail, or the postal system become unclear; different organizations make different decisions.

These assumptions emphasize that cultural descriptions always refer to the norm or stereotype; they never refer to the behavior of all people in the culture, nor do they predict the behavior of any particular person.

HOW DO CULTURES VARY?

As shown in Table 1–3, six basic dimensions describe the cultural orientations of societies: people's qualities as individuals, their relationship to nature and the world, their relationship to other people, their primary type of activity, and their orientation in space and time (29;32). The six dimensions answer the questions: Who am I? How do I see the world? How do I relate to other people? What do I do? How do I use space and time? Each orientation reflects a value with behavioral and attitudinal implications. As summarized in Table 1–4, this section presents the six value dimensions with management examples for each. Because most of us know United States business customs fairly well, I will highlight differences between the United States and various other countries.

How People See Themselves

What is the nature of the individual: good or evil? Americans traditionally see people as a mixture of good and evil, capable of choosing one over the other. They believe in the possibility of improvement through change. Other cultures see people as basically evil — as reflected in the Puritans' orientation — or as basically good — as reflected in utopian societies throughout the ages. Societies that consider people good tend to trust people a great deal, whereas societies that consider people evil tend to suspect and mistrust them. In high-trust societies, people leave doors unlocked and do not fear robbery. In low-trust soci-

TABLE 1-3 Values Orientation Dimensions

Perception of	Dimensions		
Individual	Good	Good and evil	Evil
World	Dominant	Harmony	Subjugation
Human Relations	Individuals	Laterally extended groups	Hierarchical groups
Activity	Doing	Controlling	Being
Time	Future	Present	Past
Space	Private	Mixed	Public

19

TABLE 1–4 Cultural Orientations and Their Implications for Management

Cultural Dimension		American Cultural Orientation	Contrasting Cultural Orientations
What is the nature of people?		Mixture of good and evil	Good (Evil)
		Change is possible	Change is impossible
	Example:	Emphasize training and development; give people the opportunity to learn on the job	Emphasize selection and fit; select the right person for the job, and don't expect him/her to change
What is a person's relationship to nature?		People dominant over nature	Harmony (Subjugation)
	Example:	Policy decisions made to alter nature to people's needs — i.e., build dams, roads	Policy decisions made to protect nature while meeting people's needs
What is a person's relationship to other people?		Individualistic *mperend*	Group (hierarchical or lateral)
	Example:	Personnel director reviews academic and employment records of candidates to select the best person for the job	Personnel director selects the closest relative of chief executive as the best person for the job
	Example:	Decisions are made by individuals	Decisions are made by the group

	Doing	Being (Controlling)
What is the primary mode of activity?		
Example:	Employee works hard to achieve goals; employee maximizes work.	Employee works only as much as needed to be able to live; employee minimizes work.
What is the conception of space?	Private	Public
Example:	Executive holds important meetings in a large office, behind closed doors and has the secretary screen all interruptions.	Executive holds important meetings in a moderate-sized office or in an open area, with open doors and many interruptions from employees and visitors.
What is a person's temporal orientation?	Future/Present	Past (Present)
Example:	Policy statements refer to 5-, 10-, 15-, and 20-year goals while focus is kept on this year's bottom line and quarterly reports; innovation and flexibility to meet a dynamic, changing future are emphasized.	Policy statements this year reflect policy statements 10 years ago; the company strives to use traditions to perform in the future as it has in the past.

Adapted from Kluckhohn and Strodtbeck (29), DiStefano (16); also see Lane and DiStefano (32).
Reprinted with permission from *International Journal of Intercultural Relations*, vol. 3, no. 6 (1979), p. 411.
SOURCE: Nancy J. Adler, "Women as Androgynous Managers: A Conceptualization of the Potential for American Women in International Management," Copyright 1984, Pergamon Press, Ltd.

eties, people bolt their doors. After making a purchase, people in high-trust societies expect to receive the ordered merchandise and correct change; they do not expect to be cheated. In low-trust societies, *caveat emptor* ("let the buyer beware") rules the marketplace; one can only trust oneself. In many countries people are more trusting in rural communities than in urban centers.

Today many citizens of the United States and Canada lament that their fellow citizens cannot be trusted the way they used to be. For example, a Toronto hotel now posts a sign reminding guests that "Love is leaving the towels." A Los Angeles gas station, to assure that motorists will not drive away without paying, requires customers to pay twenty dollars or sign a credit slip before filling their gas tanks. A Minneapolis firm, National Credential Verification Service, makes a profitable business of exposing résumé deception. Out of 233 personnel officers responding to a survey of Fortune 500 companies, only one said that deception by executive post applicants was diminishing (33:85). To add to this mistrust, many people find it more difficult to trust foreigners than citizens of their own country.

Managers in the People's Republic of China describe their tradition as combining the extremes of good (Confucian tradition) with evil (the tradition of Lao Tzu) — a marriage of opposites. They also describe their belief that peasants are good and rich people are not so good, giving a recent example from the People's Republic of China's fourth largest city, Tianjin:

> At the Sino-Franco joint venture wine factory in Tianjin between Remy Martin and Dynasty, a French director left his wallet filled with French francs in the ped-a-cab. The peasant ped-a-cab driver waited all day outside the factory to return the wallet to the Frenchman.

Perhaps because of our fear of the unknown, we frequently tend to misattribute evil in cross-cultural settings. For example, Canadian government officials thought the Inuits, a native people, were evil when they burned down the doors on public housing projects. The officials misinterpreted the act as vandalism and therefore evil, whereas the Inuits had actually altered the houses to fit their normal — doorless — life-style. The Canadian government condemns the destruction of property, whereas closed doors, which separate people from their families and neighbors, are condemned by the Inuits.

Apart from their tendencies toward good or evil, can human beings improve themselves? Societies and organizations vary in the extent to

---

Perception of the Individual: Good versus Evil

Can a Yugoslavian Trust a Canadian Working in Sweden?

A young Canadian in Sweden found summer employment working in a restaurant owned by Yugoslavians. As the Canadian explained, "I arrived at the restaurant and was greeted by an effusive Yugoslavian man who set me to work at once washing dishes and preparing the restaurant for the June opening.

"At the end of the first day, I was brought to the back room. The owner took an old cash box out of a large desk. The Yugoslavian owner counted out my wages for the day and was about to return the box to the desk when the phone rang in the front room. The owner hesitated: should he leave me sitting in the room with the money or take it with him? Quite simply, could he trust me?

"After a moment, the man got up to answer the phone, leaving me with the open money box. I sat there in amazement; how could he trust me, someone he had known for less than a day, a person whose last name and address he didn't even know?"

This incident contrasts perceptions of individuals as good or evil. The Yugoslavian manager saw individuals as good and inherently trustworthy. For this reason, he could leave the employee alone with the money without worrying that it would disappear before he returned. The employee's surprise that this stranger trusted him with the money is a reflection of a North American's values orientation toward individuals. Believing that people are capable of both good and evil, North Americans are cautious. If the Canadian were in the owner's shoes, he probably would have taken the cash box with him to the other room to answer the telephone, fearing that the money would be stolen.[7]

---

which they believe that adults can change or improve. For example, organizations that believe people can change emphasize training and development, whereas organizations that believe people are incapable of change emphasize selection systems. With today's microcomputer revolution, some organizations choose to hire information systems experts, while others decide to train their current employees to use the new technology. The first strategy—hiring new employees—assumes that change is not possible, and the second strategy—training present employees—implies that change is possible. North Americans' emphasis on M.B.A. education and executive seminars strongly reflects their belief that change is possible. The Chinese saying that the "Chinese man strives to become better and, when better, to become perfect" strongly reflects a belief in the ability of adults to change. As one Shanghai executive exclaimed, applying the belief to his own career path, "I was trained as an engineer and now I am an export/import manager. I changed!"

People's Relationship to Their World

What is a person's relationship to the world? Are people dominant over their environment, in harmony with it, or subjugated by it? North Americans generally see themselves as dominant over nature. Other societies, such as the Chinese and Navaho, live in harmony with nature. They see no real separation between people and their natural environment, and their beliefs allow them to live at peace with the environment. In contrast to both of these orientations, a few remote tribal societies see people as subjugated by nature. In these cultures people accept, rather than interfere with, the inevitable forces of nature.

How does an organization see its environment? Are the relevant external environments—economic, social, cultural, political, legal, and technological—seen as stable and predictable or as random, turbulent, and unpredictable? Does an organization assume that it can control its environment, that it must harmonize with it, or that it will be dominated by it?

The dominance orientation is exemplified in North Americans' approach to agriculture. Based on the assumption that people can and ethically should modify nature to enhance their own well being, dominance-oriented agribusiness executives use fertilizers and insecticides to increase crop yield. By contrast, harmony-oriented farmers attempt only to plant the "right" crops in the "right" places at the "right" time of the year in order to maintain the environment's good condition. Farmers subjugated by nature hope that sufficient rain will fall, but they do not construct irrigation systems. They hope that pests will not attack the crops, but they do not use insecticides.

Some other examples of the North Americans' dominance orientation include astronauts' conquest (dominance) of space; economists'

Perception of the World: Dominance versus Harmony

"Feng Shui"

When the Hong Kong branch of a North American bank moved to a new location, one of its expatriate executives was asked to choose between two offices. He chose the one that was larger, regularly shaped, and adjacent to the vice president's office. His Chinese clients, however, were uncomfortable visiting him in his new office. One client with whom he was particularly friendly explained why: "The room has bad *feng shui.*" *Feng shui*, or "wind water" are earth forces, which the Chinese believe can cause success or failure. *Feng shui* reflects the belief that people and their activities are affected by the layout and orientation of their workplaces and homes. The goal is to be in harmony with the environment.

The expatriate executive faced a dilemma. As a reflection of status in the North American context, he had chosen his new office because of its size and proximity to the seat of power. In contrast the Chinese clients believed that it was a poor location because it had bad *feng shui*, and predicted bad business unless he changed offices.

Ultimately, the executive moved into a smaller office, where the space was awkwardly cut by a pillar. On the advice of his Chinese clients, he placed a mirror on the pillar to overcome this drawback. There were no dire consequences or business failures; his clients were comfortable with the new office and continued to do business with him.

North American and Chinese perceptions of the world clearly differ. North Americans want to control nature, whereas the Chinese want to be in harmony with it. The expatriate executive had originally chosen his office based on reasons that appeared rational from his dominance perspective — he wanted to maximize status and influence through office size and proximity. But to the Chinese his decision was not rational; the room was unlucky because it lacked harmony with nature. The expatriate was sensitive to Chinese cultural values and changed offices.[8]

structuring of the market; sales representatives' attempts to influence buyers' decisions; and, perhaps most controversial today, bioengineering and genetic programming. Perhaps the contrasting relationships become clearer in the sayings of three societies:

Saying	Culture	Meaning
Ayorama: "It can't be helped"	Inuit — Canada	Reflects subjugation
En Shah Allah: "If God is willing"	Moslem — Arab	Reflects harmony with nature and submission to God
Can Do: "I will do it"	American	Reflects dominance

A society's orientation toward the world is pervasive. For example, in news reporting, when Sir Edmund Hillary reached the top of Mt. Everest, the Western (dominance-oriented) press reported it as "Man conquers mountain"; the Chinese (harmony-oriented) press reported it as "Man befriends mountain." Religious writings similarly reflect a people's cultural orientation. For example, the *Bible* states in Genesis, "Let them have dominion over the earth"; the Tao Te Ching states, "Those who would take over the earth and shape it to their will, I notice, never succeed"—a dominance orientation contrasted with one of harmony.

Personal Relationships: Individualism or Collectivism

Americans are individualists; they use personal characteristics and achievements to define themselves, and they value individual welfare over that of the group. By contrast, in group-oriented societies people define themselves as members of clans or communities and consider the group's welfare most important. Lateral group membership includes all who are currently part of the family, community, or organization; hierarchical group membership includes those group members from prior generations. The United States is strongly individualistic and weak on groups, teams, and communities. For example, Americans praise their sports heros by singling out individual excellence: "Mark Smith and the team trounced the opposition." Compared with people in more group-oriented societies, Americans have more geographic mobility and their relationships, especially with co-workers, are less permanent. Due to its individualistic orientation, the United States has been described as a temporary society with temporary systems, uprootedness, disconnectedness, non-permanent relationships, and mobility (6). More group-oriented societies such as Japan, China, and the Israeli Kibbutzim emphasize group harmony, unity, and loyalty. Individuals in these societies fear being personally ostracized or bringing shame to their group for behavior that deviates from the norm. Personnel policies also follow either individual or group orientations. Individual-oriented personnel directors tend to hire those best qualified to do the job based on personal skills and expertise. Individualistic applicants will therefore submit résumés listing personal, educational, and professional achievements. Group-oriented personnel directors also tend to hire those most qualified, but their prime qualifications are trustworthiness, loyalty, and compatibility with coworkers. They hire friends and relatives of people already working for the organization. Therefore, rather than sending well-prepared résumés listing individual achievements, applicants seek introductions to the personnel director through a friend or relative, and initial discussions center on mutual friends and family or community members. The management of a group-oriented company in Ghana believes that only people who are known by other employees in the company can be trusted to act responsibly.

Personnel managers' actions can appear biased, illogical, and unfair when viewed from the perspective of a contrasting culture. Many individualistic North Americans see group-oriented hiring practices as nepotism because they are only seeing these practices from their own culture's perspective.

The organization of firms in individualistic and collective societies differs. In individualistic societies such as those of Canada and the United States, organization charts generally specify individual positions, each with a detailed job description listing formal duties and responsibilities. By contrast, organization charts in more group-oriented societies such as Hong Kong, Indonesia, and Malaysia tend only to specify sections, departments, and divisions, except for the top one or two positions (41). Group-oriented societies describe assignments, responsibilities, and reporting relationships in collective terms.

The individual versus group orientation also influences decision making. In North America, individuals make decisions. Decisions, therefore, are made relatively quickly, although implementation frequently gets delayed while the decision is explained and concurrence gained from other members of the organization. By contrast in Japan, a group-oriented culture, many people make the decision rather than one. The group process of decision making is less flexible and more time-consuming than the individualistic system because concurrence must be achieved prior to making the decision. However, since all parties al-

---

Personal Relationships: Individualism versus Collectivism

The German Won't Hire His
Yugoslavian Daughter

Rad, an engineer who had immigrated to West Germany from Yugoslavia, worked for a reputable German engineering firm. His daughter, Lana, had recently graduated from a prestigious German university. Rad considered it his duty to find his daughter a job, and he wanted his German boss to hire Lana. Although the boss felt Lana was extremely well qualified for the open position, he refused to have a father and daughter working in the same office. The very suggestion of hiring family members was repugnant to him. Rad believed that his boss was acting unfairly — he saw no problem in his daughter working with him in the same office.

The unfortunate outcome was that Lana was neither considered nor hired; the boss lost respect for Rad; and Rad became so upset that he requested a transfer to a new department. Neither Rad nor his boss understood that the conflict was caused by the fundamentally different values orientations in the two countries.[9]

---

ready understand and concur, they can implement a decision almost immediately.

Activity: Doing or Being

Americans' dominant mode of activity is *doing* or *action*. They stress accomplishments measurable by standards believed to be external to the individual. Managers in doing-oriented cultures motivate employees with promotions, raises, bonuses, and other forms of public recognition. The contrasting orientations are *being* and *control*. The *being* orientation finds people, events, and ideas flowing spontaneously; the people stress release, indulgence of existing desires, and working for the moment. If managers in being-oriented cultures do not enjoy their colleagues and current projects, they quit; they will not work strictly for future rewards. People in a *control*-oriented society restrain their desires by detaching themselves from objects in order to allow each person to develop as an integrated whole. The do-er is more active, the be-er is more passive. The do-er actively tries to achieve the most in life; the be-er wants to experience life.

The doing and being orientations affect planning differently. The being orientation views time as generational, so planning should allow for the long time needed for true change to occur. Major projects often need a generation, or certainly a decade, to achieve significant results. Be-ers allow change to happen at its own — and often slow — pace. They do not push or rush things to achieve short-term results. By contrast, do-ers believe that planning can speed up the change process if plans

Activity: Doing versus Being

Kashmir versus Sweden

In 1981 the United Nations appointed a Swedish army officer as an observer in Kashmir. His job was to travel around the turbulent province situated between Pakistan and India looking for troop movements on each side. The officer and his family moved into a houseboat on the river in Sringar, the capital of the province. As is customary for Europeans working in Kashmir, the family employed a "boy" — a servant — to perform all the household services during their stay. The servant was always very polite and pleasant, cooked delicious meals, and kept the houseboat neat and clean.

The family was very pleased with his work, and after a short time decided to give him a raise. Surprisingly, the servant did not turn up for work the next day, and his little brother arrived in his place. On his new higher salary, the servant had employed his younger brother to work for the family. With the raise he could keep his desired standard of living and help his younger brother without having to work.

Because the Kashmir servant was a Hindu, he did not believe that he could improve his standard of living in his lifetime. So by being good and not disturbing the harmony of his circumstances (i.e., by simply *being*), he believed he could be reincarnated into a higher position in his next life. This natural tendency to accept life with no expectations of material goods contrasts sharply with the Swedish family's notion of working hard to achieve personal goals and improve one's material lot in this life (i.e., their doing orientation). The Swede's surprise at seeing the younger brother arrive for work reflects this contrast.[10]

are carefully outlined, specific target dates set, and frequent progress reports made (43). The be-er believes that this type of planning is possible but unwise, since it rarely works immediately and is fruitless in the long run.

The activity orientation also explains why people work. To achieve goals, do-ers maximize work; to live life fully, be-ers minimize work. Increasing the salaries of do-ers and be-ers has the opposite effect. Salary increases motivate do-ers to work more hours because of the rewards; they motivate be-ers to work fewer hours because they can earn enough money in less time and still enjoy life (see story on page 29). American expatriate managers (do-ers), using salary as a motivational tool, made a severe mistake when they raised the salaries of a group of Mexican workers (be-ers), only to discover that by doing so they had decreased the total hours that the Mexicans wanted to work. Similarly, Canadians working in Malaysia found that workers were more interested in spending extra time with their family and friends than in earning overtime pay bonuses.

Time: Past, Present, or Future

What is the temporal focus of human life? How do societies use time? Are they oriented to the *past*, the *present*, or the *future?* Past-oriented cultures believe that plans should be evaluated in terms of their fit with the customs and traditions of society and that innovation and change are justified only according to past experience. By contrast, future-oriented cultures believe that they should evaluate plans in terms of the projected future benefit to be gained. Future-oriented people justify innovation and change in terms of future economic payoffs and have less regard for past social or organizational customs and traditions.

In contrast with most North Americans, many Europeans are past-oriented. Many Europeans believe that preserving history and continuing past traditions are important, whereas North Americans give tradition less importance. North American businesspeople focus on the present and near future; they may talk about achieving five- or ten-year plans, but they work toward achieving this quarter's results. Similarly, North American employment practices are also short-term. Managers who do not perform well during their first year on a new job are fired or at best not promoted. The company does not give them ten years to demonstrate their worth. By contrast, Japan has a very long-

from India

990 L/Iope

Time: Past, Present, or Future

Bus Schedules in the Bahamas

In the Bahamas, the bus service is managed similarly to many taxi systems. Each driver owns his bus and collects fares for his salary. There is no set schedule and no set time when the bus will run or arrive at a particular location. Everything depends on the driver.

The bus drivers are present-oriented; what they feel like doing on a particular day at a particular hour dictates what they will actually do. For example, if the bus driver feels hungry, he will go home to eat lunch without waiting for a pre-set lunch hour. The drivers see no need to repeat yesterday's actions today nor to set tomorrow's schedule according to the needs and patterns of today.

This present orientation contrasts starkly with the orientation of bus drivers in New York City, Toronto, Paris, London, and most other urban centers of the Western world. Drivers in these cities have planned schedules, which drivers follow to the best of their ability.[11]

---

term, future-oriented time horizon. When large Japanese firms hire employees, the commitment of both parties is for life. Japanese firms invest in years of training for each employee because they expect the employee to work with the firm for thirty to forty years. North American firms invest less in training because a lifetime commitment is not assumed between the company and the employee.

Societies have different standards of temporal precision. What defines when people arrive late and when they are on time for work, for meetings, or for business lunches? How much variation is allowed? How long are scheduled appointments—five minutes or two hours? What is the typical length of an assignment—one week or three years? An American engineer working in Bahrain was surprised by his Arab client's response to his apologetic explanation that unfortunately, due to unforeseen delays, their planned plant would not be ready to open until six months after the orginally scheduled date. The Bahrainian's response was: "We have lived for thousands of years without this plant; we easily can wait another six months or a year. This is no problem."

Diversity exists within societies as well as between societies. Past-, present-, and future-oriented people exist within every society. Comparing lawyers and economists in the United States highlights this tem-

31

Time: Long-Term versus Short-Term Contracts

The directors of a Japanese firm and a Canadian firm met in 1984 in Vancouver to negotiate the sale of coal shipments from British Columbia to Japan. The companies reached a stalemate over the length of the contract. The Japanese, ostensibly to reduce the uncertainty in their coal supply and to assure continuous, stable production in Japan, wanted the Canadians to sign a ten-year contract. The Canadians, on the other hand, did not wish to commit themselves to such a lengthy agreement in the event that they could find a more lucrative offer in the interim. Whereas the Japanese wanted to reduce the level of risk in their coal supply, the Canadians were willing to take the risk of losing a steady buyer for the potential benefits of a more profitable future buyer.

The neogtiations had hit a snag. Unless the time frame of the contract was resolved, no contract would be signed. The deal, which would benefit both parties, had a distinct possibility of remaining unconsummated.[12]

---

poral diversity. American lawyers use a past orientation in citing precedent to adjudicate the outcome of cases, whereas economists use a future orientation in conducting cost-benefit analyses to predict the possible outcomes of alternative corporate and governmental strategies.

The People's Republic of China: A Past Orientation

While odysseys to outer space lure more future-oriented Americans to movie houses, in China historical dramas lead box-office sales, and the more ancient the story, the better. Chinese children, so far, have no space-age superman to emulate. Even at play they pretend to be the Monkey King, the supernatural hero of a famous medieval epic (35:12).

Similarly, Chinese scientists look to the past for inspiration. In the national archives, teams of Chinese meteorologists are now combing voluminous weather records of the last 300 years in an effort to discover patterns that might help them predict the droughts and floods that still plague the country. Seismologists in charge of improving China's earthquake prediction methods are doing the same thing (35).

Space: Public or Private

How do people use physical space? Is a conference room, an office, or a building seen as public or private space? When can I enter an office directly, and when must I wait outside for permission to enter? The public versus private dimension defines the arrangement of organizational space. North Americans give private offices to more important employees, and even open offices have partitions between desks. They hold important meetings behind closed doors, usually in the executive's large, private office, and generally with minimal interruptions. The Japanese, by contrast, have no partitions dividing desks; bosses often sit together with their employees in the same large room. Middle Easterners often have numerous people present during important meetings. Both Middle Easterners and Japanese have a more public orientation than do North Americans.

SUMMARY

Cultures vary in distinct and significant ways. Our ways of thinking, feeling, and behaving as human beings are neither random nor haphazard but are profoundly influenced by our cultural heritage. Until we leave our community, we are oblivious to the dynamics of our shared culture. As we come in contact with people from other cultures, we become aware of our uniqueness and begin to appreciate our differences. In interacting with foreigners, we learn to recognize and value our fundamental humanity—our cultural similarities and dissimilarities. For years people have thought that organizations were beyond the influence of culture and that they were only determined by technology and task. Today we know that work is not simply a mechanistic outgrowth of either technology or task. At every level, culture profoundly influences organizational behavior.

QUESTIONS FOR REFLECTION

1. Using the six Kluckhohn and Strodtbeck values orientations, where do you think you are individually on each of the dimensions?
2. Describe your country's culture on each of the six values orientations? On which part of the spectrum is your country's culture? What concrete evi-

dence do you have? If you were a foreigner observing your country for the first time, what could you observe that would convince you of the country's place on each of the values orientations?

3. Think about a cross-cultural situation that you have been in or are currently in (a situation in which you have to work with or negotiate with people from another culture). Describe their values orientations? Where do your and their values orientations differ? What problems have been caused or might be caused by the differences in your values orientations?

4. In reading the international press, identify a situation that involves people from more than one culture (such as the Russians negotiating a trade agreement with the Canadians). Analyze the situation using at least one of the values dimensions. Indicate how the values differences are helping or hindering the success of the situation.

5. In which ways is your culture parochial? In which ways is it ethnocentric? Give concrete examples from situations that you have actually observed or that you have read about in the press.

NOTES

1. Blaise Pascal *Pensées*, 60 (294), in Geert Hofstede, *Culture's Consequences* (Beverly Hills, Calif.: Sage Publications, 1980).

2. Unless otherwise stated, all dollar figures are in U.S. dollars.

3. Adapted from material originally appearing in the "Preface" by Nancy J. Adler in Henry W. Lane and Joseph J. DiStefano, *International Management Behavior* (Toronto: Nelson Canada, 1988), pp. xiii–xvi.

4. Although the term *American* literally refers to all peoples from North and South America, it will be used in this book as a shorthand way to refer to citizens of the United States of America.

5. As conducted and cited by Jim Cornell et al., "Cultural Aspects Influencing Advertising Messages Aimed at French Canadians" (Paper, McGill University, 1982), interview with Jacques Grenier of Publi Plus, Inc., March 10, 1982.

6. Kluckhohn and Strodtbeck reflect a North American perspective in their work. Their framework of questions is therefore most accurate in describing Western cultures.

7. Stig-Eric Gruman, BCom, McGill University, 1984.

8. Anne H. Whetham, MBA, McGill University, 1984.

9. Ismail Elkhaby, MBA, McGill University, 1984.

10. Matts Franck, MBA, McGill University, 1984.

11. Yuk Tsui Grace Seto, BComm, McGill University, 1984.

12. John Clancy, BCom, McGill University, 1984.

REFERENCES

1. Adler, N. J. "Cross-Cultural Management Research: The Ostrich and the Trend," *Academy of Management Review*, vol. 8, no. 2 (April 1983), pp. 226–232.

2. Adler, N. J. "Do MBAs Want International Careers?" *International Journal of Intercultural Relations*, vol. 10, no. 3 (1986), pp. 277–300.

3. Adler, N. J., and Ghadar, F. "International Strategy from the Perspective of People and Culture: The North American Context," in A. M. Rugman, ed., *Research in Global Strategic Management: International Business Research for the Twenty-First Century; Canada's New Research Agenda*, Vol. 1 (Greenwich, Conn.: JAI Press, 1990), pp. 179–205.

4. Ball, D. A., and McCulloch, W. H. *International Business: Introduction and Essentials* (Plano, Tex.: Business Publications, 1982).

5. Barnouw, V. *Culture and Personality* (Homewood, Ill.: Dorsey Press, 1963).

6. Bennis, W., and Slater, P. *The Temporary Society* (New York: Harper & Row, 1968), p. 124.

7. Brown, L. K. "For Women in Business, No Room in the Middle," *New York Times* (December 28, 1981), p. B18.

8. Brown, M. A. "Values—A Necessary but Neglected Ingredient of Motivation on the Job," *Academy of Management Review*, vol. 1 (1976), pp. 15–23.

9. *Business and International Education* (Washington, D.C.: American Council of Education, 1977), pp. 9–10.

10. Carrol, M. P. "Culture," in J. Freeman, ed., *Introduction to Sociology: A Canadian Focus* (Scarborough, Ont., Canada: Prentice-Hall, 1982), pp. 19–40.

11. Chandler, C. H., as quoted in C. H. Deutsch, "Losing Innocence, Abroad: American Companies Are Trying to Shake Their Provincialism by Shipping Executives Overseas," *New York Times* (July 10, 1988), Business, pp., 1,2.

12. *Chicago Tribune* (February 4, 1981), as cited in S. H. Kim, *International Business* (Richmond, Va.: Robert F. Dame, Inc., 1983).

13. Corporate Scoreboard. *Business Week* (July 21, 1980), p. 118; and *1980 World Bank Atlas* (Washington, D.C.: The World Bank, 1981).

14. Daniels, J. D.; Ogram, E. W.; and Radebaugh, L. H., *International Busi-*

ness Environments and Operations, 3d ed. (Reading, Mass.: Addison-Wesley, 1982).

15. Dhawan, K. C.; Etemad, H.; and Wright, R. W. *International Business: A Canadian Perspective*. (Reading, Mass.: Addison-Wesley, 1981).

16. DiStefano, J. "A Conceptual Framework for Understanding Cross-Cultural Management Problems" (London, Ont.: School of Business Administration, University of Western Ontario, 1972). Also see H. W. Lane and J. J. DiStefano, *International Management Behavior.* (Toronto: Nelson Canada, 1988).

17. Dun & Bradstreet, Canada, Ltd. *Canadian Book of Corporate Management*, 1980 (Toronto: Dunn & Bradstreet, Canada, Ltd., 1980).

18. Eiteman, D. K., and Stonehill, A. I. *Multinational Business Finance*, 2d ed. (Reading, Mass.: Addison-Wesley, 1979).

19. England, G. W. *The Manager and His Values: An International Perspective* (Cambridge, Mass.: Ballinger, 1975).

20. "Global Strategist," *U.S. News and World Report* (March 7, 1988), p. 50.

21. Godkin, L.; Braye, C. E.; and Caunch, C. L. "U.S.-based Cross Cultural Management Research in the Eighties," *Journal of Business and Economic Perspectives*, vol. 15, no. 2 (Fall, 1989).

22. Guth, W. D., and Taguiri, R. "Personal Values and Corporate Strategies," *Harvard Business Review*, vol. 43 (1965), pp. 123–132.

23. Hamrin, R. D. *Managing Growth in the 1980s* (New York: Praeger Publishers, 1980).

24. Hofstede, G. *Culture's Consequences: International Differences in Work-Related Values* (Beverly Hills, Calif.: Sage Publications, 1980), p. 25.

25. International Monetary Fund and ACLI International, Inc. *Wall Street Journal* (May 28, 1981), p. 50.

26. International Monetary Fund, International Financial Statistics, United Nations Monthly Bulletin of Statistics, and national statistics as cited in *International Trade, 1982/83*. Contracting Parties to the General Agreement on Tariffs and Trade, Geneva, 1983, Appendix Table A4.

27. Jelinek, M., and Adler, N. J. "Women: World Class Managers for Global Competition," *Academy of Management Executive*, vol. 2, no. 1 (1988), pp. 11–19.

28. Kim, S. H. *International Business Finance* (Richmond, Va.: Robert F. Dame, 1983).

29. Kluckhohn, F., and Strodtbeck, F. L. *Variations in Value Orientations* (Evanston, Ill.: Row, Peterson, 1961).

30. Korn. L. B. "How the Next CEO Will Be Different," *Fortune* (May 22, 1989), pp. 157–158.

31. Kroeber, A. L., and Kluckhohn, F. *Culture: A Critical Review of Concepts and Definitions, Peabody Museum Papers*, vol. 47, no. 1 (Cambridge, Mass.: Harvard University, 1952), p. 181. Reprinted with permission of the Peabody Museum of Archaeology and Ethnology, Harvard University.

32. Lane, H. W., and DiStefano, J. J. *International Management Behavior: From Policy to Practice* (Scarborough, Ont.: Nelson Canada, 1988).

33. McCain, M. "Resumes: Separating Fact from Fiction," *American Way* (December 1983), p. 85.

34. Mankoff, A. W. "Values—Not Attitudes—Are the Real Key to Motivation," *Management Review*, vol. 63, no. 12 (December 1979), pp. 23–29.

35. Mathews, J., and Mathews, L. *One Billion: A China Chronicle*. (New York: Ballantine Books, 1983).

36. Mitroff, I. I. *Business Not as Usual* (San Francisco, Calif.: Jossey-Bass, 1987).

37. Parry, T. G. "Foreign Direct Investment and the Multinational Corporation," in Ingo Walter, ed., *Handbook of International Business* (New York: John Wiley & Sons, 1982), Chapter 16, pp. 4–5.

38. Peng, T. K.; Peterson, M. F.; and Shri, Y. P. "Quantitative Methods in Cross-National Organizational Research Since 1981: A Review," *Southern Management Association Proceedings* (Atlanta, 1988).

39. Peters, T. "Competition and Compassion," *California Management Review*, vol. 28, no. 4 (1986), pp. 11–26.

40. Posner, B. Z., and Munson, J. M. "The Importance of Values in Understanding Organizational Behaviour," *Human Resource Management*, vol. 18 (1979), pp. 9–14.

41. Redding, S. G., and Martyn-Johns, T. A. "Paradigm Differences and Their Relation to Management with Reference to South-East Asia," in G. W. England, A. R. Negandhi, and B. Wilpert, eds., *Organizational Functioning in a Cross-Cultural Perspective* (Kent, Ohio: Kent State University Press, 1979).

42. Rhinesmith, S. *Cultural Organizational Analysis: The Interrelationship of Value Orientations and Managerial Behavior* (Cambridge, Mass.: McBer Publication Series Number 5, 1970).

43. Rhinesmith, S. H., and Renwick, G. W. *Cultural Managerial Analysis Questionnaire* (New York: Moran, Stahl and Boyer, 1982).

44. Rugman, A. M., and Verbeke, A. "Strategic Responses to Free Trade," in M. Farrow and A. M. Rugman, eds., *Business Strategies and Free Trade*, Policy Study No. 5. (Toronto: C. D. Howe Institute, 1988), pp. 13–29.

45. Scarangello, A., ed. *American Education through Foreign Eyes* (New York: Hobbs, Dorman, and Co., 1967). Examples contributed by Robert Kohls.

46. Simon, P. *The Tongue-Tied American: Confronting the Foreign Language Crisis* (New York: Continuum Publishing Corp., 1980).

47. Symington, J. W. "Learn Latin America's Culture," *New York Times* (September 23, 1983). Copyright © 1983 by The New York Times Company. Reprinted with permission.

48. Taylor, E. B. *Primitive Culture: Researches into the Development of Mythology, Philosophy, Religion, Language, Arts and Customs*, vol. 1 (New York: Henry Holt, 1877), p. 1.

49. Tinsley, R. L., as quoted in V. V. Merchant's book review of *The Tongue-Tied American: Confronting the Foreign Language Crisis*, in *International Psychologist*, vol. XXV, no. 1 (February 1983).

50. U.S. Department of Commerce. *Survey of Business* (February 1977).

51. Vernon, R., "International Investment and International Trade in the Product Cycle," *Quarterly Journal of Economics* (May 1966).

CHAPTER 2

▼

Do Cultural Differences Affect the Organization?

▲

Deep cultural undercurrents structure life in subtle but highly consistent ways that are not consciously formulated. Like the invisible jet streams in the skies that determine the course of a storm, these currents shape our lives; yet their influence is only beginning to be identified.

Edward T. Hall (3:12)

People dress differently, eat different foods, and celebrate different holidays in countries around the world. But do those differences affect the way people work? Do people organize, manage, and work differently from culture to culture?

WORK BEHAVIOR VARIES ACROSS CULTURES

In what ways does organizational behavior vary across cultures? Researchers have found culturally based differences in people's values, attitudes, and behaviors. Each of us has a set of attitudes and beliefs—a set of filters through which we see management situations.

Figure 2–1 shows how managers' beliefs, attitudes, and values affect their behavior. To a certain extent, beliefs, attitudes, and values cause both vicious and benevolent cycles of behavior. Douglas McGregor, an American management theorist, gave us examples of this pattern in his "Theory X" and "Theory Y" (9). Theory X managers do not trust their subordinates and believe that employees will not do a good job unless closely supervised. These managers establish tight control systems—such as punch clocks and frequent employee observation—to assure themselves that employees are working. The employees, realizing that management does not trust them, start behaving irresponsibly—they only arrive on time when the punch clock is working and only work when a manager is watching. The manager, observing this behavior, becomes more distrustful of the employees and

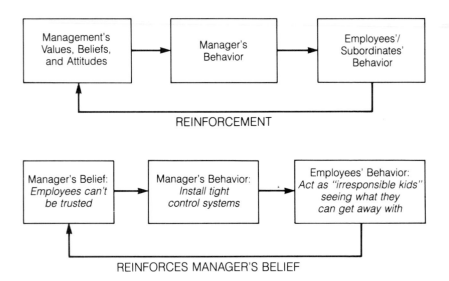

FIGURE 2–1 Managerial Attitudes and Employee Behavior: A Self-Fulfilling Prophecy
SOURCE: Based on Douglas McGregor, *The Human Side of Enterprise* (New York: McGraw-Hill, 1960).

installs even tighter control systems. According to McGregor, the manager's belief that employees cannot be trusted leads to the employees' irresponsible behavior, which in turn reinforces the manager's belief that employees cannot be trusted—a vicious circle and a self-fulfilling prophecy.

Theory X or Theory Y

Canadian Employees and Filipino Management

A Canadian bank employee gave the following description of his Filipino boss's Theory X approach to management.

"During my employment at the Royal Bank, I had a most unbearable and suspicious supervisor. As an assistant manager he had authority over all employees on the administrative side, including me. The problem was that he seemed to have a total distrust for his subordinates. He was constantly looking over our shoulders, checking our work, attitudes, and punctuality.

"Although most of his employees resented this treatment, the assistant manager was an extremely conscientious supervisor who honestly believed in what he called 'old-style' management. He believed that employees are lazy by nature. He therefore felt that they must be pressured into working. As the supervisor he felt justified in treating employees severely.

"I found his attitude condescending and counterproductive. As a group, the employees thought of themselves as basically trustworthy, but we decided that since our boss seemed to have no respect for us we would give him the same treatment in return. The result created a work environment that was filled with mistrust and hostility. The atmosphere affected everyone's work: employees became less and less willing to work, and the assistant manager increasingly believed in the employees' laziness and the need for severity. Luckily, the situation caught the manager's eye and was resolved after lengthy discussions. Only then did it become clear that we were not seeing the situation in the same way at all. From the assistant manager's perspective, he was simply showing his caring and involvement with his subordinates. As he explained, Filipino employees who were *not* treated like this might have felt neglected and unimportant. Unfortunately, we were not Filipinos and, as Canadians, did not respond as many Filipinos might have responded."[1]

McGregor's Theory Y describes a more benevolent cycle. Managers who trust their employees give them overall goals and tasks without instituting tight control systems or close supervision. The employees, believing that management trusts them, do their best work whether or not the manager is watching. The manager, seeing that the employees are present and working, becomes even more convinced that they can be trusted. Managers' attitudes influence their own behavior, which in turn influences employees' attitudes and behavior, which then reinforces the managers' original attitudes and behavior.

Worldwide Differences in Managerial Style

André Laurent (8), a French researcher, studied the philosophies and behaviors of managers in nine Western European countries, the United States, and two Asian countries (Indonesia and Japan). Laurent asked managers from each country to describe their approach to more than sixty common work situations. He found distinct patterns for managers in each of the countries.

In response to the statement, "The main reason for a hierarchical structure is so that everybody knows who has authority over whom," for example, managers from some countries strongly agreed, whereas managers from others strongly disagreed. As shown in Table 2–1, most Americans disagree with Laurent's statement; they believe that the main purpose of hierarchy is to organize tasks and facilitate problem solving

TABLE 2–1 "The Main Reason for Hierarchical Structure Is So That Everybody Knows Who Has Authority over Whom"

Agreement Rate across Countries							
United States	*Germany*	*Great Britain*	*Netherlands*	*France*	*Italy*	*Japan*	*Indonesia*
18%	24%	38%	38%	45%	50%	52%	86%

SOURCE: Based on André Laurent, "The Cultural Diversity of Western Conceptions of Management," *International Studies of Management and Organization*, vol. XIII, no. 1–2 (Spring–Summer 1983), pp. 75–96. Reprinted by permission of publisher, M. E. Sharpe, Inc., Armonk, N.Y.

around those tasks. Many Americans believe that an organization with very few hierarchical levels—in which most employees are colleagues rather than bosses and subordinates—can work. They believe that such minimal hierarchy is possible if tasks and roles are very clearly defined and the organization is small. By contrast, many southern Europeans and most Asian managers strongly agree with Laurent's statement. Eighty-six percent of the Indonesian managers surveyed believed that the main purpose of hierarchy was to have everyone know who has authority over whom. They did not believe that even a small organization could exist without a formal hierarchy.

Perhaps these different beliefs explain some potential problems when Americans work with Indonesians. Americans typically approach a project by outlining the overall goal and each of the major steps and then addressing staffing needs. Indonesians, on the other hand, first need to know who will manage the project and who will work on it. Once they know the hierarchy of people involved, they can assess the project's feasibility. Both cultures need to understand the project's goals and staffing arrangements, but the importance of each is reversed. An American would rarely discuss who will be the project director before at least broadly defining the project, while an Indonesian would rarely discuss the feasibility of a project before knowing who will be its leader.

Similarly, in response to the statement, "In order to have efficient work relationships it is often necessary to bypass the hierarchical line," Laurent found large and consistent differences across cultures. As shown in Table 2–2, Swedish managers see the least problem with bypassing. They value getting the job done, which means going to the person most

TABLE 2–2 "In Order to Have Efficient Work Relationships, It Is Often Necessary to Bypass the Hierarchical Line"

			Percent Disagreement across Countries			
Sweden	*Great Britain*	*United States*	*Netherlands*	*France*	*Germany*	*Italy*
22%	31%	32%	39%	42%	46%	75%

SOURCE: Based on André Laurent, "The Cultural Diversity of Western Conceptions of Management," *International Studies of Management and Organization*, vol. XIII, no. 1–2 (Spring–Summer 1983), pp. 75–96. Reprinted by permission of publisher, M. E. Sharpe, Inc., Armonk, N.Y.

likely to have the needed information and expertise, and not necessarily to one's boss. Most Swedish managers believe that a perfect hierarchy — in which one's boss knows everything — is impossible; they therefore see bypassing as a natural, logical, and appropriate way for employees to work in complex and changing organizations. Most Italians, by contrast, consider bypassing the boss as an act of insubordination. Most Italian managers believe that frequent bypassing indicates a poorly designed organization. Italians therefore respond to bypassing by reprimanding the employee or redesigning the hierarchical reporting structure. Imagine the frustration when Swedish employees attempt to work in a typically Italian organization. The Swedes, attempting to responsibly accomplish their work goals, continually bypass hierarchical lines and go to the people in the organization who have the necessary information and expertise. The Swedes' Italian boss, not having been consulted, thinks the Swedes are insubordinate and a threat to the organization and the project. In the reverse situation, the Swedish boss, frustrated with an Italian subordinate's constant requests for permission and information, thinks the worker lacks initiative and is unwilling both to use personal judgment and to take risks. Why else, asks the Swedish manager, would the Italian always consult the boss before acting on matters for which the boss need not be consulted? Is either side right? No, they are just different.

Laurent found little agreement across national boundaries on the nature of the managerial role. As shown in Figure 2–2, more than four times as many Japanese and Indonesian managers as American managers agreed with the statement, "It is important for a manager to have at hand precise answers to most of the questions that his subordinates may raise about their work." Most American managers believe that the role of the manager is to be a problem solver: managers should help subordinates discover ways to solve problems, rather than simply answering their questions. Furthermore, American managers believe that merely providing answers discourages subordinates' initiative and creativity and ultimately diminishes their productivity. By contrast, the French generally see the manager as an expert. Most French managers believe that they should give precise answers to subordinates' questions in order to maintain their credibility as experts and as managers and that their subordinates' sense of security depends on receiving precise answers. The French believe a person should not have a managerial position unless he or she has precise answers to most work-related ques-

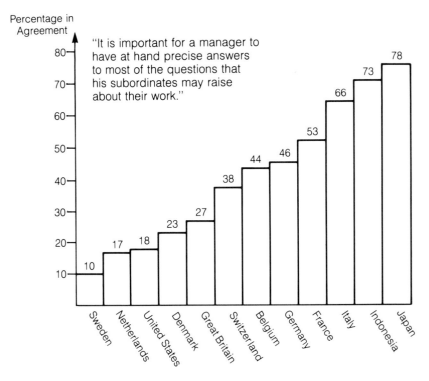

FIGURE 2-2 Manager's Role Varies across Cultures
SOURCE: Based on André Laurent, "The Cultural Diversity of Western Conceptions of Management," *International Studies of Management and Organization*, vol. XIII, no. 1-2 (Spring-Summer 1983), pp. 75-96. Reprinted by permission of publisher, M. E. Sharpe, Inc., Armonk, N.Y.

tions. (See page 79, the Iranian's view, for another example of the expert perspective.)

Is a manager primarily an expert or a problem solver? Again, there is no one right answer, because organizations from different cultures maintain different beliefs. Problems arise when managers from one culture interact with managers and employees from another. When an American manager tells French employees, "I don't know the answer, but maybe if you talk to Simon in marketing he will know," the French employees do not assume that they have received appropriate problem-solving help but rather assume that their boss is incompetent. Similarly, when American employees receive specific answers from a French boss, they may consider him egotistical rather than competent: Why didn't the French boss tell them that Simon in marketing has a better answer? Laurent concludes that the national origin of European and American managers significantly affects their views on how effective managers should manage (8:77). Overall, the extent to which managers see organizations as political, authoritarian, role-formalizing, and hierarchical-relationship systems varies according to their country to origin (8).

Dimensions of Difference

Differences in work-related attitudes exist across a very wide range of cultures. Geert Hofstede, a Dutch researcher, corroborated and integrated the results of Laurent's and others' research. In a 40-country study (4), which was later expanded to over 60 countries, including both Oriental and Occidental cultures (5;6), 160,000 managers and employees from an American multinational corporation were surveyed twice. Hofstede, like Laurent, found highly significant differences in the behavior and attitudes of employees and managers from different countries who worked for this multinational — differences that did not change over time. Hofstede found that national culture explained more of the differences in work-related values and attitudes than did position within the organization, profession, age, or gender. In summarizing the most important differences, Hofstede found that managers and employees vary on four primary dimensions: individualism/collectivism, power distance, uncertainty avoidance, and masculinity/femininity.

Individualism/Collectivism

Individualism exists when people define themselves as individuals. It implies loosely knit social frameworks in which people are supposed to take care only of themselves and their immediate families. *Collectivism* is characterized by tight social frameworks in which people distinguish between their own groups ("in-groups," such as relatives, clans, and organizations) and other groups. People expect in-groups to look after their members, protect them, and give them security in exchange for members' loyalty. For example, as reported in *The Arab Executive*, two-thirds of all surveyed Arab executives thought employee loyalty was more important than efficiency (10). This dimension resembles the individual/group values orientation discussed in chapter 1.

Determinism characterizes such collectivist cultures as Japan, where people believe that the will of the group should determine members' beliefs and behavior. This belief is reflected in the Japanese saying, "The nail that sticks out will be pounded down." By contrast, self-determination characterizes such individualistic cultures as the United States, where individuals believe that each person should determine his or her own beliefs and behavior. In each nation's case, their beliefs become self-fulfilling. People from individualistic cultures also tend to believe that there are universal values that should be shared by all. People from collectivist cultures, on the other hand, accept that different groups have different values. Being individualistic, most North Americans believe that democracy — especially North American democracy — ideally should be shared by all. People from collectivist cultures find such a view hard to understand.

Collectivist cultures control their members more through external societal pressure — shame — whereas individualistic cultures control their members more through internal pressure — guilt. Members of collectivist cultures place importance on fitting in harmoniously and saving face. Members of individualistic cultures place more emphasis on self-respect. In many ways the two orientations trade off individual freedom against collective protection: Do I do what is best for me or what is best for the group? Do I take care only of myself or does the group take care of me? Do I expect the boss to hire me because I have the right education and work experience (individual) or because I come from the right family or social class (group)? Do I expect to be promoted on the basis of my performance in the company or on the basis of my seniority with the company? In times of economic recession, do I expect the least productive workers to be laid off or every employee to take a pay cut? Figure 2–3 shows the distribution of countries on the individualism/collectivism dimension and Table 2–3 shows the abbreviations used in Figures 2–3, 2–4, and 2–5.

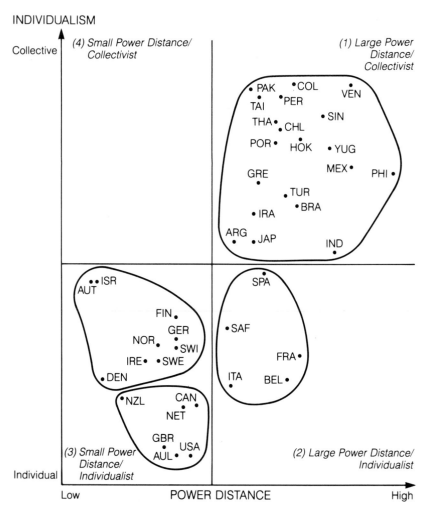

FIGURE 2-3 Position of Forty Countries on Power Distance and Individualism

SOURCE: Hofstede, Geert, "Motivation, Leadership, and Organization: Do American Theories Apply Abroad?" *Organizational Dynamics* (Summer 1980), pp. 42–63.
Note: See Table 2–3 for list of abbreviations.

TABLE 2-3 Forty Countries Showing Abbreviations Used in Figures 2-3, 2-4, and 2-5

ARG	Argentina	FRA	France	JAP	Japan	SIN	Singapore
AUL	Australia	GBR	Great Britain	MEX	Mexico	SPA	Spain
AUT	Austria	GER	Germany (West)	NET	Netherlands	SWE	Sweden
BEL	Belgium	GRE	Greece	NOR	Norway	SWI	Switzerland
BRA	Brazil	HOK	Hong Kong	NZL	New Zealand	TAI	Taiwan
CAN	Canada	IND	India	PAK	Pakistan	THA	Thailand
CHL	Chile	IRA	Iran	PER	Peru	TUR	Turkey
COL	Colombia	IRE	Ireland	PHI	Philippines	USA	United States
DEN	Denmark	ISR	Israel	POR	Portugal	VEN	Venezuela
FIN	Finland	ITA	Italy	SAF	South Africa	YUG	Yugoslavia

SOURCE: Geert Hofstede, "Motivation, Leadership, and Organization: Do American Theories Apply Abroad?" *Organizational Dynamics* (Summer 1980), p. 50.

Individualism versus Collectivism

The Pacific Area Travel Association Survey

An international market research firm in Tokyo conducted a survey of travel market potential for the Pacific Area Travel Association (PATA), an organization of national tourist offices from various nations around the Pacific Rim. Although the survey was conducted through a standard questionnaire, each nation was allowed to submit a few of its own open-ended questions.

All countries responded promptly. Of the ten countries surveyed, the U.S. Department of Commerce was the first to send in questions. Individual names were always attached to the letters and telexes from the United States.

Shortly after completing the PATA survey, the company received a contract for a similar study from the Association of Southeast Asian Nations (ASEAN). Due to the similar content, the researchers conducted the ASEAN study in an almost identical fashion to the PATA study. They requested open-ended questions from the national tourism offices of Thailand, the Philippines, Singapore, Malaysia, and Indonesia. Because they had completed the collection of questions in a little over a month for PATA, the company assumed that six weeks would be more than sufficient for the ASEAN nations. They were wrong! The ASEAN nations required a considerably longer time than did the PATA countries. Many telexes had to be exchanged between the Philippines and Tokyo before a final response was received. Moreover, every telex from the Philippines had a different individual's name on it as its sender.

In thinking over these responses, the survey researchers concluded that the contrast between the Americans' and the Filipinos' responses to the same task stemmed from the relative emphasis on the individual versus the group. While the United States office gave sole responsibility to an individual, the more group-oriented Filipinos delegated the task to a whole department. Since everyone in the office in the Philippines was included, the task naturally took longer.[2]

Power Distance

The second dimension, power distance, measures the extent to which less powerful members of organizations accept the unequal distribution of power. To what extent do employees accept that their boss has more power than they have? Is the boss right because he or she is the boss (large, or high, power distance) or only when he or she knows the correct answer (small, or low, power distance)? Do employees do their work in a particular way because the boss wants it that way (high power distance) or because they believe that it is the best way to do it (low power distance)?

In high power distance countries, such as Philippines, Venezuela, and India, superiors and subordinates consider bypassing to be insubordination; whereas in low power distance countries, such as Israel and Denmark, employees expect to bypass the boss frequently in order to get their work done. When negotiating in high power distance countries, companies find it important to send representatives with titles

---

Power Distance

An American Executive in London

An American executive went to London to manage the company's British office. Although the initial few weeks were relatively uneventful, one thing that bothered the executive was that visitors were never sent directly to his office. A visitor first spoke with the receptionist, then the secretary, then the office manager, and finally was escorted by the office manager to see the American. The American was annoyed with this practice, which he considered a total waste of time. When he finally spoke with his British employees and urged them to be less formal, sending visitors directly to him, the employees were chagrined.

After a number of delicate conversations, the American executive began to understand the greater stress on formality and hierarchy in England. He slowly learned to ignore his feelings of impatience when the British used their proper channels for greeting guests. As a result, visitors continued to see the receptionist, secretary, and office manager before being sent in to meet the American.[3]

---

equivalent to or higher than those of their bargaining partners. Titles, status, and formality command less importance in low power distance countries. As shown in Figure 2–3, the United States ranks relatively low on power distance.

Power Distance

The Chinese Dinner Party

One of Canada's leading banks invited a Chinese delegation for dinner. The Canadian host chose to share his hosting responsibilities with a colleague.

The dinner was not a success. Both the Chinese and the Canadians remained relatively uneasy throughout the meal. During the dinner, no welcoming speeches or toasts to mutual good health were

---

made. At the end of the meal, the Chinese stood up, thanked the bank officials, declined a ride back to their hotel, and left feeling slighted. The Canadians also felt upset. They found the departure of the Chinese to be very abrupt, yet they did not know what they had done wrong. Despite planning the menu carefully (avoiding such foods as beef and dairy products), providing excellent translation services, and extending normal Canadian courtesies, the Canadians knew something had gone wrong; they were worried and somewhat hurt by the lack of rapport.

When the situation was analyzed, it was clear that the Chinese expectations had not been fulfilled. First, having two people share hosting responsibilities was confusing to the hierarchically minded Chinese. Second, because age is viewed as an indication of seniority, the Chinese considered the youth of their Canadian hosts as a slight to their own status. Third, in China, it is traditional for the host to offer a welcoming toast at the beginning of the meal, which is then reciprocated by the guests; by not doing so, the Canadians were thought rude.

The specific incident that upset the Canadians—the abrupt departure of the Chinese following the banquet—was, in fact, neither unusual nor a problem: the Chinese retire early and it was getting late.

The Canadians' lack of understanding of the hierarchical nature of Chinese society and the Chinese ways of communicating respect clearly cost them in their business dealings with the visiting delegation.[4]

Uncertainty Avoidance

The third dimension, uncertainty avoidance, measures the extent to which people in a society feel threatened by ambiguous situations and the extent to which they try to avoid these situations by providing greater career stability, establishing more formal rules, rejecting deviant ideas and behavior, and accepting the possibility of absolute truths and the attainment of expertise.

Lifetime employment is more common in high uncertainty avoidance countries such as Japan, Portugal, and Greece; whereas high job mobility more commonly occurs in low uncertainty avoidance countries such as Singapore, Hong Kong, and Denmark. The United States, with its very high job mobility, ranks relatively low on uncertainty avoidance. As shown in Figure 2–4, individuals' concepts of the organization

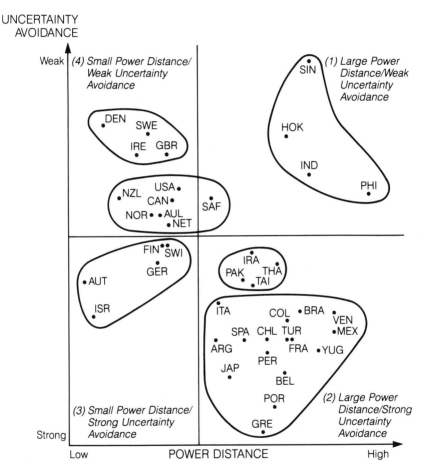

FIGURE 2–4 Position of Forty Countries on Power Distance and Uncertainty Avoidance

SOURCE: Geert Hofstede, "Motivation, Leadership, and Organization: Do American Theories Apply Abroad?" *Organizational Dynamics* (Summer 1980), pp. 42–63.

Note: See Table 2–3 for list of abbreviations.

vary markedly in their power distance and uncertainty avoidance orientations, depending on which country they are from. Organizations in countries such as Denmark that are low on both dimensions resemble village markets: they have very little hierarchy, everyone talks with everyone, and risk taking is both expected and encouraged.

Employees in high power distance and low uncertainty avoidance countries such as Singapore tend to think of their organizations as traditional families. As head of the family, the father protects family members physically and economically. In exchange, the family expects loyalty from its members.

Employees in countries such as Yugoslavia and Mexico that are high on both dimensions tend to view their organizations as pyramids of people rather than as families. Everyone in the organization knows who reports to whom, and formal lines of communication run vertically, never horizontally across the organization. In the pyramid organization, which operates vertically, management reduces uncertainty by emphasizing who has authority over whom. A pyramid organization resembles a fire department: not only is it clear who is chief, but the fire chief's word becomes law (high power distance). The department clearly defines all procedures and tolerates little or no ambiguity. When the alarm rings, fire fighters do not stop to discuss who will drive the pumper and who will drive the hook-and-ladder, because their roles and tasks have been clearly defined.

In high uncertainty avoidance and low power distance countries such as Israel and Austria, organizations tend to resemble well-oiled machines: they are highly predictable without needing a strong hierarchy. Most North American post offices provide excellent examples of these organizations: they reduce uncertainty by clearly defining roles and procedures.

Masculinity/Femininity[5]

Hofstede defines masculinity as the extent to which the dominant values in society emphasize assertiveness and the acquisition of money and things (materialism), while not particularly emphasizing concern for people. He defines femininity as the extent to which the dominant values in society emphasize relationships among people, concern for others, and the overall quality of life.

According to Hofstede's definitions, masculine societies define gender roles more rigidly than do feminine societies. For example, women may drive trucks or practice law and men may be ballet dancers or house husbands more easily in feminine societies. As shown in Figure 2–5, the Scandinavian countries are most feminine; the United States, slightly masculine; and Japan and Austria, highly masculine. In Japan and Austria people generally expect women to stay home and take care of children without working outside the home. The United States encourages women to work and gives them a certain amount of support for child care in the form of maternity leaves and day care centers. In Sweden women are expected to work; parents are given the option of paternity or maternity leave to take care of newborn children and day-mothers to care for older children.

Masculinity/Femininity

The "Inadequate" Business Commitment of Swedish Managers

Sweden has a policy that allows parents to take paternity or maternity leave at their discretion. When the policy was new, the managing director of the Swedish Postal Service created an uproar by announcing his intention to take paternity leave for a number of months to stay home with his newborn child. He explained to the press that managers do not differ from other employees: like other workers, managers also want and need to balance work with family life. In addition he said he believed that an organization that could not function for a period of time without its managing director had no *raison d'être*.

Swedish expatriate managers often do not have the opportunity to explain their desire for balancing professional and private life to their foreign colleagues. Swedes frequently surprise their international clients when they expect the work week to end at 5 P.M. on Friday or when they announce their intention to return home at the end of the day on the first plane in order to spend more time with their families. According to Swedish businesspeople, many foreigners, especially Americans, are willing to work all evening and all weekend to finish an important project; they frequently judge Swedes' behavior as demonstrating an inadequate commitment to work and quickly become annoyed. In actuality the Swedes are simply demonstrating their strong commitment to quality of life (feminine orientation), whereas the Americans and other similar foreigners behave according to their strong commitment to task (masculine orientation).[6]

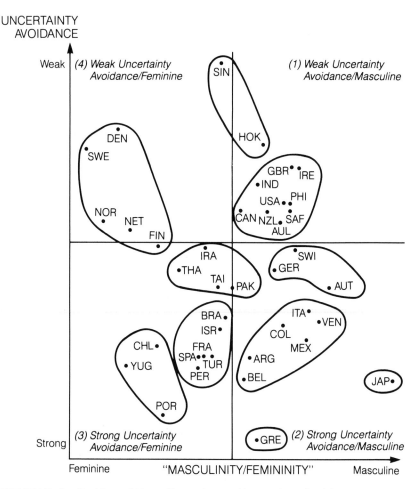

FIGURE 2-5 Position of Forty Countries on Uncertainty Avoidance and Masculinity

SOURCE: Geert Hofstede, "Motivation, Leadership, and Organization: Do American Theories Apply Abroad?" *Organizational Dynamics* (Summer 1980), pp. 42–63.

Note: See Table 2–3 for list of abbreviations.

Hofstede's masculinity/femininity dimension has important implications for motivation in the workplace. Japanese "quality circles," for example, primarily strive to achieve maximum quality (masculinity/high uncertainty avoidance); whereas the innovative Swedish work groups at Volvo attempt to enhance job satisfaction and flexibility (femininity/low uncertainty avoidance). Because feminine societies also tend to create high-tax environments, extra money often fails to strongly motivate employees (Sweden, for example). Conversely, masculine societies tend to develop into lower-tax environments in which extra money or other visible signs of success effectively reward achievement (Mexico, for example).

ARE ORGANIZATIONS BECOMING MORE SIMILAR?

Are organizations becoming more similar worldwide or are they maintaining their cultural dissimilarities? Is the world gradually creating one way of doing business; or is the world really a set of distinct markets defined by equally distinct national boundaries, each with its own culturally unique approach to business?

The question of convergence versus divergence has puzzled the international management field for years. If people around the world are becoming more similar, then understanding cross-cultural differences will become less important. If people remain dissimilar, then understanding cross-cultural differences in organizations will become increasingly important.

To clarify this issue, John Child (2), a British scholar, compared organizational research across cultures. Reviewing a myriad of cross-cultural studies, he found one group of highly reputable researchers repeatedly concluding that the world is growing more similar and another group of equally reputable researchers concluding that the world's organizations are maintaining their dissimilarity. Looking closer, Child discovered that most of the studies concluding convergence focused on macro level issues—such as the structure and technology of the organizations themselves—and most of the studies concluding divergence focused on micro level issues—the behavior of people within organizations. Therefore organizations worldwide are growing more similar, while the behavior of people within organizations is maintaining its cultural uniqueness. So organizations in Canada and Germany may look the same from the outside, but Canadians and Germans behave differently within them. Moreover, though Germans and Canadians may both install robots in their factories, each will interact with the robots differently.

57

ORGANIZATION CULTURE
AND NATIONAL CULTURE

Over the last decade, managers and researchers increasingly have recognized the importance of organization culture as a socializing influence and climate creator (1; 7; 11). Unfortunately, our understanding of organization culture has tended to limit rather than enhance our understanding of national cultures. Many managers believe that organization culture moderates or erases the influence of national culture. They assume that employees working for the same organization—even if they are from different countries—are more similar than different. They believe that national differences are only important in working with foreign clients, not in working with colleagues from the same organization.

Does organization culture erase or at least diminish national culture? Surprisingly, the answer is no: employees and managers *do* bring their ethnicity to the workplace. As described earlier, Hofstede found striking cultural differences within a single multinational corporation. In his study, national culture explained 50 percent of the differences in employees' attitudes and behaviors. National culture explained more of the difference than did professional role, age, gender, or race (4).

Even more strikingly, Laurent found cultural differences more pronounced among foreign employees working within the same multinational organization than among employees working for organizations in their native lands. After observing managers from nine Western European countries and the United States who were working for organizations in their native countries (e.g., Swedish managers working for Swedish companies, Italian managers working for Italian companies, etc.), Laurent replicated his research in one multinational corporation with subsidiaries in each of the ten original countries. He assumed that employees working for the same multinational corporation would be more similar than their domestically employed colleagues, but instead he found employees maintaining and even strengthening their cultural differences (see Figure 2–6). There were significantly greater differences between managers from the ten countries working within the same multinational corporation than there were between managers working for companies in their native countries. When they work for a multinational corporation, it appears that Germans become more German, Americans become more American, Swedes become more Swedish, and so on. Surprised by these results, Laurent replicated the research in two

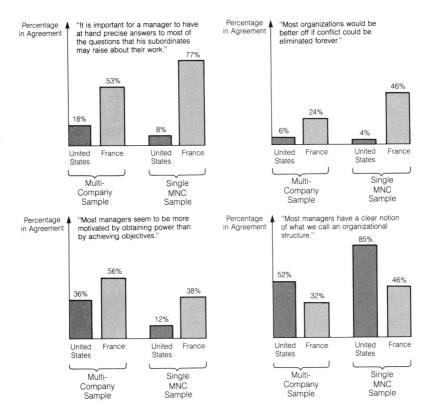

FIGURE 2-6 Organization Culture Magnifies Cross-Cultural Differences
SOURCE: André Laurent, INSEAD. Fontainebleau, France, 1981.

other multinational corporations, each with subsidiaries in the same nine Western European countries and the United States. Similar to the first company, corporate culture did not reduce or eliminate national differences in the second and third corporations. Far from reducing national differences, organizational culture maintains and enhances them.

Why might organizational culture enhance national cultural differences? At this point neither managers nor researchers know the answer. Perhaps the pressure to conform to the organization culture of a foreign-owned company brings out employees' resistance, causing them to cling more firmly to their own national identities. Perhaps our ethnic culture is so deeply ingrained in us by the time we reach adulthood that it cannot be erased by any external force. Perhaps other as yet unexplained forces are operating. The unambiguous conclusion is that employees maintain or enhance their culturally specific ways of working when placed within a multinational organization.

SUMMARY

Laurent's research documents a wide range of cultural differences in work-related behavior and beliefs. Hofstede's four dimensions — individualism/collectivism, power distance, uncertainty avoidance, and masculinity/femininity — highlight the most important differences for organizations. To manage effectively in a multinational or a domestic multicultural environment, we need to recognize the differences and learn to use them to our advantage rather than ignoring them or allowing them to cause problems. Chapter 3 investigates some of the ways in which we perceive, describe, interpret, and evaluate cultural differences. Chapter 4 then explores some of the ways in which organizations can best use those differences to their advantage. The myth of the transnational organization — the organization that is beyond nationality in its design and operation — remains, in reality, a myth.

QUESTIONS FOR REFLECTION

1. Where is your culture on Hostede's four dimensions? How is your organizational culture different from your national culture on each of the four dimensions?

2. Select a culture that you have had contact with or are currently working with. How does it differ from your own culture on Hostede's four dimensions? How might this show up in negotiations or ongoing business relationships?

3. In reading the international press, select a situation that involves two or more cultures. Analyze the situation using Hofstede's four dimensions. How does your cultural analysis help to explain the situation? Given your understanding of the cultural differences and similarities, what would you recommend that each side do (or avoid doing) to resolve the situation?

4. In what ways are you a product of the culture in which you grew up? How does your personal cultural background affect the way you think and behave? In what ways is your cultural background an advantage to working internationally? In what ways is it a disadvantage?

5. Interview a colleague about a cross-cultural situation in which he or she is currently involved. Analyze it from a cross-cultural perspective using any of the dimensions discussed in Chapters 1 and 2. What recommendations could you make to your colleague based on your cultural analysis?

NOTES

1. Ken Dang, MBA, McGill University, 1984.

2. Shigeki Iwashita, MBA, McGill University, 1984.

3. Jennifer Oakes, MBA, McGill University, 1984.

4. Anne H. Whetham, MBA, McGill University, 1984.

5. It should be noted that *masculine* and *feminine* are Hofstede's descriptions of the two poles of this fourth dimension. Neither Hofstede nor the author intend to suggest that today's male and female students and managers possess or lack certain attributes that the other gender possesses or lacks.

6. Matts Franck, MBA, McGill University, 1984.

REFERENCES

1. Burke, W., ed. "Special Issue on Organizational Culture," *Organizational Dynamics* (Autumn 1983).

2. Child, J. "Culture, Contingency and Capitalism in the Cross-National Study of Organizations," in L. L. Cummings and B. M. Staw, eds., *Research in Organizational Behavior*, vol. 3 (JAI Press, 1981), pp. 303–356.

3. Hall, E. T. *Beyond Culture.* Copyright 1976 by Edward T. Hall. Reprinted by permission of Doubleday and Company, Inc., New York.

4. Hofstede, G. *Culture's Consequences: International Differences in Work Related Values* (Beverly Hills: Sage Publications, 1980).

5. Hofstede, G. "Motivation, Leadership, and Organizations: Do American Theories Apply Abroad?" *Organizational Dynamics* (Summer 1980), pp. 42–63.

6. Hofstede, G., and Bond, M. H. "Confucius and Economic Growth: New Trends in Culture's Consequences," *Organizational Dynamics*, vol. 16, no. 4 (1988), pp. 4–21.

7. Jelinek, M.; Smircich, L.; and Hirsch, P., eds. "Organizational Culture" (Special Issue), *Administrative Science Quarterly* (September 1983).

8. Laurent, A. "The Cultural Diversity of Western Conceptions of Management." *International Studies of Management and Organization*, vol. XIII, no. 1–2 (Spring–Summer 1983), pp. 75–96.

9. McGregor, D. M. *The Human Side of Enterprise* (New York: McGraw-Hill, 1960).

10. Muna, F. A. *The Arab Executive* (New York: Macmillan, 1980), Table 6.2.

11. Uttal, B. "The Corporate Culture Vultures," *Fortune*, vol. 108, no. 8 (October 17, 1983), pp. 66–72.

CHAPTER 3

▼

Communicating
across
Cultural Barriers

▲

*If we seek to understand a people, we have to try to put our-
selves, as far as we can, in that particular historical and cultural background. . . . It is not easy for a person of one country to enter into the background of another country. So there
is great irritation, because one fact that seems obvious to us is
not immediately accepted by the other party or does not seem
obvious to him at all. . . . But that extreme irritation will go
when we think . . . that he is just differently conditioned and
simply can't get out of that condition. One has to recognize
that whatever the future may hold, countries and people differ
. . . in their approach to life and their ways of living and
thinking. In order to understand them, we have to understand
their way of life and approach. If we wish to convince them,
we have to use their language as far as we can, not language
in the narrow sense of the word, but the language of the mind.
That is one necessity. Something that goes even much further*

*than that is not the appeal to logic and reason, but some kind
of emotional awareness of other people.*

Jawaharlal Nehru, *Visit to America*

All international business activity involves communication. Within the
international and global business environment, activities such as exchanging information and ideas, decision making, negotiating, motivating, and leading are all based on the ability of managers from one
culture to communicate successfully with managers and employees from
other cultures. Achieving effective communication is a challenge to
managers worldwide even when the workforce is culturally homogeneous, but when one company includes a variety of languages and cultural backgrounds, effective two-way communication becomes even
more difficult (16:1; 10:3–5, 121–128).

CROSS-CULTURAL COMMUNICATION

Communication is the exchange of meaning: it is my attempt to let you
know what I mean. Communication includes any behavior that another human being perceives and interprets: it is your understanding
of what I mean. Communication includes sending both verbal messages
(words) and nonverbal messages (tone of voice, facial expression, behavior, and physical setting). It includes consciously sent messages as
well as messages that the sender is totally unaware of sending. Whatever I say and do, I cannot *not* communicate. Communication therefore involves a complex, multilayered, dynamic process through which
we exchange meaning.

Every communication has a message sender and a message receiver.
As shown in Figure 3–1, the sent message is never identical to the received message. Why? Communication is indirect; it is a symbolic behavior. Ideas, feelings, and pieces of information cannot be communicated directly but must be externalized or symbolized before being
communicated. *Encoding* describes the producing of a symbol message.
Decoding describes the receiving of a message from a symbol. The message sender must encode his or her meaning into a form that the receiver
will recognize — that is, into words and behavior. Receivers must then
decode the words and behavior — the symbols — back into messages that
have meaning for them.

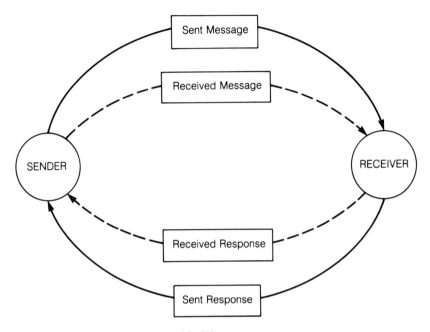

FIGURE 3-1 Communication Model

For example, because the Cantonese word for *eight* sounds like *faat*, which means prosperity, a Hong Kong textile manufacturer Mr. Lau Ting-pong paid $5 million in 1988 for car registration number 8. A year later, a European millionnaire paid $4.8 million at Hong Kong's Lunar New Year auction for vehicle registration number 7, a decision that mystified the Chinese, since the number 7 has little significance in the Chinese calculation of fortune (20).

Similarly, the prestigious members of Hong Kong's Legislative Council refrained from using numbers ending in 4 to identify their newly installed lockers. Some Chinese consider numbers ending with the digit 4 to be jinxed, because the sound of the Cantonese word *sei* is the same for *four* and *death*. The number 24, for instance, sounds like *yee sei*, or *death-prone* in Cantonese (9).

Translating meanings into words and behaviors—that is, into symbols—and back again into meanings is based on a person's cultural background and is not the same for each person. The greater the difference in background between senders and receivers, the greater the difference in meanings attached to particular words and behaviors. For example:

> A British boss asked a new, young American employee if he would like to have an early lunch at 11 A.M. each day. The employee answered, "Yeah, that would be great!" The boss, hearing the word *yeah* instead of the word *yes*, assumed that the employee was rude, ill-mannered, and disrespectful. The boss responded with a curt, "With that kind of attitude, you may as well forget about lunch!" The employee was bewildered. What had gone wrong? In the process of encoding agreement (the meaning) into *yeah* (a word symbol) and decoding the *yeah* spoken by a new employee to the boss (a word, behavior, and context symbol), the boss received an entirely different message than the employee had meant to send. Unfortunately, as is the case in most miscommunication, neither the sender nor the receiver was fully aware of what had gone wrong and why.

Cross-cultural communication occurs when a person from one culture sends a message to a person from another culture. Cross-cultural miscommunication occurs when the person from the second culture does not receive the sender's intended message. The greater the differences between the sender's and the receiver's cultures, the greater the chance for cross-cultural miscommunication. For example:

> A Japanese businessman wants to tell his Norwegian client that he is uninterested in a particular sale. To be polite, the Japanese says, "That will be very difficult." The Norwegian interprets the statement to mean that there are still unresolved problems, not that the deal is off. He responds by asking how his company can help solve the problems. The Japanese, believing he has sent the message that there will be no sale, is mystified by the response.

Communication does not necessarily result in understanding. Cross-cultural communication continually involves misunderstanding caused by misperception, misinterpretation, and misevaluation. When the sender of a message comes from one culture and the receiver from another, the chances of accurately transmitting a message are low. Foreigners see, interpret, and evaluate things differently, and consequently act upon them differently. In approaching cross-cultural situations, one should therefore assume difference until similarity is proven. It is also important to recognize that all behavior makes sense through the eyes of the person behaving and that logic and rationale are culturally relative. In cross-cultural situations, labeling behavior as bizarre usually reflects culturally based misperception, misinterpretation, and misevaluation; rarely does it reflect intentional malice or pathologically motivated behavior.

Culturally "Bizarre" Behavior:

Only in the Eyes of the Beholder

While in Thailand a Canadian expatriate's car was hit by a Thai motorist who had crossed over the double line while passing another vehicle. After failing to establish that the fault lay with the Thai driver, the Canadian flagged down a policeman. After several minutes of seemingly futile discussion, the Canadian pointed out the double line in the middle of the road and asked the policeman directly, "What do these lines signify?" The policeman replied, "They indicate the center of the road and are there so I can establish just how far the accident is from that point." The Canadian was silent. It had never occurred to him that the double line might not mean "no passing allowed."

Unwritten rules reflect a culture's interpretation of its surroundings. A foreign columnist for the English-language *Bangkok Post* once proclaimed that the unwritten traffic rule in Thailand is: "When there are more than three cars in front of you at a stop sign or intersection, start your own line!" This contravenes the Western stay-in-line ethic, of course, but it effectively portrays, albeit in slightly exaggerated fashion, a fairly consistent form of behavior at intersections in Thailand. And it drives non-Thais crazy!(14)

CROSS-CULTURAL MISPERCEPTION

Do the French and the Chinese see the world in the same way? No. Do Venezuelans and Ghanaians see the world in the same way? Again, no.

No two national groups *see* the world in exactly the same way. Perception is the process by which each individual selects, organizes, and evaluates stimuli from the external environment to provide meaningful experiences for himself or herself (2;12;16;18). For example, when Mexican children simultaneously viewed tachistoscopic pictures of a bullfight and a baseball game, they only remembered seeing the bullfight. Looking through the same tachistoscope, American children only remembered seeing the baseball game (3). Similarly, adult card players, when shown cards by researchers, failed to see black hearts and diamonds, or red clubs and spades.

Why didn't the children see both pictures? Why did the adults fail to see the unexpected playing card colors? The answer lies in the nature of perception. Perceptual patterns are neither innate nor absolute. They are selective, learned, culturally determined, consistent, and inaccurate.

▸ Perception is *selective.* At any one time there are too many stimuli in the environment for us to observe. Therefore, we screen out most of what we see, hear, taste, and feel. We screen out the overload (5) and allow only selected information through our perceptual screen to our conscious mind.

▸ Perceptual patterns are *learned.* We are not born seeing the world in one particular way. Our experience teaches us to perceive the world in certain ways.

▸ Perception is *culturally determined.* We learn to see the world in a certain way based on our cultural background.

▸ Perception tends to remain *constant.* Once we see something in a particular way, we continue to see it that way.

▸ *We therefore see things that do not exist, and do not see things that do exist.* Our interests, values, and culture act as filters and lead us to distort, block, and even create what we choose to see and hear. We perceive what we expect to perceive. We perceive things according to what we have been trained to see, according to our cultural map.

For example, read the following sentence:

FINISHED FILES ARE THE RESULT OF YEARS
OF SCIENTIFIC STUDY COMBINED WITH THE
EXPERIENCE OF YEARS

Now, quickly count the number of F's in the sentence. Most non-native English speakers see all six F's. Many native English speakers only see three F's, they do not see the F's in the word *of* because *of* is not an important word in understanding the sentence. We selectively see those words that are important according to our cultural conditioning (in this case, our linguistic conditioning). Once we see a phenomenon in a particular way, we usually continue to see it in that way. Once we stop seeing *of*s, we do not see them again (even when we look for them); we do not see things that do exist. One particularly astute manager at Canadian National railways makes daily use of perceptual filters to her firm's advantage. She gives reports written in English to bilingual Francophones to proofread and those written in French to bilingual Anglophones. She uses the fact that the English secretaries can "see" more errors—especially small typographical errors—in French and the French secretaries can "see" more errors in English.

The distorting impact of perceptual filters causes us to see things that do not exist. This phenomenon was powerfully demonstrated a number of years ago in a training session for American executives. The executives were asked to study the picture shown in Figure 3–2 and then

FIGURE 3–2 Impact of Perceptual Filters
SOURCE: Projected picture from experiment on accuracy of communication from the Anti-Defamation League of B'nai B'rith Rumor Clinic. As shown in Robert Bolton, *People Skills* (Englewood Cliffs, New Jersey: Prentice-Hall, Inc., 1979), p. 74. Copyright © 1979 by Simon & Schuster, Inc.

describe it to a colleague who had not seen the picture. The first colleague then attempted to describe it to a second colleague who had not seen the picture, and so on. Finally, the fifth colleague described his perception of the picture to the group of executives and compared it with the original picture. Among the numerous distortions, the executives consistently described the black and the white man as fighting; the knife as being in the hands of the black man; and the white man as wearing a business suit and the black man as wearing laborer's overalls. Clearly the (inaccurate) stereotypes of blacks (poorer, working class, and more likely to commit crimes) and of whites (richer, upper class, and less likely to be involved in violent crime) radically altered the executives' perceptions and totally changed the meaning of the picture (1). The executives' perceptual filters allowed them to see things that did not exist and to miss seeing things that did exist.

CROSS-CULTURAL MISINTERPRETATION

Interpretation occurs when an individual gives meaning to observations and their relationships; it is the process of making sense out of perceptions. Interpretation organizes our experience to guide our behavior. Based on our experience, we make assumptions about our perceptions so we will not have to rediscover meanings each time we encounter similar situations. For example, we make assumptions about how doors work, based on our experience of entering and leaving rooms; thus we do not have to relearn each time we have to open a door. Similarly, when we smell smoke, we generally assume there is a fire. We do not have to stop and wonder if the smoke indicates a fire or a flood. Our consistent patterns of interpretation help us to act appropriately and quickly within our day-to-day world.

Categories

Since we are constantly bombarded with more stimuli than we can absorb and more perceptions than we can keep distinct, we only perceive those images that may be meaningful. We group perceived images into familiar categories that help to simplify our environment, become the basis for our interpretations, and allow us to function in an otherwise overly complex world. For example, as a driver approaching an intersection, I may or may not notice the number of children in the back seat of the car next to me, but I will notice whether the traffic light is red or green (selective perception). If the light is red, I automatically place it in the category of all red traffic signals (categorization). This time, like prior times, I stop (behavior based on interpretation). Although people are capable of distinguishing thousands of different colors, I do not take the time to notice if the red light in Istanbul is brighter or duller than the one in Singapore or more orange or more purple than the one in Nairobi; I just stop. Categorization helps me to distinguish what is most important in my environment and to behave accordingly.

Categories of perceived images become ineffective when we place people and things in the wrong group. Cross-cultural miscategorization occurs when I use my home country categories to make sense out of foreign situations. For example, a Korean businessman entered a client's office in Stockholm and encountered a woman behind the desk. Assuming that she was a secretary, he announced that he wanted to see Mr. Silferbrand. The woman responded by saying that the secretary would be happy to help him. The Korean became confused. In assuming that most women are secretaries rather than managers, he had misinterpreted the situation and acted inappropriately. His category makes sense because most women in Korean offices are secretaries. But it proved counterproductive since this particular Swedish woman was not a secretary.

Stereotypes

Stereotyping involves a form of categorization that organizes our experience and guides our behavior toward ethnic and national groups. Stereotypes never describe individual behavior; rather, they describe the behavioral norm for members of a particular group. For example, the stereotypes of English and French businesspeople, as analyzed by Intercultural Management Associates in Paris, are described as follows:

We have found that to every set of negative stereotypes distinguishing the British and French there corresponds a particular values divergence that,

71

when recognized, can prove an extraordinary resource. To illustrate: The French, in describing the British as "perfidious," "hypocritical," and "vague," are in fact describing the Englishman's typical lack of a general model or theory and his preference for a more pragmatic, evolutionary approach. This fact is hard for the Frenchman to believe, let alone accept as a viable alternative, until, working alongside one another, the Frenchman comes to see that there is usually no ulterior motive behind the Englishman's vagueness but rather a capacity to think aloud and adapt to circumstances. For his part, the Englishman comes to see that, far from being "distant," "superior," or "out of touch with reality," the Frenchman's concern for a general model or theory is what lends vision, focus, and cohesion to an enterprise or project, as well as leadership and much needed authority (7).

Stereotypes, like other forms of categories, can be helpful or harmful depending on how we use them. Effective stereotyping allows people to understand and act appropriately in new situations. A stereotype can be helpful when it is

- ▶ *Consciously held.* The person should be aware that he or she is describing a group norm rather than the characteristics of a specific individual.
- ▶ *Descriptive* rather than evaluative. The stereotype should describe what people from this group will probably be like and not evaluate those people as good or bad.
- ▶ *Accurate.* The stereotype should accurately describe the norm for the group to which the person belongs.
- ▶ *The first best guess* about a group prior to having direct information about the specific person or persons involved.
- ▶ *Modified,* based on further observation and experience with the actual people and situations.

A subconsciously held stereotype is difficult to modify or discard even after we collect real information about a person, because it is often thought to reflect reality. If a subconscious stereotype also inaccurately evaluates a person or situation, we are likely to maintain an inappropriate, ineffective, and frequently harmful guide to reality. For example, assume that I subconsciously hold the stereotype that Anglophone Quebecois refuse to learn French and that therefore they should have no rights within the province (an inaccurate, evaluative stereotype). I then meet a monolingual Anglophone and say, "See, I told you that Anglophones aren't willing to speak French! They don't deserve to have rights here." I next meet a bilingual Anglophone and conclude, "He must be American because Canadian Anglophones always refuse to learn French." Instead of questioning, modifying, or discarding my stereotype ("Some Anglophone Canadians speak French"), I alter reality to fit the stereotype ("He must be American"). Stereotypes increase effectiveness only when used as a *first best guess* about a person or situation prior to having direct information. They never help when adhered to rigidly.

Indrei Ratiu (17), in his work with INSEAD (Institut Européen d'Administration des Affaires—European Institute of Business Administration) and London Business School, found that managers ranked "most internationally effective" by their colleagues altered their stereotypes to fit the actual people involved, whereas managers ranked "least internationally effective" continued to maintain their stereotypes even in the face of contradictory information. For example, internationally effective managers, prior to their first visit to Germany, might stereotype Germans as being extremely task oriented. Upon arriving and meeting a very friendly and lazy Herr Schmidt, they would alter their description to say that most Germans appear extremely task oriented, but Herr Schmidt seems friendly and lazy. Months later, the most internationally effective managers would only be able to say that some Germans appear very task oriented, while others seem quite relationship oriented (friendly); it all depends on the person and the situation. In this instance, the stereotype is used as a first best guess about the group's behavior prior to meeting any individuals from the group. As time goes on, it is modified or discarded entirely; information about each individual supersedes the group stereotype. By contrast, the least internationally effective managers maintain their stereotypes. They assume that the contradictory evidence in Herr Schmidt's case represents an exception, and they continue to believe that *all* Germans are highly task oriented. In drawing conclusions too quickly on the basis of insufficient information—premature closure (12)—their stereotypes become self-fulfilling (19).

Canadian psychologist Donald Taylor (4;5;21) found that most people maintain their stereotypes even in the face of contradictory evidence. Taylor asked English and French Canadians to listen to one of three tape recordings of a French Canadian describing himself. In the first version, the French Canadian used the Francophone stereotype and described himself as religious, proud, sensitive, and expressive. In the second version, he used neutral terms to describe himself. In the third version, he used terms to describe himself that contradicted the stereotype, such as not religious, humble, unexpressive, and conservative. After having listened to one of the three versions, the participants were asked to describe the Francophone on the tape (not Francophones in general). Surprisingly, people who listened to each of the three versions used the same stereotypic terms—religious, proud, sensitive, and expressive—even when the voice on the tape had conveyed the opposite information. People evidently maintain stereotypes even in the face of contradictory information.

To be effective, international managers must therefore be aware of cultural stereotypes and learn to set them aside when faced with contradictory evidence. They cannot *pretend* not to stereotype.

If stereotyping is so useful as an initial guide to reality, why do people malign it? Why do parents and teachers constantly admonish children not to stereotype? Why do sophisticated managers rarely admit to stereotyping, even though each of us stereotypes every day? The answer is that we have failed to accept stereotyping as a natural process and have consequently failed to learn to use it to our advantage. For years we have viewed stereotyping as a form of primitive thinking, as an unnecessary simplification of reality. We have also viewed stereotyping as immoral: stereotypes can be inappropriate judgments of individuals based on inaccurate descriptions of groups. It is true that labeling people from a certain ethnic group as "bad" is immoral, but grouping individuals into categories is neither good nor bad—it simply reduces a complex reality to manageable dimensions. Negative views of stereotyping simply cloud our ability to understand people's actual behavior and impair our awareness of our own stereotypes. *Everyone* stereotypes.

In conclusion, some people stereotype effectively and others do not. Stereotypes become counterproductive when we place people in the wrong groups, when we incorrectly describe the group norm, when we inappropriately evaluate the group or category, when we confuse the stereotype with the description of a particular individual, and when we fail to modify the stereotype based on our actual observations and experience.

Sources of Misinterpretation

Misinterpretation can be caused by inaccurate perceptions of a person or situation that arise when what actually exists is not seen. It can be caused by an inaccurate interpretation of what is seen; that is, by using *my* meanings to make sense out of *your* reality. An example of this type of misinterpretation (or misattribution) comes from an encounter with an Austrian businessman.

> I meet my Austrian client for the sixth time in as many months. He greets me as Herr Smith. Categorizing him as a businessman, I interpret his very formal behavior to mean that he does not like me or is uninterested in developing a closer relationship with me. (North American attribution: people who maintain formal behavior after the first few meetings do so because they dislike or distrust the associates so treated.) In fact, I have misinterpreted his behavior. I have used the norms for North American business behavior, which are more informal and demonstrative (I would say "Good morning, Fritz," not "Good morning, Herr Ranschburg"), to interpret the Austrian's more formal behavior ("Good morning, Herr Smith").

Culture strongly influences, and in many cases determines, our interpretations. Both the categories and the meanings we attach to them are based on our cultural background. Sources of cross-cultural misinterpretation include subconscious cultural "blinders," a lack of cultural self-awareness, projected similarity, and parochialism.

Subconscious Cultural Blinders. Because most interpretation goes on at a subconscious level, we lack awareness of the assumptions we make and their cultural basis. Our home culture reality never forces us to examine our assumptions or the extent to which they are culturally based, because we share our cultural assumptions with most other citizens of our country. All we know is that things do not work as smoothly or logically when we work outside our own culture as when we work with people more similar to ourselves. For example:

> A Canadian conducting business in Kuwait is surprised when his meeting with a high ranking official is not held in a closed office and is constantly interrupted. Using the Canadian-based cultural assumptions that (a) im-

75

portant people have large private offices with secretaries to monitor the flow of people into the office, and (b) important business takes precedence over less important business and is therefore not interrupted, the Canadian interprets the Kuwaiti's open office and constant interruptions to mean that the official is neither as high ranking nor as interested in conducting the business at hand as he had previously thought. The Canadian's interpretation of the office environment leads him to lose interest in working with the Kuwaiti.

The problem is that the Canadian's interpretation derives from his own North American norms, not from Middle Eastern cultural norms. The Kuwaiti may well have been a high-ranking official who was very interested in doing business. The Canadian will never know.

Cases of subconscious cross-cultural misinterpretation occur frequently. For example a Soviet poet, after lecturing at American universities for two months, said, "Attempts to please an American audience are doomed in advance, because out of twenty listeners five may hold one point of view, seven another, and eight may have none at all" (10). The Soviet poet confused Americans' freedom of thought and speech with his ability to please them. He assumed that one can only please an audience if all members hold the same opinion. Another example of well-meant misinterpretation comes from the United States Office of Education's advice to teachers of newly arrived Vietnamese refugee students (22):

> Students' participation was discouraged in Vietnamese schools by liberal doses of corporal punishment, and students were conditioned to sit rigidly and speak out only when spoken to. This background . . . makes speaking freely in class hard for a Vietnamese student. Therefore, don't mistake shyness for apathy.

Perhaps the extent to which this is a culturally based interpretation becomes clearer if we imagine the opposite advice the Vietnamese Ministry of Education might give to Vietnamese teachers receiving American children for the first time.

> Students' proper respect for teachers was discouraged by a loose order and students were conditioned to chat all the time and to behave in other disorderly ways. This background makes proper and respectful behavior in

class hard for an American student. Therefore, do not mistake rudeness for lack of reverence.

Lack of Cultural Self-Awareness.   Although we think that the major obstacle in international business is in understanding the foreigner, the greater difficulty involves becoming aware of our own cultural conditioning. As anthropologist Edward Hall has explained, "What is known least well, and is therefore in the poorest position to be studied, is what is closest to oneself (8:45)." We are generally least aware of our own cultural characteristics and are quite surprised when we hear foreigners' descriptions of us. For example, many Americans are surprised to discover that they are seen by foreigners as hurried, overly law-abiding, very hard working, extremely explicit, and overly inquisitive (see the example that follows). Many American businesspeople were equally surprised by a *Newsweek* survey reporting the characteristics most and least frequently associated with Americans (see Table 3-1). Asking a foreign national to describe businesspeople from your country is a powerful way to see yourself as others see you.

Cross-Cultural Awareness

Americans as Others See Them

People from other countries are often puzzled and intrigued by the intricacies and enigmas of American culture. Below is a selection of actual observations by foreigners visiting the United States. As you read them, ask yourself in each case if the observer is accurate, and how you would explain the trait in question.

India "Americans seem to be in a perpetual hurry. Just watch the way they walk down the street. They never allow themselves the leisure to enjoy life; there are too many things to do."

Kenya "Americans appear to us rather distant. They are not really as close to other people — even fellow Americans — as Americans overseas tend to portray. It's almost as if an American says, 'I won't let you get too close to me.' It's like building a wall."

Turkey   "Once we were out in a rural area in the middle of nowhere and saw an American come to a stop sign. Though he could see in both directions for miles and no traffic was coming, he still stopped!"

TABLE 3-1 How Others See Americans

				Industrious

Characteristics Most Often Associated with Americans* by the Populations of

France	Japan	West Germany	Great Britain	Brazil	Mexico
Industrious	Nationalistic	Energetic	Friendly	Intelligent	Industrious
Energetic	Friendly	Inventive	Self-indulgent	Inventive	Intelligent
Inventive	Decisive	Friendly	Energetic	Energetic	Inventive
Decisive	Rude	Sophisticated	Industrious	Industrious	Decisive
Friendly	Self-indulgent	Intelligent	Nationalistic	Greedy	Greedy

Characteristics Least Often Associated with Americans* by the Same Populations

Lazy	Industrious	Lazy	Lazy	Lazy	Lazy
Rude	Lazy	Sexy	Sophisticated	Self-indulgent	Honest
Honest	Honest	Greedy	Sexy	Sexy	Rude
Sophisticated	Sexy	Rude	Decisive	Sophisticated	Sexy

SOURCE: *Newsweek* (July 11, 1983), p. 50, copyright © 1981 by Newsweek, Inc. All rights reserved, reprinted by permission.

*From a list of fourteen characteristics.

Colombia "The tendency in the United States to think that life is only work hits you in the face. Work seems to be the one type of motivation."

Indonesia "In the United States everything has to be talked about and analyzed. Even the littlest thing has to be 'Why, Why, Why?'. I get a headache from such persistent questions."

Ethiopia "The American is very explicit; he wants a 'yes' or 'no.' If someone tries to speak figuratively, the American is confused."

Iran "The first time . . . my [American] professor told me, 'I don't know the answer, I will have to look it up,' I was shocked. I asked myself, 'Why is he teaching me?' In my country a professor would give the wrong answer rather than admit ignorance."[1]

Another very revealing way to understand the norms and values of a culture involves listening to common sayings and proverbs. What does a society recommend, and what does it avoid? Following is a list of a number of the most common North American proverbs and the values each teaches.

North American Values: Proverbs

It is evidently much more potent in teaching practicality, for example, to say, "Don't cry over spilt milk" than, "You'd better learn to be practical." North Americans have heard this axiom hundreds of times, and it has made its point. Listed below are North American proverbs on the left and the values they seem to be teaching on the right.[2]

Proverb	Value
Cleanliness is next to godliness.	*Cleanliness*
A penny saved is a penny earned.	*Thriftiness*
Time is money.	*Time Thriftiness*
Don't cry over spilt milk.	*Practicality*
Waste not; want not.	*Frugality*
Early to bed, early to rise, makes one healthy, wealthy and wise.	*Diligence; Work Ethic*
God helps those who help themselves.	*Initiative*

It's not whether you win or lose, but how you play the game.	*Good Sportsmanship*
A man's home is his castle.	*Privacy; Value of Personal Property*
No rest for the wicked.	*Guilt; Work Ethic*
You've made your bed, now sleep in it.	*Responsibility*
Don't count your chickens before they're hatched.	*Practicality*
A bird in the hand is worth two in the bush.	*Practicality*
The squeaky wheel gets the grease.	*Aggressiveness*
Might makes right.	*Superiority of Physical Power*
There's more than one way to skin a cat.	*Originality; Determination*
A stitch in time saves nine.	*Timeliness of Action*
All that glitters is not gold.	*Wariness*
Clothes make the man.	*Concern of Physical Appearance*
If at first you don't succeed, try, try again.	*Persistence; Work Ethic*
Take care of today, and tomorrow will take care of itself.	*Preparation of Future*
Laugh, and the world laughs with you; weep, and you weep alone.	*Pleasant Outward Appearance*

To the extent that we can begin to see ourselves clearly through the eyes of foreigners, we can begin to modify our behavior, emphasizing our most appropriate and effective characteristics and minimizing those least helpful. To the extent that we are culturally self-aware, we can begin to predict the effect our behavior will have on others.

Projected Similarity. Projected similarity refers to the assumption that people are more similar to you than they actually are, or that a situation is more similar to yours when in fact it is not. Projecting similarity reflects both a natural and a common process. American researchers Burger and Bass (6) worked with groups of managers from fourteen different countries. They asked each manager to describe the work and life goals of a colleague from another country. As shown in Figure 3–3, in every case the managers assumed that their foreign col-

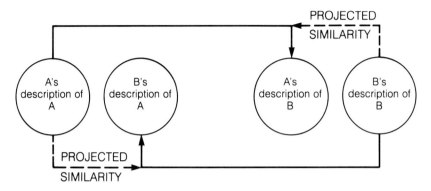

FIGURE 3-3 Projected Similarity

leagues were more like themselves than they actually were. Projected similarity involves assuming, imagining, and actually perceiving similarity when differences exist. Projected similarity particularly handicaps people in cross-cultural situations. As a South African, I assume that my Greek colleague is more South African than he actually is. As an Egyptian, I assume that my Chilean colleague is more similar to me than she actually is. When I act based on this assumed similarity, I often find that I have acted inappropriately and thus ineffectively.

At the base of projected similarity is a subconscious parochialism. I assume that there is only one way to be: my way. I assume that there is only one way to see the world: my way. I therefore view other people in reference to me and to my way of viewing the world. People may fall into an

> illusion of understanding while being unaware of . . . [their] misunderstandings. "I understand you perfectly but you don't understand me" is an expression typical of such a situation. Or all communicating parties may fall into a collective illusion of mutual understanding. In such a situation, each party may wonder later why other parties do not live up to the "agreement" they had reached (13:3).

Most international managers do not see themselves as parochial. They believe that as world travelers they are able to see the foreigner's point of view. This is not always true.

81

EXAMPLE

When a Danish manager works with a Saudi and the Saudi states that the plant will be completed on time, "En shah allah" ("If God is willing"), the Dane rarely believes that God's will is really going to influence the construction progress. He continues to see the world from his parochial Danish perspective and assumes that "En shah allah" is just an excuse for not getting the work done, or is meaningless altogether.

Similarly, when Balinese workers' families refuse to use birth control methods, explaining that it will break the cycle of reincarnation, few Western managers really consider that there is a possibility that they too will be reborn a number of times. Instead, they assume that the Balinese do not understand or are afraid of Western medicine.

While it is important to understand and respect the foreigner's point of view, it is not necessary to accept or adopt it. A rigid adherence to our own belief system is a form of parochialism, and parochialism underlies projected similarity.

One of the best exercises for developing empathy and reducing parochialism and projected similarity is *role reversal*. Imagine that you are a foreign businessperson. Imagine the type of family you come from, the number of brothers and sisters you have, the social and economic conditions you grew up with, the type of education you received, the ways in which you chose your profession and position, the ways in which you were introduced to your spouse, your goals in working for your organization, and your life goals. Asking these questions forces you to see the other person as he or she really is, and not as a mere reflection of yourself. It forces you to see both the similarities and the differences, and not to imagine similarities when differences actually exist. Moreover, role reversal encourages highly task-oriented businesspeople, such as Americans, to see the foreigner as a whole person rather than someone with a position and a set of skills needed to accomplish a particular task.

CROSS-CULTURAL MISEVALUATION

Even more than perception and interpretation, cultural conditioning strongly affects evaluation. Evaluation involves judging whether someone or something is good or bad. Cross-culturally, we use our own culture as a standard of measurement, judging that which is like our own culture as normal and good and that which is different as abnormal and bad. Our own culture becomes a *self-reference criterion:* since no other culture is identical to our own, we judge all other cultures as inferior. Evaluation rarely helps in trying to understand or communicate with people from another culture. The consequences of misevaluation are exemplified in the following:

> A Swiss executive waits more than an hour past the appointed time for his Latin colleague to arrive and sign a supply contract. In his impatience, he concludes that Latins must be lazy and totally unconcerned about business. He has misevaluated his colleague by negatively comparing him to his own cultural standards. Implicitly, he has labeled his own group's behavior as good (Swiss arrive on time and that is good) and the other group's behavior as bad (Latins do not arrive on time and that is bad).

COMMUNICATION: GETTING THEIR MEANING, NOT JUST THEIR WORDS

Effective cross-cultural communication is possible, but international managers cannot approach it in the same way as do domestic managers. First, effective international managers "know that they don't know." They assume difference until similarity is proven rather than assuming similarity until difference is proven.

Second, in attempting to understand their foreign colleagues, effective international managers emphasize description, by observing what is actually said and done, rather than interpreting or evaluating it. Describing a situation is the most accurate way to gather information about it. Interpretation and evaluation, unlike description, are based more on the observer's culture and background than on the observed situation. To that extent, my interpretations and evaluations tell me more about myself than about the situation. Although managers, as decision makers, must evaluate people (e.g., performance appraisals) and situations (e.g., project assessments) in terms of organizational standards and objectives, effective international managers delay judgment until they have had sufficient time to observe and interpret the situation from the perspective of all cultures involved.

Third, when attempting to understand or interpret a foreign situation, effective international managers try to see it through the eyes of their foreign colleagues. This role reversal limits the myopia of viewing situations strictly from one's own perspective.

Fourth, once effective international managers develop an explanation for a situation, they treat the explanation as a guess (as a hypothesis to be tested) and not as a certainty. They systematically check with other foreign and home country colleagues to make sure that their guesses — their interpretations — are plausible. This checking process allows them to converge meanings — to delay accepting their interpretations of the situation until they have confirmed them with others.

Understanding: Converging Meanings

There are many ways to increase the chances for accurately understanding foreigners. The excerpt that follows suggests what to do when business colleagues are not native speakers of your language. Each technique is based on presenting the message through multiple channels (for example, stating your position and showing a graph to summarize the same position), paraphrasing to check if the foreigner has understood your meaning (and not just your words), and converging meanings (always double-checking with a second person that you communicated what you intended).

What Do I Do If They Do Not Speak My Language?

VERBAL BEHAVIOR
▸ *Clear, slow speech.* Enunciate each word. Do not use colloquial expressions.
▸ *Repetition.* Repeat each important idea using different words to explain the same concept.
▸ *Simple sentences.* Avoid compound, long sentences.
▸ *Active verbs.* Avoid passive verbs.

NON-VERBAL BEHAVIOR
▸ *Visual restatements.* Use as many visual restatements as possible, such as pictures, graphs, tables, and slides.
▸ *Gestures.* Use more facial and hand gestures to emphasize the meaning of words.
▸ *Demonstration.* Act out as many themes as possible.

▶ *Pauses.* Pause more frequently.

▶ *Summaries.* Hand out written summaries of your verbal presentation.

ATTRIBUTION

▶ *Silence.* When there is a silence, wait. Do not jump in to fill the silence. The other person is probably just thinking more slowly in the non-native language or translating.

▶ *Intelligence.* Do not equate poor grammar and mispronunciation with lack of intelligence; it is usually a sign of second language use.

▶ *Differences.* If unsure, assume difference, not similarity.

COMPREHENSION

▶ *Understanding.* Do not just assume that they understand; assume that they do not understand.   *even if they not* *[handwritten]*

▶ *Checking comprehension.* Have colleagues repeat their understanding of the material back to you. Do not simply ask if they understand or not. Let them explain what they understand to you.

DESIGN

▶ *Breaks.* Take more frequent breaks. Second language comprehension is exhausting.

▶ *Small modules.* Divide the material into smaller modules.

▶ *Longer time frame.* Allocate more time for each module than usual in a monolingual program.

MOTIVATION

▶ *Encouragement.* Verbally and nonverbally encourage and reinforce speaking by non-native language participants.

▶ *Drawing out.* Explicitly draw out marginal and passive participants.

▶ *Reinforcement.* Do not embarrass novice speakers.[3]

Standing Back from Yourself

Perhaps the most difficult skill in cross-cultural communication involves standing back from yourself, or being aware that you do not know everything, that a situation may not make sense, that your guesses may be wrong, and that the ambiguity in the situation may continue. In this sense the ancient Roman dictum "knowledge is power" becomes true. In knowing yourself, you gain power over your perceptions and reactions; you can control your own behavior and your reactions to others' behavior. Cross-cultural awareness complements in-depth self-awareness. A lack of self-awareness negates the usefulness of cross-cultural awareness.

One of the most poignant examples of the powerful interplay between description, interpretation, evaluation, and empathy involves a Scottish businessman's relationship with a Japanese colleague. The following story recounts the Scottish businessman's experience.

Cross-Cultural Communication

Japanese Pickles and Mattresses, Incorporated

It was my first visit to Japan. As a gastronomic adventurer, and because I believe cuisine is one route which is freely available and highly effective as a first step towards a closer understanding of another country, I was disappointed on my first evening when the Japanese offered me a Western meal.

As tactfully as possible I suggested that some time during my stay I would like to try a Japanese menu, if that could be arranged without inconvenience. There was some small reluctance evident on the part of my hosts (due of course to their thought that I was being very polite asking for Japanese food which I didn't really like, so to be good hosts they had to politely find a way of not having me eat it!). But eventually, by an elegantly progressive route starting with Western food with a slightly Japanese bias through to genuine Japanese food, my hosts were convinced that I really wanted to eat Japanese style and was not "posing."

From then on they became progressively more enthusiastic in suggesting the more exotic Japanese dishes, and I guess I graduated when, after an excellent meal one night (apart from the Japanese pickles) on which I had lavished praise, they said, "Do you like Japanese pickles?" To this, without preamble, I said, "No!," to which reply, with great laughter all round, they responded, "Nor do we!"

During this gastronomic getting-together week, I had also been trying to persuade them that I really did wish to stay in traditional Japanese hotels rather than the very Westernized ones my hosts had selected because they thought I would prefer my "normal" lifestyle. (I should add that at this time traditional Japanese hotels were still available and often cheaper than, say, the Osaka Hilton.)

Anyway, after the pickles joke it was suddenly announced that Japanese hotels could be arranged. For the remaining two weeks of my stay, as I toured the major cities, on most occasions a traditional Japanese hotel was substituted for the Western one on my original schedule.

Many of you will know that a traditional Japanese room has no furniture except a low table and a flower arrangement. The "bed" is a mattress produced just before you retire from a concealed cupboard, accompanied by a cereal-packed pillow.

One memorable evening my host and I had finished our meal together in "my" room. I was expecting him to shortly make his "goodnight" and retire, as he had been doing all week, to his own room.

However, he stayed unusually long and was, to me, obviously in some sort of emotional crisis. Finally, he blurted out, with great embarrassment, "Can I sleep with you?!"

As they say in the novels, at this point I went very still! My mind was racing through all the sexual taboos and prejudices my own upbringing had instilled, and I can still very clearly recall how I analyzed: "I'm bigger than he is so I can fight him off, but then he's probably an expert in the martial arts, but on the other hand he's shown no signs of being gay up until now and he is my host and there is a lot of business at risk and there's no such thing as rape, et cetera. . . . !

It seemed a hundred years, though it was only a few seconds, before I said, feeling as if I was pulling the trigger in Russian roulette, "Yes, sure."

Who said that the Orientals are inscrutable? The look of relief that followed my reply was obvious. Then he looked worried and concerned again, and said, "Are you sure?"

I reassured him and he called in the maid, who fetched his mattress from his room and laid it on the floor alongside mine. We both went to bed and slept all night without any physical interaction.

Later I learned that for the traditional Japanese one of the greatest compliments you can be paid is for the host to ask, "Can I sleep with you?" This goes back to the ancient feudal times, when life was cheap, and what the invitation really said was, "I trust you with my life. I do not think that you will kill me while I sleep. You are my true friend."

To have said "No" to the invitation would have been an insult — "I don't trust you not to kill me while I sleep" — or, at the very least, my host would have been acutely embarrassed because he had taken the initiative. If I refused because I had failed to perceive the invitation as a compliment, he would have been out of countenance on two grounds: the insult to him in the traditional context and the embarrassment he would have caused me by "forcing" a negative, uncomprehending response from me.

As it turned out, the outcome was superb. He and I were now "blood brothers," as it were. His assessment of me as being "ready for

Japanization" had been correct and his obligations under ancient Japanese custom had been fulfilled. I had totally misinterpreted his intentions through my own cultural conditioning. It was sheer luck, or luck plus a gut feeling that I'd gotten it wrong, that caused me to make the correct response to his extremely complimentary and committed invitation.[4]

SUMMARY

Cross-cultural communication confronts us with limits to our perceptions, our interpretations, and our evaluations. Cross-cultural perspectives tend to render everything relative and slightly uncertain. Entering a foreign culture is tantamount to knowing the words without knowing the music, or knowing the music without knowing the beat. Our natural tendencies lead us back to our prior experience: our default option becomes the familiarity of our own culture, thus precluding our accurate understanding of others' cultures.

Strategies to overcome our natural parochial tendencies exist: with care, the default option can be avoided. We can learn to see, understand, and control our own cultural conditioning. In facing foreign cultures, we can emphasize description rather than interpretation or evaluation, and thus minimize self-fulfilling stereotypes and premature closure. We can recognize and use our stereotypes as guides rather than rejecting them as unsophisticated simplifications. Effective cross-cultural communication presupposes the interplay of alternative realities: it rejects the actual or potential domination of one reality over another.

QUESTIONS FOR REFLECTION

1. The most effective international managers use stereotypes. What are some of the ways that you can use stereotypes to your advantage when working with people from other countries?

2. Today many managers must work with people from other cultures, both at home and when traveling abroad. What are some of the ways that your organization could train people to communicate more effectively with foreigners?

3. What stereotypes do you have concerning lawyers? How about South Africans? If you had an appointment with a South African lawyer, what would you expect and how would you prepare for the meeting?

4. In seeking to understand the importance of nonverbal communication, we must start by examining ourselves. List four examples of nonverbal communication that you commonly use and what each means to you. Then indicate how each might be misinterpreted by someone from a foreign culture.

5. List four examples of nonverbal communication that are used by managers in other parts of the world but not in your country. Indicate how each might be misinterpreted by colleagues from your country.

NOTES

1. John P. Feig and G. Blair, *There Is a Difference*, 2d ed. (Washington, D.C.: Meridian House International, 1980).

2. L. Robert Kohls, *Survival Kit for Overseas Living* (Yarmouth, Me: Intercultural Press, Inc., 1979), pp. 30–31.

3. Based on Nancy J. Adler and Moses N. Kiggundu, "Awareness at the Crossroad: Designing Translator-Based Training Programs," in D. Landis and R. Brislin, *Handbook of Intercultural Training: Issues in Training Methodology*, vol. II (New York: Pergamon Press, 1983), pp. 124–150.

4. A Scottish executive participating in the 1979 Managerial Skills for International Business Program at INSEAD, in Fontainebleau, France.

REFERENCES

1. Anti-Defamation League of the B'nai B'rith Rumor Clinic as cited in Robert Bolton, *People Skills* (Englewood Cliffs, N.J.: Prentice-Hall, 1979), pp. 73–74.

2. Asch, S. "Forming Impressions of Persons," *Journal of Abnormal and Social Psychology*, vol. 40 (1946), pp. 258–290.

3. Bagby, J. W. "Dominance in Binocular Rivalry in Mexico and the United States," in I. Al-Issa and W. Dennis, eds., *Cross-Cultural Studies of Behavior* (New York: Holt, Rinehart and Winston, 1970), pp. 49–56. Originally in *Journal of Abnormal and Social Psychology*, vol. 54 (1957), pp. 331–334.

4. Berry, J.; Kalin, R.; and Taylor, D. "Multiculturalism and Ethnic Atti-

tudes in Canada," in *Multiculturalism as State Policy* (Ottawa: Government of Canada, 1976).

5. Berry, J.; Kalin, R.; and Taylor, D. *Multiculturalism and Ethnic Attitudes in Canada* (Ottawa: Minister of Supply and Services, 1977).

6. Burger, P., and Bass, B. M. *Assessment of Managers: An International Comparison* (New York: Free Press, 1979).

7. Gancel, C., and Ratiu, I. Internal document, Inter Cultural Management Associates, Paris, France, 1984.

8. Hall, E. T. *Beyond Culture.* (Garden City, N.Y.: Anchor Press/Doubleday and Company, 1976). Also see E. T. Hall's *The Silent Language* (Doubleday, 1959, and Anchor Books, 1973) and *The Hidden Dimension* (Doubleday, 1966, and Anchor Books, 1969).

9. Ho, A. "Unlucky Numbers are Locked out of the Chamber," *South China Morning Post* (December 26, 1988), p. 1.

10. Kanungo, R. N. *Biculturalism and Management* (Ontario: Butterworth, 1980).

11. Korotich, V. "Taming of a Desert of the Mind," *Atlas* (June 1977).

12. Lau, J. B., and Jelinek, M. "Perception and Management," in *Behavior in Organizations: An Experiential Approach* (Homewood, Ill.: Richard D. Irwin, 1984), pp. 213–220.

13. Maruyama, M. "Paradigms and Communication," *Technological Forecasting and Social Change*, vol. 6 (1974), pp. 3–32.

14. Miles, M. *Adaptation to a Foreign Environment* (Ottawa: Canadian International Development Agency, to be published).

15. Miller, J. G. "Adjusting to Overloads of Information," in The Association for Research in Nervous and Mental Disease, *Disorders of Communication*, vol. 42 (Research Publications, A.R.N.M.D., 1964).

16. Prekel, T. "Multi-Cultural Communication: A Challenge to Managers," paper delivered at the International Convention of the American Business Communication Association, New York, November 21, 1983.

17. Ratui, I. "Thinking Internationally: A Comparison of How International Executives Learn," *International Studies of Management and Organization*, vol. XIII, no. 1–2 (Spring–Summer 1983), pp. 139–150. Reprinted by permission of publisher, M. E. Sharpe, Inc., Armonk, N.Y.

18. Singer, M. "Culture: A Perceptual Approach," in L. A. Samovar and R. E. Porter, eds., *Intercultural Communication: A Reader* (Belmont, Calif.: Wadsworth Publishing Company, 1976), pp. 110–119.

19. Snyder, M. "Self-Fulfilling Stereotypes," *Psychology Today* (July 1982), pp. 60–68.

20. *South China Morning Post*, "Mystery Man Gives a Fortune for Lucky '7'" (January 22, 1989), p. 3; and "Lucky '7' to Go on Sale" (January 4, 1989), p. 4.

21. Taylor, D. "American Tradition," in R. C. Gardner and R. Kalin, eds., *A Canadian Social Psychology of Ethnic Relations* (Toronto: Methuen Press, 1980).

22. U.S. Office of Education. *On Teaching the Vietnamese* (Washington, D.C.: General Printing Office, 1976).

PART II

▾

Managing
Cultural Diversity

▲

CHAPTER 4

▼

Cultural Synergy

▲

Bhinneka Tunggal Ika
("Unity through diversity")

National Motto of Indonesia

E Pluribus Unum
("Out of many one")

Motto on all coins
in the United States of America

Is culture visible? Do managers think that cultural diversity has an impact on organizations? If an impact exists, is it positive or negative, helpful or harmful to the organization? How should businesspeople manage diversity? Should they ignore it, minimize it, or use it? This chapter investigates the invisibility of culture and our own cultural blindness. It describes the potential problems and advantages of working in a culturally diverse environment, and it presents alternative strategies for managing cultural diversity and its outcomes.

INVISIBLE CULTURE: STRATEGIES FOR RECOGNIZING CULTURE

Culture Is Invisible

Do managers see culture? No; neither managers nor academics generally see culture as affecting day-to-day operations of organizations. Very often good managers see themselves as beyond passport, and good organizations as beyond nationality.

In the 1980s a study to determine the impact of cultural diversity on organizations was conducted (5). Montreal was selected as an ideal location for the study since it has the largest English-speaking population in the predominantly French Canadian province of Quebec. In the study 60 organizational development (OD) consultants described the impact, good and bad, of cultural diversity on their organizations and jobs. Two-thirds said they saw no impact whatsoever. Of the remaining one-third, only one consultant saw the impact as positive. Interestingly, although TV, radio, and newspaper reports daily attest to Montrealers' recognition of bilingualism's and biculturalism's influence on the social, political, and economic environment of Quebec, the majority of the surveyed consultants saw no influence in the world of work.

Management professors seem to demonstrate an equivalent cultural blindness. A survey of management research published in 24 academic and professional journals over the last decade documented that less than 5 percent of the articles refer to either international or domestic multiculturalism in their research designs or results. American researchers conduct the vast majority of the studies in the United States and yet assume their findings to be universally true. Management researchers, perhaps to an even greater extent than their corporate colleagues, have ignored the influence of culture on organizations (2).

Cultural Blindness: Is Seeing Culture Illegitimate?

Cultural diversity does exist and affects the ways in which we operate within an organization (11;12 among others). As one corporate executive recognized, "Local culture affects virtually every aspect of our business." Yet according to two South African managers interviewed for a study of organization communication, "Interest in cultural differences is offensive " (15).

In many instances, people associate recognizing cultural differences with simplistic, primitive, immoral thinking. They label managers who recognize the diversity within organizations as prejudiced, racist, sexist, ethnocentric, and unprofessional. Cultural norms, especially in North America, encourage managers to blind themselves to gender, race, and ethnicity, and to see people only as individuals and to judge them according to their professional skills. This approach causes problems because it confuses recognition with judgment. Recognition occurs when a manager realizes that people from different cultural groups behave differently and that that difference affects their relationship to the organization. People from one ethnic group are not inherently any better or worse (judgment) than those from another group; they are simply different. To ignore cultural differences is unproductive. Judging colleagues and clients based on their membership in particular groups fosters prejudice — a prejudgment based on group rather than individual characteristics. *Judging* cultural differences as good or bad can lead to inappropriate, offensive, racist, sexist, ethnocentric attitudes and behaviors. *Recognizing* differences does not. Choosing not to see cultural diversity limits our ability to manage it — that is, to minimize the problems it causes while maximizing the advantages it allows.

When we blind ourselves to cultural diversity, foreigners become mere projections of ourselves. As explained in chapter 3, research has demonstrated that we frequently see similarity even when difference exists; we project similarity. As one Canadian manager stated, "It is very easy to work with people from other cultures. People are basically the same and have the same needs and aspirations" (6). In a fascinating study involving 14 countries, managers described the work and career goals of their foreign colleagues. In every paired combination of the 14 countries, managers described their foreign colleagues as more similar to themselves than they actually were (7). Although people are not the same, we perceive them to be the same — to have the same needs and aspirations. Cultural blindness is therefore both perceptual and conceptual: we neither see nor want to see differences. Any form of effective cross-cultural management must start with a concerted effort to recognize cultural diversity without judging it — to see difference where difference exists.

Diversity Causes Problems

Culture remains generally invisible and, when visible, we usually think it causes problems: people rarely think that cultural diversity benefits the organization. For example, international executives attending management seminars in France listed the advantages and disadvantages of cultural diversity to their organizations. While every executive could list disadvantages, less than a third (30 percent) could list an advantage (13). As a French executive summarized, "I have been involved in many situations over the years, but I can't think of one made easier because it involved more than one culture." His Danish colleague agreed, "I can think of no situation in my experience where managing ordinary business became easier or more effective because it involved people from more than one culture."

In the Montreal study described earlier (5), only one of the 60 organizational development consultants mentioned an advantage to the organization from cultural diversity. Similarly, the 52 corporate and academic experts participating in the McGill International Symposium on Cross-Cultural Managment had a considerably harder time identifying the benefits to be gained from diversity than the problems it causes. Every manager and academic present could identify a series of diversity-related problems (1).

What types of problems does diversity cause? As shown in Table 4–1, problems most frequently occur in convergent processes, at times when the organization needs employees to think or act in similar ways. Communication (converging on similar meanings) and integration (converging on similar actions) become more difficult. People from different cultures fail to understand one another; they do not work in the same ways or at the same pace. The potential for increased ambiguity, complexity, and confusion becomes highest when the organization or project requires clarity and direction — convergence.

Diversity also results in problems when employees overgeneralize organizational practices and processes. For example, problems result when managers export marketing campaigns developed in one country without adapting them to another country:

Africa

[One multinational] tried to sell baby food in an African nation by using its regular label showing a baby and stating the type of baby food in the jar. Unfortunately, the local population took one look at the labels and interpreted them to mean the jars contained ground-up babies! Sales, of course, were terrible (16:31).

Cultural diversity causes problems when the organization must reach a single agreement—whether formal or informal:

Switzerland/Japan
[The settlement of a licensing agreement between a Japanese and a Swiss company] became much more difficult due to big differences in the de-

TABLE 4-1 Advantages and Disadvantages of Diversity

Advantages	*Disadvantages*
Culturally Synergistic Advantages: *Organizational Benefits from* *Multiculturalism*	*Disadvantages Due to Cultural* *Diversity: Organizational Costs* *Due to Multiculturalism*
Expanding meanings 　Multiple perspectives 　Greater openness to new ideas 　Multiple interpretations Expanding alternatives 　Increasing creativity 　Increasing flexibility 　Increasing problem-solving skills	Diversity increases 　Ambiguity 　Complexity 　Confusion Difficulty converging meanings 　Miscommunication 　Hard to reach a single agreement Difficulty converging actions 　Hard to agree on specific actions
Culture-Specific Advantages: *Benefits in Working with a Particular* *Country or Culture*	*Culture-Specific Disadvantages:* *Costs in Working with a Particular* *Country or Culture*
Better understanding of foreign employees Ability to work more effectively with particular foreign clients Ability to market more effectively to specific foreign customers Increased understanding of political, social, legal, economic, and cultural environment of foreign countries	Overgeneralizing 　Organizational policies 　Organizational strategies 　Organizational practices 　Organizational procedures Ethnocentrism

99

cision-making and legal systems between the two countries, the inability of the Swiss to understand the Japanese language, the long distances, and the lack of spontaneity. In one's own country, these difficulties would not exist or could easily be overcome (13).

Cultural diversity increases the complexity and difficulty in developing overall procedures:

Personnel Records in Europe

In line with the American parent company's policies, European subsidiaries attempted to design a common system for developing historical medical data on all employees. Personnel managers from the United Kingdom, Germany, Holland, Sweden, Luxembourg, Spain, and Italy convened a meeting to agree on how and what could be accomplished. Despite good procedures from the American parent company, limitations imposed by the variety of national legislation, cultural concerns, and the need for consultation with work councils and trade unions prior to reaching an agreement imposed limitations on the scope of information available. In a domestic setting, the variety of constraints would be reduced and (those remaining) clearly understood by all persons involved in developing the system. The system would have been developed much more quickly (13).

Diversity Provides Advantages

Whereas diversity causes the most problems in convergent processes, it leads to the most advantages in divergent processes. Diversity becomes most advantageous when the organization wants to expand — to expand its perspective, its approach, its range of ideas, its operations, its product line, or its marketing plans. Diversity is an advantage in repositioning the organization starting a new project, creating a new idea, developing a new marketing plan, planning a new operation, or assessing trends from a new perspective.

As outlined in Table 4–1, some managers describe multicultural organizations as more flexible and open to new ideas. Others stress the ability of multicultural organizations to understand customers' needs better — for example, to tailor their marketing campaigns to the nationality of their clients. Still others note the multiple perspectives brought to problem solving and the increased ability to avoid "groupthink." Overall, advantages include enhanced creativity, flexibility, and problem-solving skills — especially on complex problems involving large numbers of qualitative factors (10;18), improved effectiveness in working with culturally distinct client groups, and a heightened awareness of the dynamics and communication patterns within the organization. Advantages come from using cultural diversity as a resource rather than treating it as a liability to the organization. International managers attending executive programs in France described the following benefits from diversity to their corporations:

New Product Development

A U.S. pharmaceutical firm developed a new competitive anti-cancer drug based on an initial discovery made in their Italian subsidiary, research conducted in conjunction with the best-equipped institute for therapeutical research in the world (the U.S.–based National Cancer Institute), new creativity techniques coming out of Sweden, specific new therapy indications from Japan and China, and a major cash flow from Germany and the United States (13).

Accepting New Ideas

New ideas that seemed threatening or absurd when mentioned by someone from one's own country were easier to "hear" when suggested by foreigners. For example, during the energy crisis, American and British workers found the low maximum thermostat settings restrictive. When an ex-British-Leyland team then went to Korea to design the Pony car, they found it amazing that the Koreans broke the ice before they could wash their products. Thereafter, the low thermostat setting no longer seemed so restrictive (13).

New Perspectives, Better Communication and Cooperation

A European firm created a Technical and Field Support Center with the involvement of all their European subsidiaries. By involving all countries in defining the "where, how, and why" of operations, the Center avoided one-nation dictatorial decisions which, in the past, had caused continuous conflicts between countries (13).

New Perspectives — Neutrality

An American/French partnership required an outside audit of their Algerian subsidiary. The American partner unsuccessfully proposed an American firm. Similarly, the French partner failed in proposing a French firm. The two finally agreed on a French-affiliated office of an American accounting firm that agreed to assign two French-speaking British citizens to do the job. Everybody was happy (13).

Recognizing the Advantages from Diversity

Culture is not one of the ideas readily used by managers or employees to explain organizational behavior. Unless presented with the idea of culture, they often fail to consider it as a possible explanation for variations in organizational functioning. They attribute patterns and changes in behavior to influences other than culture.

The follow-up to the Montreal organizational development (OD) study demonstrated the need to give managers a model showing cultural diversity as leading to both organizational advantages *and* disadvantages (5). The organizational development study became particularly interesting because the follow-up did not replicate the results of the original interviews. Following the initial 60 interviews, a similar group of 75 Canadian OD consultants received questionnaires. The consultants again described the impact of culture on their organizations. However, this time the structured questionnaire gave the consultants the idea of culture and a model highlighting its possible positive and negative impacts. Unlike the interviewees, the majority of the questionnaire respondents did see an impact of cultural diversity on the organization and almost half saw the potential for the impact being positive.

As shown in Figure 4–1, the original interviewees had seen the impact of culture as (a) nonexistent, (b) only ranging from negative to neutral (being more or less negative), or (c) only ranging from negative to positive (being either negative or positive, but not both). Interviewees had not seen the possibility of simultaneous negative and positive impacts. By contrast, the questionnaire respondents saw the possibility of the impact of cultural diversity being simultaneously highly positive and highly negative within the same organization. A positive impact was not necessarily related to the lack of a negative impact. Similarly, they saw the possibility of the impact of cultural diversity being *neither* positive nor negative (5).

The two parts of the study differed in that the interviewees were given neither the idea of culture nor a model of its possible positive and negative impacts, whereas the questionnaire respondents were explicitly given both. Although it did not occur naturally, it appears that managers can see culture and its positive and negative impacts if given the idea. If culture is not pointed out, managers remain culture-blind.

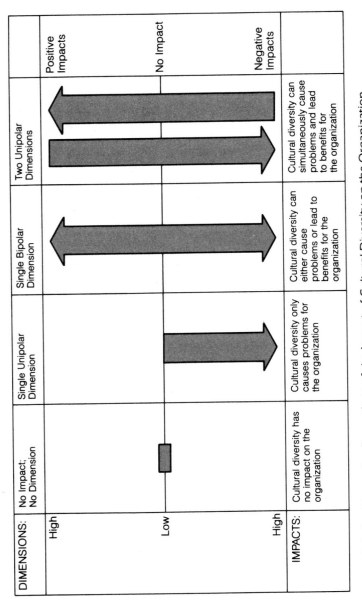

FIGURE 4-1 Alternative Perceptions of the Impact of Cultural Diversity on the Organization

SOURCE: Reprinted with permission from *Journal of Applied Behavioral Science*, "Organizational Development in a Multicultural Environment," by Nancy J. Adler, vol. 19, no. 3 (Summer 1983), pp. 349–365, copyright 1983 by NTL, Institute.

Strategies for Managing Cultural Diversity

The extent to which managers recognize cultural diversity and its potential advantages and disadvantages defines the organization's approach to managing that diversity (5). As shown in Table 4-2, the most common response of organizational members to cultural diversity is *parochial*—they do not recognize cultural diversity or its impact on the organization. In parochial organizations, members believe that "our way is the *only* way" to organize and manage. The second most common response is *ethnocentric*—members recognize diversity, but only as a source of problems. In ethnocentric organizations, members believe that "our way is the *best* way" to organize and work; they view all other ways as inferior. Only in those cases in which organization members explicitly recognize the concept of culture can the response to cultural diversity be *synergistic*—seeing cultural diversity as leading to both advantages and disadvantages. In synergistic organizations, members believe that "our way and their way differ, but neither is inherently superior to the other." Members of synergistic organizations believe that creative combinations of our ways and their ways produce the best ways to organize and work.

The various perceptions and assumptions have different implications for organizations' approaches to managing diversity. If organizations assume the impact of culture to be negligible, as in the case of parochial organizations, the selected strategy is to ignore cultural diversity. As some parochial managers describe, "Cultural diversity is just not important enough to consider; it's irrelevant." This strategy precludes the effective management of diversity. It precludes the possibility of minimizing negative impacts and enhancing positive impacts.

If organization members assume that the only impacts of culture are negative, as in the case of ethnocentric organizations, then their strategy is to minimize the sources and impacts of cultural diversity within the organization. They can implement this strategy in a number of ways: for example, by attempting to select a culturally homogeneous workforce or socializing all workers into behavior patterns of the dominant culture. Ethnocentric organizations, by minimizing diversity, preclude the possibility of benefiting from the many cultures present.

If organization members see the impacts of cultural diversity as both positive and negative, as in the case of synergistic organizations, then their strategy is to manage the *impacts* of cultural diversity rather than the diversity itself. Synergistic organizations minimize potential problems by managing the impacts, not by minimizing the diversity. Similarly, they maximize the potential advantages by managing the impacts, rather than ignoring the diversity. Synergistic organizations train their members to recognize cultural differences and to use those differences to create advantages for the organization.

The first two strategies—ignoring and minimizing cultural differences—occur naturally and are therefore quite common. Only when members of the organization recognize both the cultural diversity and its potential positive impacts is it probable that an organization will select to manage the diversity rather than ignore or minimize it. Cultural diversity can potentially have both positive or negative impacts on the organization. The approach to diversity, and not the diversity itself, determines the actual positive and negative outcomes.

CULTURAL SYNERGY

According to Buckminster Fuller, synergy involves "a new way of thinking . . . which helps to free one from outdated patterns and can break the shell of permitted ignorance" (7). Synergy is "the behavior of whole systems that cannot be predicted by the behavior of any parts taken separately. . . . In order to really understand what is going on, we have to abandon starting with parts, and we must work instead from whole to particular." (9). In their book *Managing Cultural Synergy*, Moran and Harris emphasize that "the very differences in the world's people can lead to mutual growth and accomplishment that is more than the single contribution of each party to the intercultural transaction." They suggest that we can

> go beyond awareness of our own cultural heritage to produce something greater by cooperation and collaboration. Cultural synergy builds upon similarities and fuses differences resulting in more effective human activities and systems. The very diversity of people can be utilized to enhance problem solving by combined action. Those in international management have unique opportunities to foster synergy on a global basis (14).

Cultural synergy, as an approach to managing the impact of cultural diversity, involves a process in which managers form organiza-

TABLE 4-2 Perceiving and Managing the Impact of Cultural Diversity on the Organization

Type of Organization	Perception	Strategy	Most Likely Outcomes	Frequency
	What is the perceived impact of cultural diversity on the organization?	*How should the impact of cultural diversity on the organization be managed?*	*What can be expected with this perception and this strategy?*	*How common is each of these perceptions and strategies?*
Parochial Our way is the only way.	**No impact:** Cultural diversity is seen as having no impact on the organization.	**Ignore differences:** Ignore the impact of cultural diversity on the organization.	**Problems:** Problems will occur but they will not be attributed to culture.	Very common
Ethnocentric Our way is the best way.	**Negative impact:** Cultural diversity will cause problems for the organizations.	**Minimize differences:** Minimize the source and the impact of cultural diversity on the organization. If possible, select a monocultural workforce.	**Some problems and few advantages:** Problems will be reduced as diversity is decreased while the possibility of creating advantages will be ignored or eliminated. Problems will be attributed to culture.	Common

Synergistic	Potential negative *and* positive impacts:	Manage differences:	Some problems and many advantages:	Very uncommon
Creative combinations of our way and their way may be the best way.	Cultural diversity can simultaneously lead to problems and advantages for the organization.	Train organization members to recognize cultural differences and use them to create advantages for the organization.	Advantages to the organization from cultural diversity will be recognized and realized. Some problems will continue to occur which will need to be managed.	

SOURCE: Nancy J. Adler, "Organizational Development in a Multicultural Environment," *Journal of Applied Behavioral Science*, vol. 19, no. 3 (Summer 1983), pp. 349–365.

tional policies, strategies, structures, and practices based on, but not limited to, the cultural patterns of individual organization members and clients. Culturally synergistic organizations create new forms of management and organization that transcend the individual cultures of their members (3:172). This approach recognizes both the similarities and differences among the nationalities that compose a multicultural organization and suggests that we neither ignore nor minimize cultural diversity, but rather that we view it as a resource in designing and developing organizations (3:172).

A set of assumptions that differ from the most commonly held assumptions about cross-cultural interaction within work settings form the basis of the cultural synergy approach (4). First, as shown in Table 4–3, although the most common assumption especially in the United States (based on the "melting pot" myth) is *homogeneity*—the belief that all people are basically the same—cultural synergy assumes *heterogeneity*. The synergy approach assumes that we are not all the same—that many different cultural groups exist within society and that each maintains its distinctness. The image of a pluralistic, rather than a homogeneous, society underlies the synergy approach. Second, whereas the most common assumption is that the similarities among people are most important, cultural synergy assumes that similarities and differences share equal importance. Third, whereas the most common assumption posits that our way is the only way of living and working (parochialism), cultural synergy assumes *equifinality*—that many equivalent ways (*equi*) to reach a final goal (*finality*) exist, and that no culture's way is inherently superior. Fourth, whereas most people are, to some extent, ethnocentric (believing that their way is the best way to live and work), the synergy approach assumes *cultural contingency* —that the best way depends on the culture of the people involved.

In a survey of 145 international executives from around the world, 83 percent preferred the synergy approach, yet only 33 percent described their organizations as currently using a synergistic approach to multinational and multicultural problem solving (6). Although international managers clearly recognize the value of approaching problem solving from a synergistic perspective, they realize that the approach is neither easy nor the traditional approach taken. The following section describes a three-step process for creating synergistic solutions to dilemmas faced by culturally diverse organizations.

TABLE 4–3 Misleading Assumptions in a Multicultural World

	Common and Misleading Assumptions	Less Common and More Appropriate Assumptions
Homogeneity	*Melting Pot Myth:* We are all the same.	*Heterogeneity* *Image of Cultural Pluralism:* We are not all the same; there are many culturally different groups in society.
Similarity	*Similarity Myth:* "They" are all just like me.	*Similarity and Difference* *They are not just like me:* Many people are culturally different from me. Most people have both cultural similarities and differences when compared to me.
Parochialism	*The Only-One-Way Myth:* Our way is the only way. We do not recognize any other way of living, working, or doing things.	*Equifinality* *Our way is not the only way:* There are many culturally distinct ways of reaching the same goal, of working, and of living one's life.
Ethnocentrism	*The One-Best-Way Myth:* Our way is the best way. All other ways are inferior versions of our way.	*Cultural Contingency* *Our way is one possible way:* There are many other different and equally good ways to reach the same goal. The best way is contingent on the culture of the people involved.

SOURCE: Nancy J. Adler, "Domestic Multiculturalism: Cross-Cultural Management in the Public Sector," in William Eddy, ed., *Handbook of Organization Management* (New York: Marcel Dekker, Inc., 1983), pp. 481–499. Reprinted from *Handbook of Organization Management*, p. 363 by courtesy of Marcel Dekker, Inc.

Culturally Synergistic Problem Solving

Culturally synergistic organizations reflect the best aspects of all members' cultures in their strategy, structure, and process without violating the norms of any single culture. Managers in synergistic organizations use diversity as a key resource in solving problems. As outlined in Figure 4–2, the process of developing culturally synergistic solutions to organizational problems involves situation description, cultural interpretation, and cultural creativity (3:173).

Step 1: Situation Description

What dilemma faces the organization? Can organization members describe it from each of the cultural perspectives represented? Situation description involves one of the most difficult and critical steps in finding solutions to complex problems. Across cultures, people's divergent values and perceptions magnify the difficulty in problem definition. Some examples involving North Americans include (3:178):

Japan

An American sales manager conveyed the following concern: "I'm an 'open-door manager.' I expect my employees to come to me when they have a problem. But these Japanese never come to you until it's a crisis . . . until it's too late to do anything." To the American manager, the "problem" had begun weeks earlier. To the Japanese sales representative, the situation only became a "problem" that morning. When questioned later about his behavior, the Japanese salesman replied that "Americans see everything as a problem!" In analyzing the situation, it became clear that one's cultural perspective determines the definition of a *problem*. Westerners often see life as a series of problems to be resolved, whereas non-Westerners frequently view life as a series of situations to be accepted (17). Americans therefore define situations as problems much earlier than do the Japanese (3:178).

Egypt

An Egyptian executive, after entertaining his Canadian guest, offered joint partnership in a business venture. The Canadian, delighted with the offer, suggested that they meet again the next morning with their respective laywers to fill in the details. The Egyptians never arrived. Was the problem that Egyptians lack punctuality, that the Egyptian was expecting a counteroffer, or that lawyers are not available in

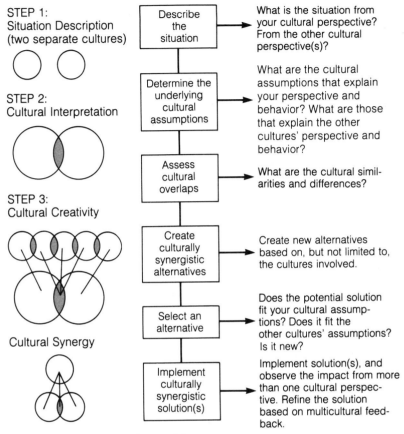

FIGURE 4-2 Creating Cultural Synergy
SOURCE: Reprinted from W. Warner Burke and Leonard D. Goodstein, eds., *Trends and Issues in OD: Current Theory and Practice.* San Diego, Calif. Copyright 1980, University Associates, Inc. Used with permission.

Cairo? None of these explanations was true, although the Canadian executive suggested each of them. At issue was the perceived meaning of inviting lawyers. The Canadian saw the lawyers' presence as facilitating the successful completion of the negotiation; the Egyptian interpreted it as signaling the Canadian's mistrust of his verbal commitment (3:178). Canadians often use the impersonal formality of a lawyer's services to finalize an agreement. Egyptians more frequently depend on a personal relationship developed between bargaining partners for the same purposes.

111

The first step in the cultural synergy process involves recognizing that a conflict situation exists. Organization members must recognize that a potential problem exists even when the problem does not make sense from their own cultural perspective (3:178). They must then describe it from each culture's perspective, while refraining from interpreting or evaluating it from any one culture's point of view.

Step 2: Cultural Interpretation

Why do members of different cultures think, feel, and act the way they do? What historical and cultural assumptions must be made to understand the present situation? Once organization members recognize a problem, they can use the synergy approach to analyze it from each culture's perspective. Organization members identify and interpret similarities and differences in thoughts, feelings, and actions among cultures (3:178). Logically, the second step in the cultural synergy process involves role reversal—this approach assumes that all behavior is rational and understandable from the perspective of the person behaving, but that cultural biases lead us to misunderstand the logic of another culture's behavioral patterns (3:179). Whereas single-culture perspectives limit managers' flexibility in international situations, multiple perspectives enhance their understanding and options.

During cultural interpretation, members of each culture attempt to understand the underlying assumptions that lead those in other cultures ("foreigners") to behave as they do. During this process, the group identifies similarities and differences between their culture's assumptions and behaviors and those of the other culture.

EXAMPLE

Iran

An American engineer who was teaching Persians to use a complex machine was disappointed in the achievement of his trainees and therefore gave them poor reviews. One Persian came to the American and said, "But I thought that you were my friend. Why don't you give me a better review?" The American was furious. In analyzing and interpreting the underlying cultural assumptions, the American came to understand the importance Persians place on friendship relative to task accomplishment, while the Persian came to recognize that Americans base their system of equity on competence rather than relationship (17). While both cultures value friendship and achievement, they differ in the relative importance they attach to each (3:179).

Step 3: Cultural Creativity

Organizations create synergistic alternatives by searching for ways to solve problems—that is, for ways to help people from different cultures enhance their productivity and job satisfaction. The question "What can people from one culture contribute to people from another culture?" initiates the search. The answer should be compatible with, but not imitative of, the cultural assumptions of all represented groups. It should be novel and transcend the behavioral patterns of each of the root cultures (3:179). Selecting the best alternative—evaluation—only becomes possible when preceded by adequate description and interpretation (see chapter 3).

EXAMPLE

Creating Cultural Synergy

Uruguay and the Philippines

Situation Description. A Uruguayan doctor at a major California hospital became concerned when he realized that a Filipina nurse was improperly using a particular machine for patient treatment. He instructed the nurse on the proper procedure and asked if she understood. She said she did. Two hours later the patient was doing poorly because the nurse had continued to improperly administer the treatment. The doctor again queried the nurse, and she again affirmed her understanding of the procedure. What went wrong?

Interpretation. In analyzing the situation, the doctor came to understand that many Filipinos will not contradict people in respected positions. To the Filipina nurse, the doctor's status was clearly above hers. He was a man; she was a woman. He was older; she was younger. He was a doctor; she was a nurse. Based on her cultural assumptions, she could not tell the doctor that she did not understand without implying that he had given poor instructions and thus causing him to lose face. The doctor, based on his cultural assumptions, expected "open communication"; he expected the nurse to say whether she understood his instructions and to ask questions if she did not. He considered it a sign of incompetence to assume responsibility for a patient's care without fully understanding the manner of treatment.

Synergistic Solution. After analyzing the situation, the hospital administrator suggested a culturally synergistic solution. Upon giving his initial instructions, the doctor was to ask the nurse to describe the procedure that she would follow. As the doctor listened, he could assess the accuracy of the nurse's understanding and identify areas that needed further explanation. The nurse, never having been asked directly if she understood, would not be forced to say "no" to a superior. The hospital administrator solved the problem without violating either culture's assumptions (3:179–180). The organization could achieve its goal — the delivery of excellent medical care — without violating the norms of either culture.

Implementation

Organizations must plan the implementation of synergistic solutions carefully. Before organization members will understand the need for changes based on synergistic problem solving, they must develop cultural self-awareness (an understanding of their own cultural assumptions and patterns of behavior) as well as cross-cultural awareness (an understanding of the other cultures' assumptions and patterns of behavior). Without some understanding of the cultural dynamics involved, proposed changes often appear absurd; with cultural understanding, the organization can solve its problems and implement the changes needed to foster client service, employee effectiveness, and job satisfaction (3:180). The following example highlights the synergistic scheduling plan implemented by an American air freight company for its routes between Japan and the United States:

Creating Cultural Synergy[1]

Japanese and American Scheduling

Situation Description. American sales representatives of a United States–based air freight company with extensive Asian operations generally promised customers specific dates and hours for flight arrivals of freight shipments. However, shipments often arrived late. American customers would usually understand and forgive these delays if given an adequate explanation, whereas Japanese customers expected the company to keep its promises and lost faith in the company when they did not adhere to the promised arrival times. Unlike the Americans, the Japanese sales representatives often refused to promise delivery times until, as the Americans explained, "the plane had arrived on the runway" or, as the Japanese explained, they could be certain that their promises would be kept. Yet American clients expect definite timetables; when not given, they tend to distrust the company's ability to perform its services.

Interpretation. The company needed to design a uniform "promising" system that would be culturally appropriate for both American and Japanese employees and clients. From the American perspective, the system had to be definite enough to develop credibility with American customers. From the Japanese perspective, the promises to customers had to conform to reality sufficiently so that no one would lose face.

Synergistic Solution. After analyzing the underlying cultural dynamics in both systems, the sales representatives agreed that they should begin promising delivery within a range of time, rather than at specific times. For instance, they would promise clients delivery "early afternoon Thursday," rather than at 2:03 P.M. (scheduled flight arrival time). Thus Americans could continue to promise and the Japanese would rarely promise something that the company could not deliver.

The solution recognizes the values of both cultures without upsetting either cultures' management practices. As a synergistic solution, it is new and acceptable to both cultures (3:180–181).

SUMMARY

In *Fortune's* cover story on "What the Leaders of Tomorrow See," Corning's Kaiser asserts, "Future leaders will have to learn how to manage cultural diversity." (8:59) Cultural synergy is an approach to managing the impact of cultural diversity and allows organizations to solve problems effectively when working in cross-cultural environments. Synergistic solutions create new forms of management and organization by recognizing and transcending the individual ethnic cultures of employees and clients. The synergy approach, far from ignoring the presence of cultural diversity within the organization, recognizes both its potentially positive and negative impacts. Unlike the more common cultural dominance and compromise approaches, cultural synergy emphasizes managing the impacts of diversity, rather than attempting to eliminate the diversity itself.

The synergy approach to problem solving involves three fundamental steps: situation description, cultural interpretation, and cultural creativity. Organization members first define the problem from the perspective of all cultures involved. Second, they analyze the patterns that make each culture's behavior logical from within its own perspective. Third, they create solutions that foster the organization's productivity without violating the norms of any culture involved.

The synergy approach creates organizational solutions to problems by using cultural diversity as a resource and an advantage to the organization. The approach is designed to be used in organizations in which cross-cultural interaction among employees and clients occurs daily. However, organizations need not implement a synergistic solution all at once; instead, they can introduce it gradually as the need for cross-cultural problem solving becomes evident. Although no current organization is fully synergistic, a number of organizations employ this strategy in sovling many of their key cross-cultural and multinational problems.

In introducing culturally synergistic problem solving to an organization for the first time, line managers and human resource professionals must realize that they are involved fundamentally in the process of managing change. The major change is that of perspective: senior executives and human resource managers must guide the organization from a domestic to a global world view. Most organizations find it helpful to begin the cultural synergy process with cross-cultural communications workshops, during which employees have the opportunity to become more culturally self-aware (recognizing and understanding their own culture's patterns of doing business) and more cross-culturally aware (recognizing and understanding the culturally based styles of working of clients and colleagues from other cultures). Following these initial cross-cultural communications workshops, organizations can begin to address their culturally based conflict situations. As the organization addresses more problems from a synergistic perspective, it accumulates the sophistication and body of knowledge needed to address future problems. Whereas initial problems must be addressed explicitly, formally (through workshops, seminars, and formal meetings), and slowly (developing awareness prior to attempting to solve problems), later problem-solving sessions can become more implicit, more informal, and less time-consuming. The learning acquired during the initial stages becomes a part of the organzation's increasingly global perspective and cross-cultural body of knowledge.

The synergistic problem-solving process is not a "quick fix." It is a systematic process for moving an organization from a domestic to an international perspective; it becomes an effective approach for competing successfully in the increasingly multicultural domestic environment and in the now all-important world of global business.

QUESTIONS FOR REFLECTION

1. Select an organizational problem that you are currently facing or that you have faced in the past. Describe the process you would recommend for developing a culturally synergistic solution to that problem.

2. What are the advantages of using a multicultural senior management team for a domestically based company that conducts a substantial part of its business abroad? What are the advantages of using a team of senior executives selected primarily from the local area? Which type of senior executive team would you recommend and why?

3. For many corporations, a major problem is cultural blindness. In the organizations that you know, what factors cause managers to be blind to the impact of cultural diversity? What would you recommend to decrease managers' work-related cultural blindness?

4. Select a cross-cultural conflict situation that is currently on the news or that is currently occurring in an organization in which you are familiar. As a consultant what would you recommend in order to help the parties involved create a culturally synergistic solution? What might a final culturally synergistic solution look like?

5. Reflecting on your own personality and work style, what do you see as your greatest skills in being able to create culturally synergistic solutions? In which areas do you need to work in order to improve your skills at creating culturally synergistic solutions?

NOTES

1. Clifford Clarke, President, Clarke Consulting Group, was instrumental in interpreting this cross-cultural air freight situation. His insight and creativity in creating cultural synergy with Japanese organizations continues to advance the insight of the field.

REFERENCES

1. Adler, N. J. "Cross-Cultural Management: Issues to Be Faced," *International Studies of Management and Organization*, vol. 13, no. 1–2 (Spring–Summer 1983), pp. 7–45.

2. Adler, N. J. "Cross-Cultural Management Research: The Ostrich and the Trend," *Academy of Management Review*, vol. 8, no. 2 (April 1983), pp. 226–232.

3. Adler, N. J. "Cultural Synergy: The Management of Cross-Cultural Organizations," in W. W. Burke and L. D. Goodstein, eds., *Trends and Issues in OD: Current Theory and Practice* (San Diego, Calif.: University Associates, 1980) pp. 163–184.

4. Adler, N. J. "Domestic Multiculturalism: Cross-Cultural Management in the Public Sector," in W. Eddy, ed., *Handbook on Public Organization Management* (New York: Marcel Dekker, 1983), pp. 481–499.

5. Adler, N. J. "Organizational Development in a Multicultural Environment," *Journal of Applied Behavioral Science*, vol. 19, no. 3 (Summer 1983), pp. 349–365.

6. Adler, N. J., and Laurent, A. Unpublished results from the Cultural Synergy Survey collected at INSEAD in 1980–1983 and in 1982 at major American and Canadian multinationals ($n = 145$).

7. Burger, P., and Bass, B. M. *Assessment of Managers: An International Comparison* (New York: Free Press, 1979).

8. Dumaine, B. "What the Leaders of Tomorrow See," *Fortune* (July 3, 1989), pp. 48–62.

9. Fuller, R. B. *Critical Path* (Washington D.C.: St. Martin's Press/World Future Society, 1981).

10. Hayles, R. "Costs and Benefits of Integrating Persons from Diverse Cultures in Organization," paper presented at the 20th International Congress of Applied Psychology, Edinburgh, Scotland, July 25–31, 1982.

11. Hofstede, G. *Culture's Consequences: International Differences in Work-Related Values* (Beverly Hills, Calif.: Sage Publications, 1980).

12. Laurent, A. "The Cultural Diversity of Western Conceptions of Management," *International Studies of Management and Organization*, vol. 13, no. 1–2 (Spring–Summer 1983), pp. 75–96.

13. Laurent, A., and Adler, N. J. "Managerial Skills for International Business," executive seminars held at INSEAD in Fontainebleau, France, August, 1981–1983.

14. Moran, R. T., and Harris, P. R. *Managing Cultural Synergy* (Houston, Tex.: Gulf Publishing Company, 1981), Chapter 15, p. 3.

15. Prekel, T. "Multicultural Communication: A Challenge to Managers," paper delivered at the International Convention of the American Business Communication Association, New York, November 21, 1983, p. 11.

16. Ricks, D. A. *Big Business Blunders: Mistakes in Multinational Marketing* (Homewood, Ill.: Dow Jones-Irwin, 1983).

17. Stewart, E. C. *American Cultural Patterns: A Cross-Cultural Perspective* (Chicago: Ill.: Intercultural Press, 1979).

18. Ziller, R. C. "Homogeneity and Heterogeneity of Group Membership," in C. G. McClintock, ed., *Experimental Social Psychology* (New York: Holt, Rinehart, and Winston, 1972), pp. 385–411.

CHAPTER 5

▼

Multicultural Teams

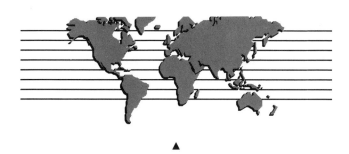

▲

It was once said that the sun never set on the British Empire. Today the sun does set on the British Empire, but not on the scores of global corporate empires including those of IBM, Unilever, Volkswagen, and Hitachi.

Lester Brown, President of Worldwatch Institute (43:320)

International management used to be a minor component of industrial activity; now it is a major one. International management used to involve simply sending one of "our" managers "over there" to sell products to foreign clients; now the foreigners are working within our companies. International management used to involve sending expatriates overseas to direct foreign operations; now members of corporate boards, executives, and workers represent every nationality. Today, more than 10,000 firms headquartered in high-technology, non-Communist countries have operations outside their home nations (see 43:320).

In the 1990s global business is bringing cross-cultural contact home to every business. Without leaving their own communities, managers may work for a foreign-owned firm, sell to non-native clients, and purchase components from abroad, while regularly attending meetings with colleagues from around the world. Design teams routinely develop revolutionary new products in electronic meetings among experts on three continents, none of whom ever leaves home to participate in the telephone, fax, computer, and electronic mail dialogues. Cross-cultural dialogue has become the very foundation on which global business is based.

MANAGING A MULTICULTURAL WORKFORCE

Both domestically and internationally, the multicultural workforce has become a reality. However, the impact of multiculturalism varies significantly with the type of environment and the firm's overall strategy. As shown in Figure 5–1, international cultural diversity traditionally has had a minimal impact on Phase 1 domestic organizations; and yet domestic multiculturalism has a highly significant impact. In international organizations (Phase 2 firms that export to foreign clients), the impact of culture is highly significant. The international firm must adapt its approach and its products and services to that of the local culture. In the Phase 3 multinational firm, because price tends to dominate all other considerations, the impact of culture lessens slightly.

By the time corporations become global (Phase 4), the impact of culture becomes extremely important. Global firms need an understanding of cultural dynamics to plan their strategy, to locate production facilities and suppliers worldwide, to design and market culturally appropriate products and services, as well as to manage cross-cultural interaction throughout the organization—from senior executive committees to the shop floor. As more firms today move from domestic, international, and multinational organizations to operating as truly global organizations and alliances, the importance of cultural diversity increases markedly. What once was "nice to understand" becomes imperative for survival, let alone success (2). (See chapter 1 for a review of the four phases.)

Similar to its increasing importance, the location of the impact of cultural diversity varies with the firm's environment and strategy. As shown in Figure 5–2, international culture diversity has traditionally affected neither the domestic firm's organizational culture nor its relationship with its clients. Domestic firms work domestically, and only domestic multiculturalism has a direct impact on the internal dynamics of the firm as well as on its relationship to its external environment.

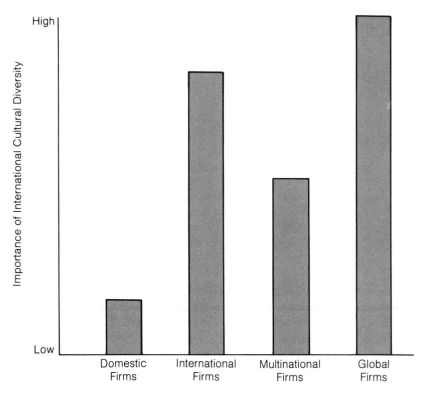

FIGURE 5-1 The Importance of Cultural Diversity

In international firms, which focus primarily on exporting and producing abroad, cultural diversity strongly affects external relationships, especially with potential buyers and foreign workers. As the organization becomes multinational, there is less emphasis on managing cultural differences outside of the firm but an increasing need to manage the growing cultural diversity within the firm. Whereas international firms use primarily expatriate managers to sell and work abroad, multinational firms hire people from all over the world as employees and managers. In the international firm, only expatriates have a high need for developing cultural sensitivity and cross-cultural management skills. Whereas in multinational firms, because the location of the impact of cultural diversity has moved inside the organization and up the levels of hierarchy, many more regular employees and managers must develop cross-cultural management skills.

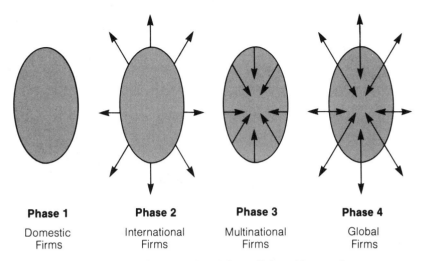

Phase 1	**Phase 2**	**Phase 3**	**Phase 4**
Domestic Firms	International Firms	Multinational Firms	Global Firms

FIGURE 5-2 Location of International Cross-Cultural Interaction

Global firms must manage cultural diversity both within the firm and between the firm and its external environment. To work effectively, everyone — from the CEO to the newest worker employed — needs cross-cultural management skills. This progression from culture's relative lack of importance to its critical importance, both with respect to the firm's external environment as well as to its internal organizational culture, underlies the growing recognition that today's executives and managers must work effectively in multinational and multicultural teams to succeed (2).

How do we manage people who differ from us? Research has shown that the styles of leadership, motivation, decision making, planning, organizing, staffing, and controlling vary among different countries (see chapter 6). What happens when people from dissimilar cultures work together on a day-to-day basis within the same organization? How should a multicultural workforce be managed?

This chapter investigates ways of managing cultural diversity within the organization. It begins with a review of the increasing levels of domestic multiculturalism, an important source of multicultural task groups. It then focuses on cross-cultural interaction within task groups: What types of problems does diversity cause within executive and work teams? What potential benefits emerge from culturally diverse teams? And, most importantly, what does management need to do to maximize the benefits and minimize the problems caused by diversity?

123

DOMESTIC MULTICULTURALISM

You do not have to go overseas to meet someone with a cultural background different from your own. With increasing immigration, third country nationals searching for work, and the presence of indigenous ethnic communities, managers who never leave home often face a multicultural workforce in local organizations and plants.

Culturally distinct populations populate all countries of the world. Singapore, for example, has four cultural and linguistic groups: Chinese, Malay, Indian, and Eurasian. Belgium has two linguistic groups, French and Flemish. Switzerland has four distinct ethnic communities: French, German, Italian, and Romansh. Canada, a multicultural country by national policy, uses two official languages, English and French. Many countries, including Israel and the United States, have developed historically as havens for immigrants from around the world.

Each population exhibits a culturally unique lifestyle. Most of us are familiar with the typical foods of the major ethnic groups: no one thinks that spaghetti is Russian, that tortillas are Chinese, or that sushi is Senegalese. But many of us remain unaware of how extensively other cultures' lifestyles differ from our own. Even if we consider ourselves internationally sophisticated, many of us fail to recognize the culturally distinct attitudes and behaviors that our fellow citizens bring to the workplace (1).

The city of Los Angeles highlights the pervasiveness of domestic multiculturalism and its impact on the workplace. Since 1970, more than two million foreign immigrants have settled in Los Angeles; during 1982 alone, more than 90,000 became Los Angeles residents (7:17). Of Los Angeles 550,000 school children, 117,000 speak one of 104 languages more fluently than English — including 35 fluent only in Gujarati, a language of western India (7:18). Los Angeles no longer has a majority population but must constantly "adjust to the quirky, polyglot rhythms of 60,000 Samoans and 30,000 Thais, 200,000 Salvadorans and 175,000 Armenians" (7:18). Los Angeles is the second largest Mexican agglomeration after Mexico City (23:52), more Samoans live in Los Angeles than on the island of Samoa four thousand miles away (42:1), and more Israelis live there than in any other city outside of Israel (45). As a former lieutenant governor of California said, there is one central, inevitable fact: "If the present trends continue, the emerging ethnic groups will constitute more than half the population of California by 1990, and . . . [California] will become the country's first Third World state" (26:35).

The story reflects the same pattern in other cities and states in the United States. Of the 700,000 largely middle-class Cubans who left Cuba by 1978, more than 430,000 have settled in Dade County, Florida (23:51). More than 1.3 million Puerto Ricans now live in the greater New York City area (23:55). Hawaii has become a domestic microcosm of Eastern and Western cultures. Moreover, there has been a resurgence of ethnic self-identity among both new immigrants and European populations that had seemed all but assimilated (35). Observing these and dozens of other statistics, multiculturalism has become a dominant fact of domestic life in the United States. Americans can no longer forget multiculturalism nor relegate it to the domain of international managers and diplomats.

Perhaps William Somerset Maugham best captured the essence of domestic multiculturalism in 1921 in *The Trembling Leaf* when he described Hawaii, a state whose 900,000 residents represent 29 percent Caucasians, 27.5 percent Japanese, 18 percent Hawaiian and part-Hawaiian, 10 percent Filipino, 4.5 percent Chinese, 1 percent each Korean, Samoan, and black, and 8 percent mixed or miscellaneous (20:97).

It is a meeting place of East and West, the very new rubs shoulders with the immeasurably old . . . you have come upon something singularly intriguing. All these strange people live close to each other, with different languages and different thoughts; they believe in different gods and they have different values; two passions alone they share, love and hunger. And somehow as you watch them, you have an impression of extraordinary vitality.

TASK GROUPS:
THE ORGANIZATION IN MICROCOSM

Organizations consist of groups, and groups form the basic structure of organizations. Companies organize their employees into many forms of temporary and permanent work groups—departments, offices, teams, task forces, subcommittees, committees, commissions, and boards. Groups vary in quality from poor to excellent, from completely unproductive to highly productive. They can have societally desirable values and goals, or society can view their objectives as destructive. They can accomplish much that is good, or they can cause great harm. From the organization's perspective, they can be highly effective or totally ineffective. There is nothing implicitly good or bad, weak or strong, about a group (29).

A group's productivity depends on its task, its available resources, and its process. The group's goal defines its task, and this task can involve a decision, recommendation, project, report, action, or series of actions (i.e., a plan). The group's resources include the people, information, materials, time, money, and energy available for accomplishing the task. For example, a task force may have three or five people available; it may have one week or five months; it may have a large budget or no budget at all; it may have unlimited computer time or no computer access. The group's process "consists of the actual steps taken by an individual or group when confronted by a task. It includes all those intrapersonal and interpersonal actions by which people transform their resources into a product, and all those nonproductive actions that are prompted by frustration, competing motivations, and inadequate understanding" (41:8).

The actual productivity of a group is its potential productivity minus the losses due to faulty process (41:9):

> **Actual productivity = Potential productivity**
> **— Losses due to faulty process**

Actual productivity depends on how well the group works together and uses its resources to accomplish the task.

TYPES OF DIVERSITY
IN GROUPS

Group members can have very similar or quite different backgrounds, perspectives, and training (8). Although diversity can refer to many characteristics (gender, race, profession, nationality, age, and experience), this chapter focuses on ethnic differences (46). Therefore groups with all members from the same culture will be referred to as *homogeneous*, and those which have more than one culture as *multicultural*. Multicultural groups can be divided into three categories: those with one member from a different culture (token groups), those with members representing two cultures (bicultural groups), and those with members from three or more cultures (literally multicultural groups).

Homogeneous Groups

In homogeneous groups, all members share similar backgrounds. Homogeneous group members generally perceive, interpret, and evaluate the world more similarly than do members of heterogeneous groups. For example, a group of male Finnish bankers is homogeneous, based on gender, culture, and profession. A group of Mexican and Panamanian stockbrokers is professionally but not culturally homogeneous.

Token Groups

In token groups, all but one member comes from the same background. For example, in a group of Australian lawyers and one British attorney, the British attorney would be the token member. In such a token group the British attorney would probably see and understand situations somewhat differently from the Australians. In the last decade, male management teams began to pay considerable attention to the new token female members. Today, corporations focus significantly more attention on the contributions of their token ethnic members.

Bicultural Groups

In bicultural groups, two or more members represent each of two distinct cultures; for example, a fifty-fifty partnership between Peruvians and Bolivians, or a task force composed of Saudi Arabians and Jordanians, or a committee with seven Spanish and three Portuguese executives. Bicultural groups must recognize and integrate the perspectives of both represented cultures.

Multicultural Groups

In multicultural groups, members represent three or more ethnic backgrounds. United Nations agencies are good examples of multicultural organization structures, as are the committees of the European Economic Community (EEC) and the Association of Southeast Asian Nations (ASEAN). Although often moderated by the economic and political power structure of the represented members, multicultural groups, to work effectively, should recognize and integrate all represented cultures.

Although little research exists describing cross-cultural interaction within groups, there has been considerable research on the conditions for effective group functioning within the United States (18;31;41). A sizable literature also exists describing group behavior in countries around the world (often with American comparisons) (39). Studies include research on such diverse peoples as Hispanics (12), black and white Americans (37), Indians (5;32), Hong Kong and American Chinese (33), Lebanese (14), New Zealanders (6), Arabs (10), Canadians (40), British (30), South Africans, Nigerians, Filipinos (17), and Japanese (11;34). As with other types of organizational behavior, the behavior of people in groups has been found to vary across cultures.

CULTURAL DIVERSITY'S IMPACT ON GROUPS

Cultural diversity has positive and negative impacts. Diversity augments potential productivity while greatly increasing the complexity of the process that must occur in order for the group to realize its full potential (41:107). Multicultural groups have more potential for higher productivity than do homogeneous groups, but they also bear the risk of greater losses due to faulty process. As shown in the following model, the actual productivity of multicultural groups can therefore be higher, lower, or the same as that of homogeneous groups:

$$(\uparrow \text{ or } \downarrow) \ \frac{\text{Actual}}{\text{productivity}} = (\uparrow) \ \frac{\text{Potential}}{\text{productivity}} - (\uparrow) \ \frac{\text{Losses due to}}{\text{faulty process}}$$

For example, multicultural groups can have many perspectives on a problem (thus increasing potential productivity), but they frequently experience greater difficulty in pooling and evaluating these perspectives (thus causing losses in productivity due to faulty process).

Process Losses in Culturally Diverse Groups

Diversity makes group functioning more difficult because it becomes more difficult to see situations in similar ways, understand them in similar ways, and act on them in similar ways. Diversity makes reaching agreement more difficult. Employees from the same culture are gen-

and to trust each other more readily. In culturally diverse groups, misperception, misinterpretation, misevaluation and miscommunication abound (see chapter 3). Stress levels increase, and employees frequently disagree, implicitly and explicitly, on expectations, the appropriateness of information, and the particular decisions that must be taken. Diversity increases the ambiguity, complexity and inherent confusion in the group's process (see chapter 4, Table 4-1). These process losses diminish productivity.

Cohesiveness involves the ability of individual group members to act as one; the ability of group members, when necessary, to perceive, interpret, and act on the world in similar or mutually agreed upon ways. Because they begin with a less substantial base of similarity, multicultural groups are initially less cohesive than homogeneous groups.

As shown in Table 5-1, the higher levels of mistrust, miscommunication, and stress present in multicultural groups diminish cohesion. More importantly, these attitudinal and perceptual communication problems can also diminish productivity. The main "process problems" experienced by multicultural groups are discussed here.

Attitudinal Problems: Dislike and Mistrust. Culturally diverse groups possess higher levels of mistrust than do their more homogeneous counterparts. Group members often find themselves less drawn to people from other cultures than to those from their own culture (44). For example, researchers in Belgium found Walloon and Flemish individuals speaking more frequently to colleagues of their own than the opposite culture (36). In some cases mistrust results primarily from cross-cultural misinterpretation rather than dislike. For example, many Indian employees look down when acknowledging authority, an attitude that many North American and European managers misinterpret as untrustworthiness. As a result, these North American and European managers may fail to develop sufficient trust in their Indian colleagues to delegate or share more than trivial responsibilities.

Perceptual Problems: Stereotyping. Team members often inappropriately stereotype foreign colleagues rather than accurately seeing and assessing skills and potential contributions for accomplishing the present task (15). For instance, when some members come from high status cultures and others from low status cultures, group members tend to talk more to those from the higher status cultures. They assume, usually

129

TABLE 5-1 Advantages and Disadvantages of Group Diversity

Advantages	*Disadvantages*
Diversity Permits Increased Creativity	*Diversity Causes Lack of Cohesion*
Wider range of perspectives	Mistrust
More and better ideas	Lower interpersonal
Less "groupthink"	attractiveness
Diversity Forces Enhanced	Stereotyping
Concentration to Understand Others'	More within-culture
Ideas	conversations
Meanings	Miscommunication
Arguments	Slower speech: Non-native
	speakers and translation
	problems
	Less accurate
	Stress
	More counterproductive behavior
	Less disagreement on content
	Tension
Increased Creativity Can Lead to	*Lack of Cohesion Causes Inability to*
Better problem definitions	Validate ideas and people
More alternatives	Agree when agreement is needed
Better solutions	Gain consensus on decisions
Better decisions	Take concerted action
Groups Can Become	*Groups Can Become*
More effective	Less efficient
More productive	Less effective
	Less productive

subconsciously, that national stereotypes apply to each individual in the group. Thus, in initial meetings, group members frequently judge those colleagues from the most developed and economically strongest countries more favorably (15). On one particular management team, members assumed that their American colleagues had more technological expertise than did their Moroccan colleagues simply because Morocco is the economically and technologically less developed country. In a parallel situation an Indian manager described the lack of respect granted him by many of his British colleagues who, he believed, "assume that I am underdeveloped simply because I come from an economically underdeveloped country." Both the initial stereotype and the

Indian's resulting frustration diminished the organization's productivity.

Communication Problems: Inaccuracy, Misunderstanding, Inefficiency. Diversity causes communication problems (41). It slows down communication when all members are not fluent in the group's working language (19). In linguistically diverse groups, some members must use a foreign language or employ translators. In both cases communication speed decreases and the chance for errors increases as compared with unilingual groups (19).

Group members from different cultures often disagree over important meanings, such as the causes of events, the determination of admissible evidence, the relevance of specific information, and the possible conclusions that can be drawn (19). In some cases, disagreement remains implicit or hidden; members assume they interpret things similarly when, in fact, the opposite is true.

INDIAN / AUSTRIAN EXAMPLE

When asked if his department could complete a project by a given date, a particular Indian employee said "Yes" even when he knew he could not complete the project, because he believed that his Austrian supervisor wanted "yes" for an answer. When the completion date arrived and he had not finished the project, his Austrian supervisor showed dismay. The Indian's desire to be polite — to say what he thought his supervisor wanted to hear — seemed more important than an accurate assessment of the completion date. Unfortunately, the supervisor considered accurate information more important than politeness. Cross-cultural miscommunication interrupted the smooth functioning of work.[1]

Stress.   Stress and tension levels in culturally diverse groups often exceed those in homogeneous groups (44) due to a lack of trust and communication inaccuracies. For example, the deductive, analytical discussion style of the French often causes stress for the more inductive, pragmatic North Americans: the French continually want to discuss principles and historical precedent whereas the North Americans focus on the details of the immediate situation. Multicultural groups often exhibit symptoms of considerable social stress, including bickering, apathy, single-party (or single-culture) domination of discussions, stubbornness, and reprimanding (19). Multicultural groups can also show "a quiet climate of politeness and gradually increasing friendliness" (36), but according to some researchers, "these [rituals of politeness] have to be seen as the superficial defense of a weak group cohesiveness" (36). This ritual politeness leaves members frustrated and becomes yet another hindrance to group productivity.

Decresed Effectiveness. As has been demonstrated in the previous examples, cultural diversity diminishes effective group functioning in a number of serious ways. Studies show that members of multicultural groups use "more of their time and effort in creating cohesion and solidarity than members of homogeneous groups" (25;36). If unmanaged, cultural differences can paralyze a group's ability to act. For example, as described by one European manager,

> In attempting to plan a new project, a three-person team composed of managers from Britain, France, and Switzerland failed to reach agreement. To the others, the British representative appeared unable to accept any systematic approach; he wanted to discuss all potential problems before making a decision. The French and Swiss representatives agreed to examine everything before making a decision, but then disagreed on the sequence and scheduling of operations. The Swiss, being more pessimistic in their planning, allocated more time for each suboperation than did the French. As a result, although everybody agreed on its validity, we never started the project. If the project had been discussed by three Frenchmen, three Swiss, or three Britons, a decision, good or bad, would have been made. The project would not have been stalled for lack of agreement.[2]

Potential Productivity: Advantages in Culturally Diverse Groups

Although encountering more process problems, culturally diverse groups also have the potential to work more productively than do homogeneous groups because their wide range of human resources allows them to function more creatively. Groups need to perceive, interpret, and evaluate situations in numerous ways and then agree on the best decisions and directions. To function effectively, the input into the group's process should include many alternatives (the result of divergence). Managers in any organization constantly balance divergence with convergence, gathering new ideas and gaining agreement on particular decisions and actions. This balancing of creativity and cohesion particularly challenges leaders of multicultural groups.

As summarized in Table 5-1, multicultural groups invent more options and create more soultions than do single culture groups. Diversity makes it easier for groups to create more and better ideas. It allows them to avoid the trap of "groupthink" (24). It often forces members to pay closer attention to the contributions of colleagues. Each of these advantages will be discussed in the following sections (also see Table 4–1).

More and Better Ideas.   Due to the varied backgrounds present in multicultural groups, members are able to create more ideas, alternatives, and potential problem solutions than homogeneous groups (22). Researchers have found that heterogeneous groups also propose more inventive alternatives (21) and higher quality solutions to problems (22), but they only realize their potential when they adequately manage the process problems associated with diversity. For example, as described by a manager in a Swedish pharmaceutical firm,

> Product design was traditionally carried out at our Stockholm headquarters. Once, by accident or design, we brought in an international team to discuss the design of a new allergy product. Due to extreme differences in opinion on what constitutes good medical practice, the team designed the new product with maximum flexibility to suit the major demands of each country. Later we discovered this flexibility to be a great advantage in developing and marketing internationally competitive products.[3]

Limited "Groupthink."   "Groupthink" describes "a mode of thinking that people engage in when they are deeply involved in a cohesive ingroup, when the members' striving for unanimity overrides their motivation to realistically appraise alternative courses of action. . . . Groupthink refers to a deterioration of mental efficiency, reality testing, and moral judgment that results from in-group pressures" (24:9). It constitutes one of the major sources of task group ineffectiveness.

The three major symptoms of groupthink are (24): overestimates of the group's power and morality, closed-mindedness, and pressures toward uniformity. Compared with their homogeneous counterparts, multicultural groups have less chance of premature agreement caused by such counterproductive behaviors as (24:175)

1. *Self-censorship* of deviations from the apparent group consensus, reflecting each member's inclination to minimize to himself the importance of his doubts and counterarguments.

133

2. *A shared illustion of unanimity* concerning judgments conforming to the majority view (partly resulting from self-censorship of deviations, augmented by the false assumption that silence means consent).

3. *Direct pressure* on any member who expresses strong arguments against any of the group's stereotypes, illusions, or commitments, making clear that this type of dissent is contrary to what is expected of all loyal members.

4. The emergence of *self-appointed mindguards* — members who protect the group from adverse information that might shatter their shared complacency about the effectiveness and morality of their decisions.

The consequences of groupthink include incomplete survey of objectives and alternatives, failure to examine risks of preferred choices, failure to reappraise initially rejected alternatives, poor information search, selective bias in processing the information at hand, and failure to work out contingency plans (24:175). Multicultural groups find themselves less susceptible to groupthink because they are less likely to subconsciously limit their perspectives, ideas, conclusions, and decisions to that of the majority or group leadership.

CONDITIONS FOR TEAM EFFECTIVENESS

Multicultural teams have the potential to become the most effective and productive teams in an organization. Unfortunately they frequently become the least productive. Figure 5–3 shows the relative productivity of a series of four- to six-member problem-solving teams. Culturally diverse teams tended to be the most or least effective, whereas the homogeneous teams tended to be average (27). What differentiates the most from the least effective teams? Why are culturally diverse teams either more or less effective than homogeneous teams but rarely equally effective?

Highly productive and less productive teams differ in how they manage their diversity, not, as is commonly believed, in the presence or absence of diversity. When well managed, diversity becomes a productive resource to the team. When ignored, diversity causes process problems that diminish the team's productivity. Since diversity is more frequently ignored than managed (see chapter 4), culturally diverse

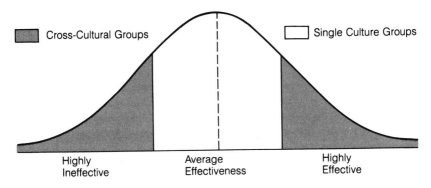

FIGURE 5-3 Group Effectiveness
SOURCE: Based on Dr. Carol Kovach's research conducted at the Graduate School of Management, University of California at Los Angeles (UCLA).

teams often perform below expectations and below the organization's norms.

As shown in Table 5-2, a multicultural team's productivity depends on its task, its stage of development, and the ways in which diversity is managed. Diversity becomes most valuable when the need for agreement (cohesion) remains low relative to the need for invention (creativity), and when creativity and agreement can be balanced. The manager must accurately assess each situation and emphasize those aspects that best fit the group's current function and structure.

TABLE 5-2 Effectively Managing Diversity

	Effective	*Ineffective*
Task	Innovative	Routine
Stage	Divergence (earlier)	Convergence (later)
Conditions	Differences recognized	Differences ignored
	Members selected for task-related abilities	Member selected on basis of ethnicity
	Mutual respect	Ethnocentrism
	Equal power	Cultural dominance
	Superordinate goal	Individual goals
	External feedback	No feedback (complete autonomy)

135

Task: Innovative or Routine

Whether and how much diversity is desirable depends on the nature of the task. When a task requires participants to perform highly specialized roles, it is more advantageous to have a diverse group. When everyone must do exactly the same thing, it is easier if members think and behave very similarly (41:106). For example, corporate consulting teams generally work most effectively when they include many specialities — finance, marketing, production, and strategy experts. Teams assembling radios, on the other hand, generally perform better when all members have the same level of manual dexterity and coordination.

For some tasks the ability of the most or the least competent member determines the group's potential productivity. For other tasks the group's potential productivity is determined by the combination of the abilities of all members. For example, if a manager decides to give workers a bonus based on the best employee's performance, the group's objective is to see that the best employee performs outstandingly. Olympic teams work in this way: a country receives the gold medal for an individual event based on the performance of its top team member. Alternatively, if the manager decides to give the entire department a bonus based on the best performance of the worst employee (that is, based on all employees, including the worst, exceeding a certain minimal level), the group's objective is to increase the productivity of the weakest employee. This approach reflects the philosophy behind the saying, "A chain is only as strong as its weakest link." In another instance, if the manager chooses to give all employees a bonus based on the department's average productivity, all department members must individually and collectively strive to perform as well as possible. Managers are very frequently assessed using this average scheme — their performance appraisal depends on their department's overall (or average) productivity. Finally, if a manager allows employees to select a reward system, the department members must assess the range of abilities within the department and select a reward scheme accordingly. In this case the team's process becomes discretionary.

Cultural diversity provides the biggest asset for teams with difficult, discretionary tasks requiring innovation. Diversity becomes less helpful when employees are working on simple tasks involving repetitive or routine procedures. Therefore, diversity generally becomes more valuable during the planning and development of projects (the "work" stage referred to in the next section) and less helpful during their implementation (the "action" stage). The more senior the team members, the more likely they are to be working on projects that can benefit from diversity. Diversity is therefore extremely valuable to senior executive teams, both within and across companies.

Stages: Entry, Work, and Action

Work groups progress through three basic stages: entry, work, and action. Early in its life, a team must develop cohesiveness. Members need to begin to know and trust each other. After this initial entry stage, creativity becomes central. The team must create ways of defining its objectives, gathering and analyzing information, and developing alternative forms of action. Although tending to hinder the team's initial development, diversity becomes most valuable during this work stage. The team needs creativity (facilitated by divergence) to succeed. During the third and final stage, convergence again becomes important. Teams need to agree, or converge, on which decisions and actions to take. Cohesion, not creativity, fosters agreement. Table 5–3 describes the advantages and disadvantages contributed by diversity at each stage of the group's development.

TABLE 5–3   Diversity and the Group's Stage of Development

Stage	Process	Diversity Makes the Process	Process Based On
Entry: Initial group formation	Trust building (developing cohesion)	More difficult	Using similarities and understanding differences
Work: Problem description and analysis	Ideation (creating ideas)	Easier	Using differences
Action: Decision making and implementation	Consensus building (agreeing and acting)	More difficult	Recognizing and creating similarities

Entry: Initial Group Formation.   In the initial stages group members need to develop relationships and build trust. Members from more task-oriented cultures such as Germany, Switzerland, and the United States, spend relatively little time getting to know each other. Members from more relationship-oriented cultures such as Latin America, the Middle East, and Southern Europe, generally spend more time getting to know their teammates. When groups from these different orientations work together, problems can result. While the task-oriented members are impatient to get down to business, the more relationship-oriented members feel rushed and distrustful of their more hurried colleagues.

On first meeting, group members are generally drawn to people who are most similar to themselves. They initially trust those people to whom they feel most attracted. Similarity therefore facilitates initial group formation and visible differences hinder it. For this reason, multicultural groups often find building initial relationships and trust more difficult than do their homogeneous counterparts. To counteract this tendency, experienced multicultural managers often focus initially on team members' equivalent professional qualifications and status rather than their dissimilar cultural backgrounds. Once they establish professional similarity and respect, they can acknowledge the cultural diversity as a potential group resource and not as an imminent threat.

Work: Problem Description and Analysis.   The group next defines its work goals and objectives and assesses its problem-solving potential. During this work stage, the group uses its diversity to collect new perspectives and ideas in order to create alternative problem definitions and solutions. Although diversity often hinders the group's initial trust building, it can enhance this second, work phase. As discussed previously, diverse gorups generally are able to see situations in more ways, interpret their perceptions in more ways, and create more alternatives than can homogeneous groups. Multicultural groups rarely succumb to groupthink, to all members blindly accepting a single definition of the situation.

Action: Decision Making and Implementation.   In this third stage the group must decide what to do and how to do it. Members must agree on which alternatives appear best and which action plans would probably be most effective. Groups reach agreement by building a consensus around a particular perspective. Implementation also depends on consensus: the group must agree on the best ways to act. These convergent processes — consensus building, agreement, and concerted action (or implementation) — are usually easier for homogeneous than heterogeneous groups. The very diversity that makes creating new ideas easier at the second stage makes consensus building and achieving agreement more difficult at this third stage.

MANAGING CULTURALLY DIVERSE GROUPS

Will a group be productive or unproductive? Multicultural teams must learn to use their diversity when it enhances productivity and minimize it when it diminishes productivity. Managers must therefore learn to minimize diversity-related losses due to faulty process by following the guidelines below.

Managing Cultural Diversity

Task-Related Selection. While acknowledging the group's diverse cultural background, leaders should not select members solely for their ethnicity but rather for their task-related abilities. "To maximize team effectiveness, members should be selected to be homogeneous in ability levels (thus facilitating accurate communication) and heterogeneous in attitudes (thus ensuring a wide range of solutions to problems)" (44).

Recognition of Differences. Groups should not ignore or minimize cultural differences: "Many barriers to intercultural communication are due to ignorance of cultural differences rather than a rejection of those differences" (13). Similarly, communication is facilitated by a better understanding of cross-cultural differences (9). Some research indicates that "culturally trained leader[s], regardless of leadership style . . . achieve a generally high[er] level of performance and rapport than do non-trained leaders" (16.) To recognize differences, team members should describe the range of cultures present without initially interpreting or evaluating the nature of any particular culture. Team members should become aware of their own stereotypes without allowing them to limit their expectations, understandings, and actions. Once they begin to recognize actual differences (to differentiate their stereotypes from the actual personality and behavior of groups members — cultural description), they should attempt to understand why the people from other cultures think, feel, and act the way they do (cultural interpre-

139

tation). Subsequently, they should begin to ask what people from each culture can contribute to those of the other cultures (cultural creativity). In this way, creating effective multicultural teams follows the same process as creating cultural synergy (see chapter 4).

A Vision or Superordinate Goal. Members of diverse groups generally have more trouble agreeing on their purpose and task than do members of homogeneous groups. This is especially true since groups set their overall purpose and superordinate goals during the initial stage of group development—the stage during which individual differences tend to dominate and often interfere with group cohesion. To maximize effectiveness, the team leader must help the group to agree on a vision or superordinate goal—a goal that transcends their individual differences. Superordinate goals are often very broad in definition and give general direction and focus to the group's subsequent activities. Superordinate goals in which success depends on collaboration and cooperation tend to decrease prejudice and increase mutual respect (38). This is particularly true when members require the continued help of their colleagues to achieve results important to each culture, as well as to the overall organization.

Equal Power. Teams generally produce more and better ideas if all members participate. Cultural dominance (disproportionate power vested in members of one culture over those from other cultures) is therefore counterproductive, because it stifles nondominant group members' contributions. In international teams, leaders must guard against vesting disproportionate power in host country members, members of the same nationality as the employing organization, members from the most technologically advanced or economically developed countries, or those with ideologies most consonant with their own. Managers should distribute power according to each member's ability to contribute to the task, not according to some preconceived gradient of relative cultural superiority.

Mutual Respect. Ethnocentrism reflects a "view of things in which one's own group is the center of everything and all others are scaled and rated with reference to it." (28:8) Prejudice refers to the judging of other groups as inferior to one's own. Equal status, close contact, and cooperative efforts toward a common goal decrease prejudice (3; 4). "The greater the opportunity for interethnic contacts, the less prejudiced and more frequent the development of cross-ethnic acceptance and friendship" (44:110). For most teams to work effectively, members must respect each other. Managers can enhance mutual respect by selecting members of equal ability, making prior accomplishments and task-related skills known to the group, and minimizing early judgments based on ethnic stereotypes.

Feedback. Given the different perspectives present, culturally diverse teams have more trouble than homogeneous teams in collectively agreeing on what constitutes a good or bad idea or decision. Whereas homogeneous teams rapidly develop judgment criteria based on their similar values, multicultural teams usually cannot. To encourage effective functioning, managers should give teams positive feedback on their process and output—as individuals and as groups—early in the team's life together. External feedback (given by a manager outside of the team) helps the group see itself as a team and serves the function of teaching the team to value its diversity, recognize contributions made by each member, and trust its collective judgment.

SUMMARY

The potential productivity of culturally diverse teams is high—they have the additional breadth of resources, insights, perspectives, and experiences that facilitate the creation of new and better ideas. Regrettably, culturally diverse groups rarely actualize their full potential. Process losses due to mistrust, misunderstanding, miscommunication, stress, and a lack of cohesion often negate the potential benefits of diversity to the team. Only if well managed can culturally diverse teams hope to achieve their potential productivity.

For effective functioning, multicultural teams must therefore (1) use their diversity to generate multiple perspectives, problem definitions, ideas, action alternatives, and solutions, (2) learn to achieve consensus (agree on specific decisions and directions, despite the diversity), and (3) balance the simultaneous needs for creativity (divergence) with those for cohesion (convergence). If teams fail to generate many ideas, they become no more effective than individuals working alone. If teams fail to achieve consensus, their diversity paralyzes them. If teams fail to balance creativity and cohesion, they become awkwardly inefficient structures having little value to the organization.

QUESTIONS FOR REFLECTION

1. As a manager, what can you do to help a multinational team work more effectively than a domestic team? What are the major problems that might occur and how best could you handle them?

2. Think of the teams you have worked with or heard about. How have the group dynamics differed in multinational teams, bicultural teams, token teams, and homogeneous teams?

3. As a senior manager in the automotive industry in charge of two Canadians, a Frenchman, a German, and three Japanese, would you rather manage them in the research division or on the production line? Why? What differences in management approach would you employ for the two situations?

4. What are some of the losses in productivity caused by faulty process? Give examples from the teams that you have worked with or observed.

5. Select a multinational political or economic team that is currently being reported in the business press. Using a synergistic management approach, how would you manage the situation? What outcomes would you strive to achieve?

6. Select a multicultural work team that you are currently involved in or aware of. Analyze the underlying cultural values affecting the situation. Suggest ways to manage the situation that would lead to synergy.

NOTES

1. A similar situation between an Indian and an American is dramatized in the movie *Going International*, Part 2, by Copeland Griggs Productions, San Francisco.

2. Based on a story told to Nancy J. Adler by a European manager attending the "Managerial Skills for International Business" executive seminar at INSEAD, Fontainebleau, France.

3. Same as Note 2.

REFERENCES

1. Adler, N. J. "Domestic Multiculturalism: Cross-Cultural Management in the Public Sector," in W. Eddy, ed., *Handbook of Organization Management* (New York: Marcel Dekker, 1983), pp. 481–499.

2. Adler, N. J., and Ghadar, F. "International Strategy from the Perspective of People and Culture: The North American Context," in A. M. Rugman, ed., *Research in Global Strategic Management: International Business Re-*

search for the Twenty-First Century; Canada's New Research Agenda, vol. 1. Greenwich, Conn.: JAI Press, 1990), pp. 179–205.

3. Allport, G. W. The Nature of Prejudice (Reading, Mass.: Addison-Wesley, 1954), p. 281.

4. Amir, Y. "Contact Hypothesis in Ethnic Relations," Psychological Bulletin, vol. 71 (1969), pp. 319–342; and Amir, Y. "The Role of Intergroup Contact in Change of Prejudice and Ethnic Relations," in P. A. Katz, ed., Toward the Elimination of Racism (New York: Pergamon, 1976).

5. Anderson, K. "The New Ellis Island," Time (June 13, 1983), pp. 16–23.

6. Anderson, L. R. "Leader Behavior, Member Attitudes and Task Performance of Intercultural Discussion Groups," Journal of Social Psychology, vol. 69 (1966), pp. 305–319.

7. Anderson, L. R. "Management of the Mixed-Cultural Work Group," Organizational Behavior and Human Performance, vol. 31, no. 3 (1983), pp. 303–330.

8. Bass, B. M. "A Plan to Use Programmed Group Exercises to Study Cross-Cultural Differences in Management Behavior," International Journal of Psychology, vol. 1, no. 4 (1966), pp. 315–322.

9. Brislin, R. W. Cross-Cultural Encounters (New York: Pergamon, 1981).

10. Chemers, M. M.; Fiedler, F. E.; Lekhyananda, D.; and Stolurow, L. M. "Some Effects of Cultural Training on Leadership in Heterocultural Task Groups," International Journal of Psychology, vol. 1, no. 4 (1966), pp. 301–314.

11. Davidson, W. H. "Small Group Activity at Musashi Semiconductor Works," Sloan Management Review, vol. 23, no. 3 (Spring 1982), pp. 3–14.

12. Delgado, M. "Hispanic Cultural Values: Implications for Groups," Small Group Behavior, vol. 12, no. 1 (February 1981), pp. 69–80.

13. Devonshire, C., and Kremer, J. W. Towards a Person-Centered Resolution of Intercultural Conflicts (La Jolla, Calif.: Center for the Whole Person).

14. Diab, L. "A Study of Intragroup and Intergroup Competition among Experimentally Produced Small Groups," Genetic Psychology Monographs, vol. 82 (1970), pp. 325–332.

15. Ferrari, S. "Human Behavior in International Groups," Management International Review, vol. XII no. 6 (1972), pp. 31–35.

16. Fielder, F. E.; Meuwese, W. A. T.; and Oonk, S. "Performance on Laboratory Tasks Requiring Group Creativity," Acta Psychology, vol. 18 (1961), pp. 110–119.

17. Hare, A. P. "Cultural Differences in Performances in Communication Networks in Africa, United States and the Philippines," Sociology and Social Research (1969), pp. 77–92.

18. Hare, A. P. *Handbook of Small Group Research* (New York: Free Press, 1976).

19. Hayles, R. "Costs and Benefits of Integrating Persons from Diverse Cultures into Organizations." Paper presented at the 21st International Congress of Applied Psychology, Edinburgh, Scotland, July 1982.

20. Hoefer, H. J. *Hawaii*, 4th ed. (Hong Kong: APA Productions, 1983).

21. Hoffman, L. R. "Homogeneity of Member Personality and Its Effect on Group Problem-Solving," *Journal of Abnormal Psychology*, vol. 58 (1959), pp. 27–32.

22. Hoffman, L. R. and Maier, N. R. F. "Quality and Acceptance of Problem Solutions by Members of Homogeneous and Heterogeneous Groups," *Journal of Abnormal Psychology*, vol. 62, no. 2 (1961), pp. 401–407.

23. "It's Your Turn in the Sun: Now 19 Million and Growing Fast, Hispanics are Becoming a Power," *Time*, vol. 112, no. 16 (October 16, 1978), pp. 48–61.

24. Janis, I. L. *Groupthink*, 2nd ed. Copyright © 1982 by Houghton Mifflin Company. Used with permission.

25. Katz, J.; Goldston, J.; and Benjamin, L. "Behavior and Productivity in Biracial Work Groups," *Human Relations*, vol. 11 (1958), pp. 123–151.

26. Kirsch, J. (citing former Lieutenant Governor of California M. Cymally). "Chicano Power," *New West*, vol. 3, no. 19 (September 11, 1978), pp. 35–46.

27. Kovach, C. Based on observations of 800 second-year MBAs in field study teams at UCLA, 1977–1980. Evaluation of teams was conducted by corporate clients and business faculty members in Los Angeles, California, 1980. Originally based on Kovach's paper, "Some Notes for Observing Group Process in Small Task-Oriented Groups," Graduate School of Management, University of California at Los Angeles, 1976.

28. Levine, R. A., and Campbell, D. T. *Ethnocentrism* (New York: John Wiley & Sons, 1972).

29. Likert, R. "The Nature of Highly Effective Groups," in *New Patterns of Management* (New York: McGraw-Hill, 1961).

30. Maier, N. R. F., and Hoffman, L. R. "Group Decision in England and the United States," *Personnel Psychology*, vol. 15, no. 2 (1962), pp. 75–87.

31. Mann, L. "Cross-Cultural Studies of Small Groups," in H. Triandis, ed., *Handbook of Cross-Cultural Psychology*, vol. 5 (Boston: Allyn & Bacon, 1980).

32. Meade, R. "An Experimental Study of Leadership in India," *Journal of Social Psychology*, vol. 72 (1967), pp. 35–43.

33. Meade, R. "Leadership Studies of Chinese and Chinese-Americans," *Journal of Cross-Cultural Psychology*, vol. 1 (1970), pp. 325-332.

34. Misumi, J. "Experimental Studies on Group Dynamics in Japan," *Psychologia*, vol. 2 (1959), pp. 229-235.

35. Novack, M. *The Rise of the Unmeltable Ethnics* (New York: Macmillan, 1972).

36. Rombauts, J. "Gedrag en Groepsbeleving in Etnisch-Homogene en Etnisch-Heterogene Groepen," *Tijdschrift Voor Opvoedkunde*, nr. 1 (1962-1963).

37. Ruhe, J., and Eastman, J. "Effects of Racial Composition on Small Work Groups," *Small Group Behavior*, vol. 8, no. 4 (November 1977), pp. 479-486.

38. Sherif, M.; Harvey, O.; White, B.; Hood, W.; and Sherif, C. *Inter-Group Conflict and Cooperation: The Robers Cave Experiment* (Norman, Okla.: Institute of Group Relations, 1961).

39. Shuter, R. "Cross-Cultural Small Group Research: A Review, an Analysis, and a Theory," *International Journal of Intercultural Relations*, vol. 1, no. 1 (Spring 1977), pp. 90-104.

40. Simard, L. M., and Taylor, D. M. "The Potential for Bicultural Communication in a Dyadic Situation," *Canadian Journal of Behavioral Science*, vol. 5 (1973), pp. 211-225.

41. Steiner, I. D. *Group Process and Productivity* (New York: Academic Press, 1972).

42. "The Samoans among Us," *The Los Angeles Times* (January 2, 1979), p. 1.

43. Toffler, A. *The Third Wave* (New York: William Morrow, 1980).

44. Triandis, H. C.; Hall, Eleanor R.; and Ewen, R. B. "Some Cognitive Factors Affecting Group Creativity," *Human Relations*, vol. 18, no. 1 (February 1965), pp. 33-35.

45. United States Office of Immigration. Personal conversation with immigration official (Los Angeles, Calif., November 1979).

46. Ziegler, S. "The Effectiveness of Cooperative Learning Teams for Increasing Cross-Ethnic Friendship: Additional Evidence," *Human Organization, The Journal of the Society for Applied Anthropology*, vol. 40, no. 3 (Fall 1981), pp. 264-268.

47. Ziller, R. C. "Homogeneity and Heterogeneity of Group Membership, in C. G. McClintock, ed., *Experimental Social Psychology* (New York: Holt, Rinehart and Winston, 1972), pp. 385-411.

CHAPTER 6

▼

Cross-Cultural Leadership, Motivation, and Decision Making

▲

For all practical purposes, all business today is global. Those individual businesses, firms, industries, and whole societies that clearly understand the new rules of doing business in a world economy will prosper; those that do not will perish.

Ian Mitroff (56:ix)

Organizations worldwide strive to fulfill their missions. They select leaders to guide them toward achieving long-term goals and short-term objectives. They expect their leaders to motivate the workforce in consistent and effective ways. The leader's prime tool is decision making: corporate managers continually make decisions that influence the success of entire operations.

This chapter looks at some of the ways corporate vision and leadership vary across cultures, how culture influences motivation, and what the implications are for managerial decision making. Although some of the principles of leadership, motivation, and decision making apply almost everywhere, the ways in which we adapt them to the local culture and work situation determine most principles' success or failure (29). Although the three are highly interrelated, they will be presented separately.

Most organization theories, while not influenced by Bruce Springsteen, were "Made in the U.S.A." and therefore influenced by the political, economic, and cultural context of the United States (10). Because the research does not yet exist explaining the specific ways in which initially American-based management theories must be altered to become internationally applicable, this chapter cannot be as comprehensive as its subject warrants. Until such knowledge is available, it is best to resist the temptation of assuming universality. As Triandis (79:139) astutely observed, culture's

> influence for organizational behavior is that it operates at such a deep level that people are not aware of its influences. It results in unexamined patterns of thought that seem so natural that most theorists of social behavior fail to take them into account. As a result, many aspects of organizational theories produced in one culture may be inadequate in other cultures.

The prudent manager can only assume that the current American-based theories are applicable to the United States; not, as is so tempting, to the world at large.

LEADERSHIP

What is our vision of success? What do we want our society to look like? How do we want our organizations to function? Who do we want to lead us? Leadership and vision remain fundamental to the understanding of a people and their institutions. The questions involved are universal, the answers often culturally specific. For example, *The Way of Lao Tzu* captures a traditional Chinese vision of leadership (81:214).

> I have three treasures. Guard and keep them.
> The first is deep love,
> The second is frugality,
> And the third is not to dare to be ahead of the world.
> Because of deep love, one is courageous.

> Because of frugality, one is generous.
> Because of not daring to be ahead of the world,
> one becomes the leader of the world.

The American Arthur Schlesinger expresses a different leadership vision in *A Thousand Days*, that of former U.S. President John F. Kennedy (67).

> Above all he [Kennedy] gave the world for an imperishable moment a vision of a leader who greatly understood the terror and the hope, the diversity and the possibility, of life on this planet and who made people look beyond nation and race to the future of humanity.

Both visions, although from different cultures and centuries, express the tension between one's immediate national concerns and the broader interests of humanity and the future. Research suggests that perceptions of what managers should be doing vary more than descriptions of what managers actually do (82). It is that tension between our world today and where we would like to be tomorrow that gives rise to the need for societies to articulate visions and select leaders to guide them toward their visions. In *Beyond National Borders*, Kenichi Ohmae (60) captures that vision as Japan moves into the twenty-first century.

> Of all the conceivable goals and achievements that Japan might seek to accomplish in the next century, only one, I believe, is worthy of Japan. It is to prove that without wielding military might, by human strength and resourcefulness alone, a major global power can alleviate the earth's disparities and injustices. . . . Now we must begin to think beyond national borders (60:11).

Traditionally, corporate visions have reflected the values and goals of the society in which they were a part. Today, with the dominant presence of multinational and global firms, corporate visions are becoming transnational. As witnessed with the 1992 integration of European Economic Community, national borders are vanishing. Whereas historical feuds remain nationally defined at government levels, economic pragmatism vanquishes them at a corporate level. Corporate leaders have chosen to transcend national boundaries in ways that remain outside the realm of government diplomats: if it is good for business, it is worth learning and doing. Corporations consequently are facing the difficult questions involved in integrating visions based on divergent values. Their success defines the global corporation's success.

Leadership Theories

Leadership involves the ability to inspire and influence the thinking, attitudes, and behavior of people (4;5;6;7;20;40). In the past, many people assumed that leaders were born, not made, and they attempted to identify the traits of great leaders. Although every society has had its great leaders, researchers have found no consistent set of traits differentiating leaders from other people (76). For example, North Americans value charisma in their leaders and identify such business and political leaders as Lee Iacocca, CEO of Chrysler Corporation (32), and Ronald Reagan, former president of the United States, as charismatic (13;14). By contrast, West Germans do not value charisma in their contemporary leaders as they associate it with the evil Hitler was able to perpetrate on the world during World War II, in part through his negative charisma.

Researchers have therefore focused on behavior, examining the types of behavior leaders display in various work settings to motivate employees. As described by Levinson in the book *Executive* (44:50), leaders' attitudes and behaviors are strongly influenced by the culture in which they grow up.

Consider the implications for leadership of individual attitudes and expectations towards power. As a result of extended experiences with people who have wielded power over them when they were children, adults have expectations about how they should relate to others who have power and how they should behave in return. These attitudes are somewhat modified as a consequence of experiences and teachers, ministers, scout leaders, and other authority figures, but fundamental attitudes toward power are derived from the earliest and most intense experiences with authority figures. . . .

In spite of individual differences, however, these experiences reflect a strong common element in any given culture. As a result, there are generalized expectations about how authority is to be wielded, how the more powerful people should act toward the weaker, and what kinds of behavior the latter might expect from the former. It is expected that one will use social strength according to culturally established norms. Therefore, when acquiring control over others, one also incurs the effects of these expectations about power figures. In short, in a particular culture a person who becomes authoritative in direct relationships to others is expected to act in much the same way as a parent acts in the family. It means that as people develop their expectations of power and attitudes toward it based on their earliest experiences with it, they will tend to work from these attitudes in every encounter. A superior who fails to conform to these expectations will be seen as an inadequate, unfair, or unjust leader.

McGregor's "Theory X" and "Theory Y" describe two different sets of assumptions about the nature of human beings and what they want from their work environment (50; also see chapter 2). Theory X leaders believe they must direct, control, and coerce people in order to motivate them to work. They assume that the more basic needs for safety and security motivate people. By contrast, Theory Y leaders believe that they must give employees freedom, autonomy, and responsibility in order to motivate them to work. Theory Y leaders assume that the higher order needs for achievement and self-actualization fundamentally motivate people.

Leaders from different cultures vary in their reasons for making Theory X and Theory Y assumptions. For example, in the United States, many Theory Y managers assume that workers' basic physiological needs for safety and security have been met and that therefore only opportunities to satisfy higher order needs will motivate workers. Moreover, they believe that the denial of these opportunities leads to alienation and lower productivity. Theory Y managers believe that most people can and want to develop interpersonal relationships characterized by trust and open communication. They therefore assume that workers produce more when the workplace is most democratic.

Theory Y managers in China act similarly, but for very different reasons. According to Oh (59), the pre-1949 Chinese saw satisfaction of lower needs as the main objective of the masses, with higher order needs going unrecognized for all but upper social class people. After the revolution two types of managers emerged: "Reds" and "Experts." "Experts," skilled in the management of things and possessing extensive technical expertise, tended to use Theory X. "Reds," skilled in the management of people and possessing political and ideological expertise, tended to use Theory Y. The "Reds," believing that Theory Y assumptions were closely tied to the philosophy of Chairman Mao, felt the workplace had to become egalitarian—that all employees had to rise together both economically and culturally. The management system must give workers' welfare prominence over the production of things. It must discourage material incentives that promote self-interest and competition. Managers had to stress collaboration by replacing individual rewards with collective rewards, encouraging participation in decision making, and emphasizing democracy and decentralization. Both Americans and Chinese agree, for different reasons, that Theory Y organizations can perform efficiently and productively—that industrialization without dehumanization is possible.

Two other very well known behavioral theories developed in the United States—Likert's "System 4" management (45;46) and Blake and Mouton's "Managerial Grid" (8;9)—advocate employee participation in decision making initiated by management. The assumption behind each theory—Theory Y, System 4, and the Managerial Grid—is that people are basically good and trustworthy. Managers can therefore delegate tasks, allow employees to structure their own work, and feel no need to supervise closely or control the work flow. Managers combine a strong concern for task with an equally strong concern for people.

Cultural Contingency

Some researchers suggest that American management theories apply abroad—for example, in the People's Republic of China (59) and Yugoslavia (37). Most managers, however, believe that they must adapt their style of leadership to the culture of the employees; that is, they believe that leadership is culturally contingent. In their groundbreaking research in 1963, Haire, Ghiselli, and Porter (22) found that, although the fourteen countries they studied had more similarities than differences, the countries clustered along ethnic rather than industrial lines. Almost two decades later, Hofstede (29) concluded that participative management approaches—including Theory Y, System 4, and the Managerial Grid—which were strongly encouraged by American theorists and managers, were not suitable for all cultures. Employees in high power distance cultures expect managers to lead, and they become uncomfortable with the delegation of discretionary decisions. Some cultures want their managers to act as decisive, authoritarian experts; others want managers to act as participative problem solvers (see Figure 2–4). For example, Laurent (41:75–76) describes his difficulty explaining matrix management to French managers:

> The idea of reporting to two bosses was so alien to these managers that mere consideration of such organizing principles was an impossible, useless exercise. What was needed first was a thorough examination and probing of the holy principle of the single chain of command and the managers' recognition that this was a strong element of their own belief system rather than a constant element in nature.

151

Even among countries culturally well suited to participative management (such as the United States, England, and Sweden), organizations must adapt the form of participation to the local culture (19). While studies vary in the extent to which appropriate leadership styles are seen to be similar to the accepted American models (see, for example, descriptions of managers in Israel [83], Europe [58], India [36], and Germany [80]), today's conclusion is that global managers must be flexible enough to alter their approach when crossing national borders and working with people from foreign cultures.

MOTIVATION

Beyond culturally appropriate leadership, what causes high employee productivity and job satisfaction? What energizes employees to behave in certain ways? What directs and channels their behavior to accomplish organizational goals? How do organizations maintain desired behavior? What forces in employees and their environment reinforce or discourage them in their course of action (74)?

One global high-technology firm based in the Silicon Valley in California thought it had the answer. The firm created the "Dragon Slayer Campaign" with posters encouraging employees to "Slay the Dragon." Unfortunately, the American management had not realized that dragons symbolized good luck to the Chinese and that their campaign was not encouraging Chinese employees to cut costs and beat the competition but rather to destroy their good luck. Understandably, Chinese employees forced the firm to take down the posters and to end the campaign.

Numerous motivation theories address these questions and, like the majority of leadership theories, most have been developed and tested in the United States (23). Each attempts to explain why human beings behave in the ways they do and what managers can do to encourage certain types of behavior while discouraging others. Let's look at a few of the historically better-recognized motivation theories and determine if they are universal or culture bound.

Maslow's Need Hierarchy

Maslow (51;52;53), an American psychologist, suggested that human beings' five basic needs form a hierarchy: from physiological, to safety, to social, to esteem, to self-actualization needs. According to Maslow, the higher order needs (i.e., esteem and self-actualization) only become activated, and thus motivate behavior, after lower order needs have been satisfied.

Does Maslow's theory, which he based on Americans, hold for employees outside of the United States?[1] Hofstede (29; see chapter 2) suggests that it does not. For instance, in countries high on uncertainty avoidance (such as Greece and Japan) as compared with lower uncertainty avoidance (such as the United States), security motivates most employees more strongly than does self-actualization. Employees in high uncertainty avoidance countries tend to consider job security and lifetime employment more important than holding a very interesting or challenging job. Social needs tend to dominate the motivation of workers in countries (such as Sweden, Norway, and Denmark) that stress the quality of life (Hofstede's femininity dimension) over productivity (Hofstede's masculinity dimension). Workers in more-collectivist countries, such as Pakistan, tend to stress social needs over the more individualistic ego and self-actualization needs. Viewing the conflicting motivations of individual and group-oriented cultures, managers using Americans' highly individualist motivation theories must ask

> In what cultural and historical context does the greatest good involve being able to break apart from one's collective base to stand alone, self-sufficient and self-contained? In the context of an individualistic society in which individualism and self-containment is the ideal, the person who most separates self from the group is thereby seen as embodying that ideal most strongly; the person who remains wedded to a group is not our (American) esteemed ideal (66:776).

By contrast, community dominates individualism in most East African nations. As explained by Mutiso (57:35), the community

> dominates all aspects of African thought. Dances are communal and worship is communal. Property was held communally before the colonial era and there are attempts today to reinstate that practice. This inbuilt bias toward the community means that *individualism is always seen as a deviance.*

"The [African] value most clearly approved . . . is traditional communal responsibility revealed partly in the condemnation of self-seeking individualism" (68:358). Clearly the motivation of employees from more collective oriented cultures differs from that of their more individualistic, American counterparts.

Numerous research studies testing Maslow's hierarchy demonstrate similar but not identical rank ordering of needs across cultures. Studies include research on such diverse cultures as Peru (75; 86), India (34), the Middle East (2;3), Mexico (65), and Anglophone and Francophone Canada (35). For example, one study shows that Liberian managers express needs similar to those of managers in South Africa, Argentina, Chile, India, and other developing countries, while demonstrating higher security and self-esteem needs than managers in more developed countries (30). In another study the need hierarchy of Libyan executives failed to replicate the rank ordering of needs in the United States; the conclusion was that Maslow's hierarchy varies from culture to culture (12). Another study found results more consistent with Maslow's findings: in a study involving the United States, Mexico, Puerto Rico, Venezuela, Japan, Thailand, Turkey, and Yugoslavia, workers in the twenty-six surveyed industrial plants ranked self-actualization most highly and security among the two least important needs. In all eight countries the more highly educated managers ranked self-actualization as more important and security as less important than did their less educated colleagues (64). In a fourteen-country study, Haire et al. (22) found that although managers in each culture want similar things from their jobs, they differ in what they think their jobs are currently giving them.

Although the conflicting patterns of research fail to be definitive, it strongly indicates that we should not assume Maslow's hierarchy to hold universally. As aptly summarized by researchers O'Reilly and Roberts (61),

> Studies have found that an individual's frame of reference will determine the order of importance of his needs. It has also been found that his frame of reference is in part determined by his culture. Therefore, it can be said that an individual's needs are partially bound by culture.

Human needs may well include fundamental or universal aspects, but their importance and the ways in which they express themselves differ in different cultures.

McClelland's Three Motives

McClelland, another American theorist, suggested that three important motives drive workers: the needs for achievement, power, and affiliation (49). Although McClelland has focused more recently on executives' needs for power (48), he initially emphasized the need for achievement as fundamental in explaining why some societies produce more than others (47). For example, in his famous studies in India, he found that entrepreneurs trained in the need for achievement did better than did untrained entrepreneurs (also see 31).

Comparative research on McClelland's achievement motivation has shown it to be relatively robust across cultures. For example, managers in New Zealand appear to follow the pattern developed in the United States (27). However, similar to his analysis of Maslow's need hierarchy, Hofstede questions the universality of McClelland's three needs (29). Hofstede begins by pointing out that the word *achievement* itself is hardly translatable into any language other than English (29:55). In his research, Hofstede found that countries with a high need for achievement also have a high need to produce (Hofstede's masculinity dimension) and a strong willingness to accept risk (Hofstede's weak uncertainty avoidance). As shown in Figure 2–6, Anglo-American countries such as the United States, Canada, and Great Britain (weak uncertainty avoidance combined with masculinity) follow the high achievement motivation pattern; and countries such as Chile and Portugal (strong uncertainty avoidance combined with femininity) follow the low achievement motivation pattern. Although helpful in explaining human behavior, McClelland's three motives have not been shown to be universal (see boxed example).

What Motivates a Person

The New Hotel in Tahiti

A major hotel chain chose to develop a new hotel in Tahiti. The developer contracted with a native skilled in carving large wooden totems. The hotel desired a number of these totems to provide the site with "atmosphere." The native quoted a price for carving the first totem, and then higher and higher prices for each succeeding totem. This, of course, astonished the hotel developer; it was "No way to do business." Didn't the Tahitian understand quantity discounts? The Tahitian artisan, equally mystified, also tried to explain, "No, you don't understand. The first one is fun. Each additional one becomes less so" (55:134).

Herzberg's Two-Factor Theory

Herzberg (24;25) suggested that certain extrinsic factors (those associated with the environment surrounding a job) only have the power to demotivate while intrinsic factors (those associated with the job itself) ✝ have the power to energize, or motivate, behavior. The extrinsic, or hygiene, factors largely correspond to Maslow's lower order physiological and safety needs. They include factors associated with job dissatisfaction such as working conditions, supervision, relations with co-workers, salary, company policy, and administration. Intrinsic factors, or motivators, largely corresponding to Maslow's higher order needs, include the work itself, responsibility, recognition for work well done, advancement, and achievement.

Recent research has questioned Hertzberg's two categories and shown that people sometimes continue a particular course of action because they have made a prior public commitment to it (impression management) and not because it continues to be rewarding (73). Similarly, some people, who gained intrinsic satisfaction from a particular activity, switch to explaining their motivation in extrinsic terms after having been given an extrinsic reward (retrospective sense-making, see [73], among others). Others indicate that some behavior is random, and not as goal oriented and rational as many American models and theories would suggest (63).

Hofstede (29) again points out that culture influences factors that motivate and demotivate behavior. According to his dimensions, it is not surprising that the highly individualistic, productivity-oriented (masculine) American culture has focused on job enrichment (the restructuring of individual jobs to increase productivity); whereas the more feminine and slightly more collective societies of Sweden and Norway developed socio-technical systems and new approaches to the quality of working life (the restructuring of employees into work groups to achieve the same ends).

Herzberg's two-factor theory has also been tested outside of the United States (28). Results in New Zealand failed to replicate those in the United States: in New Zealand, supervision and interpersonal relationships appear to contribute significantly to satisfaction and not merely to reducing dissatisfaction (27). Similarly, in a Panama Canal Zone study, researchers found non-United States citizens (including those of the Republic of Panama, the West Indies, Latin America, Europe, Asia, and Canada) cited certain hygiene factors as satisfiers with greater frequency than did their American counterparts (15).

MOTIVATION

Similar to other motivation theories, the universality of Herzberg's two-factor theory cannot be assumed. In every culture certain factors act as motivators; others act as hygiene factors. The specific factors and their relative importance appear particular to each culture and, all too frequently, to each situation. Managers should enter a new culture asking which factors are important and not assuming that their prior experience is transferable. ✳

Vroom's Expectancy Theory

Expectancy theories (84, 85; also see 42) claim that people are driven by the expectation that their acts will produce results. Workers assess both their ability to perform a task and the probable type of reward for successful performance (for example, continued employment or a paycheck). According to expectancy theories, the likelihood that an action will lead to certain outcomes or goals (E), multiplied by attractiveness of the outcome $(V$, its valence) equals motivation $(M = E \times V)$ (43). Expectancy theories depend on the extent to which employees believe they have control over the outcomes of their efforts as well as the manager's ability to identify desired rewards, both of which vary across cultures. Although expectancy theories have clearly advanced our understanding of motivation, they are equally clearly culturally dependent.

A recent review of our understanding of motivation (72:650–651) underscores that "whether the driving force is thought to be prior reinforcement, need fulfilment, or expectancies of future gain, the individual is assumed to be a rational maximizer of personal utility." Unfortunately, this individual, calculative view of motivation has questionable applicability outside of the United States and "could be a fundamental omission in our motivation theories." (72:651; also see 10).

For example, in countries where individualism dominates, employees see their relationship with the organization from a calculation perspective, whereas in collectivist societies, the ties between the individual and the organization have a moral component (10;1;58). Clearly people become committed to organizations for very different reasons in individualistic than in collectivist societies (73). Employees with collectivist values make organizational commitments due to their ties with managers, owners, and co-workers (collectivism); and much less because of the nature of the job or the particular compensation scheme (individualistic incentives [10]). Given its individualistic orientation, it is not surprising that the United States has the most executive search firms and the highest level of executive and managerial mobility in the world (10).

As discussed in chapter 1 (see the dominance-harmony dimension, pages 23–25), people in different cultures vary in the amount of control they believe they have over their environment. Most Americans strongly believe that they control their environment. American managers believe that they directly influence the world in which they work (that is, they have a high level of internal attribution). Americans believe that "Where there is a will, there is a way." By contrast, many managers in other parts of the world believe that they only partially control their work environment and the outcomes of their own behavior (that is, they attribute the causes of some events to external circumstances). For example, Moslem managers believe that things will happen only if God wills them to happen (external attribution); Latin American managers believe that it is important to be from the right family and social class (external attribution); Hong King Chinese believe that there is an element of "joss," or luck, involved in all transactions (external attribution); whereas most American managers believe hard work will get the job done (internal attribution). Expectancy theories work best in explaining cultures that emphasize internal attribution.

The rewards people want from work also vary greatly across cultures. As discussed in reference to Maslow, security is very important to some people, congenial relationships are paramount to others, and individual status and respect (career advancement) are dominant for others. In a classic study, Sirota and Greenwood (71) investigated the work goals of 19,000 employees in a large multinational electrical equipment manufacturer operating in forty-six countries and reported the results for the twenty-five countries with at least forty employees, including Argentina, Australia, Austria, Belgium, Brazil, Canada, Chile, Colombia, Denmark, Finland, France, Germany, India, Israel, Japan, Mexico, New Zealand, Norway, Peru, South Africa, Sweden, Switzerland, the United Kingdom, the United States, and Venezuela.

In these countries the five most important goals concerned achievement, especially individual achievement. Next in importance were the immediate environment, general features of the organization, and employment conditions such as pay and work hours. Some of the major differences among the culture groups included

1. English-speaking countries were higher on individual achievement and lower on the desire for security.

2. French countries, although similar to the English-speaking countries, gave greater importance to security and somewhat less to challenging work.

3. Northern European countries expressed less interest in "getting ahead" and work recognition goals and put more emphasis on job accomplishment; in addition, they showed more concern for people and less for the organization as a whole (it was important for them that the job not interfere with their personal lives).

4. Latin countries found individual achievement somewhat less important, especially southern Europeans who placed the highest emphasis on job security. Both groups of Latin countries emphasized fringe benefits.

5. Germany was high on security and fringe benefits and among the highest on "getting ahead".

6. Japan was low on advancement but was also second highest on challenge and lowest on autonomy, with strong emphasis on good working conditions and a friendly working environment (71).

Expectancy theories are universal to the extent that they do not specify the types of rewards that motivate a given group of workers. Managers themselves must determine the level and type of rewards most sought after by a particular people. While Sirota and Greenwoods' conclusions support the idea that basic human needs are similar, they highlight that culture and environment determine how these needs can best be met.

The international management literature is replete with examples of overgeneralization, due to the dominance of American reward structures. For example (as described in chapter 1), raising the salaries of a particular group of Mexican workers motivated them to work *fewer*, not more, hours. As the Mexicans explained, "We can now make enough money to live and enjoy life [one of their primary values] in less time than previously. Now, we do not have to work so many hours." In another example, an expatriate manager in Japan decided to promote one of his Japanese sales representatives to manager (a status reward). To the surprise of the expatriate boss, the promotion diminished the new Japanese manager's performance. Why? Japanese have a high need for harmony—to fit in with their work colleagues. The promotion, an individualistic reward, separated the new manager from his colleagues, embarrassed him, and therefore diminished his motivation to work.

When modified for the extent to which managers believe they control their work environment and for the specific types of rewards desired, expectancy theories appear to hold outside of the United States, even in countries as culturally dissimilar to the United States as Japan (54).

Motivation Is Culture Bound

Most motivation theories in use today were developed in the United States by Americans and about Americans. Of those that were not, many have been strongly influenced by American theoretical work. Americans' strong emphasis on individualism has led to the expectancy and equity theories of motivation: theories that emphasize rational, individual thought as the primary basis of human behavior. The emphasis placed on achievement is not surprising given Americans' willingness to accept risk and their high concern for performance. The theories therefore do not offer universal explanations of motivation; rather, they reflect the values system of Americans (see 29).

Unfortunately, American as well as non-American managers have tended to treat American theories as the best or only way to understand motivation. They are neither. American motivation theories, although assumed to be universal, have failed to provide consistently useful explanations outside the United States. Managers must therefore guard against imposing domestic American management theories on their multinational business practices (see 33).

DECISION MAKING

In the United States, "It could be argued that the essence of living is free choice—the process of making decisions. To be deprived of choices is to lose all meaning." (17:59) Decision making plays a central role in managing; for some, decision making *is* managing (70). The higher the level of management, the greater the number and complexity of the decisions made. Leadership involves making decisions that affect a whole organization or a unit within an organization. Motivation, when viewed from the perspective of decision making, simply becomes the series of choices leaders make in order to influence the behavior of their colleagues and subordinates. Moreover, planning becomes the making of sets of related decisions. Ian Wilson captures the ultimate dilemma faced by all decision makers in observing that "no amount of sophistication is going to allay the fact that all your knowledge is about the past and all your decisions are about the future." Decision makers will always act on the basis of inadequate and incomplete knowledge. Good decision makers in every culture are those who learn to cope with this reality. In the past, managers could base their decisions on their own experience and culture; today that is no longer true.

Oganization theorists have argued for years about the theory and reality of how people make decisions. Some believe that managerial decision making reflects a conscious, rational process in which the manager selects a set of criteria and uses it to evaluate alternative solutions to a particular problem. For example, in choosing profit maximization as a prime criterion, managers might assess a range of business opportunities relative to their potential to generate profit. Alternatively, an equally rational decision rule might be satisficing (i.e., meeting acceptable standards on several criteria rather than maximum standards on a single criterion). When satisficing, managers might assess alternatives until they identify at least one projected to generate a certain acceptable profit. Without further search, they would then select that alternative. Unfortunately, our contact with other cultures has created new problems for us in attempting to use these objective, rational processes. As futurist Robert Theobold (78:42) observed, "We are all having increasing problems as we come to understand that different people have profoundly different visions of reality, and that there is no objective way of sorting out which of these visions is correct."

Other theorists, such as the noted psychoanalyst Sigmund Freud, believe that human decision making is an irrational process—that forces outside of our conscious control drive decision making. Herbert Simon (69;70), in his administrative theory of individual decision making, describes the process managers use to make decisions as "bounded rationality." According to Simon, managers make choices based on simplified rather than real situations. This "subjective rationality" narrows and alters the objective facts. Since managers from different cultures perceive the world differently, their subjective rationalities are different, as are their ways of simplifying complex realities into environments in which they are capable of making choices.

Along this rational/irrational spectrum, some theorists believe that one best way exists to make decisions; others believe that the best way depends on the particular situation. For example, in certain situations companies should profit maximize, in others they should satisfice, and in still others they should base their decisions on intuition rather than on rational economic analysis. In this section we will look at some of the ways in which decision making is culturally contingent; that is, the ways in which the "best way" depends on the values, beliefs, attitudes, and behavioral patterns of the people involved. In this sense, cultural contingency becomes one more contingency in the fit-models of decision making; the decision-making style must fit the culture.

Decision making involves five basic steps (17, based on 16 & 70):

1. Problem recognition
2. Information search
3. Construction of alternatives
4. Choice
5. Implementation

These steps ask the following questions: Do managers from different cultures perceive problems in the same way? Do they gather similar types and amounts of information while investigating the problem? Do they construct similar types of solutions? Do they use similar strategies for choosing between alternatives? Do managers implement their decisions in the same ways? The answer to each question is *no*. At each step, as illustrated in Table 6–1, culture influences the ways managers make decisions and solve problems.

Problem Recognition

When is a problem a problem? When do people from different cultures recognize that a problem exists? Based on differences in a society's orientation to activity—to "getting things done" (see chapter 1)—some cultures emphasize solving problems; others focus on accepting situations as they are. In certain cultures, such as the United States, managers perceive most situations as problems to be solved; as opportunities for improvement through change. Other cultures, such as the Thai, Indonesian, and Malaysian cultures, tend to see no need to change situations but rather attempt to accept situations as they are. If problem-solving managers receive notice that a prime supplier will be three months late in delivering needed construction materials, they will immediately attempt to speed up delivery or to find an alternative supplier. If, on the other hand, situation-accepting managers were to re-

TABLE 6-1 The Cultural Contingencies of Decision Making

Five Steps in Decision Making	Cultural Variations	
1. Problem Recognition	*Problem Solving* Situation should be changed.	*Situation Acceptance* Some situations should be accepted rather than changed.
2. Information Search	*Gathering "Facts"*	*Gathering ideas and possibilities*
3. Construction of Alternatives	*New, future-oriented alternatives* Adults can learn and change.	*Past-, present-, and future-oriented alternatives* Adults cannot change substantially.
4. Choice	*Individual decision making* Decision making responsibility is delegated. Decisions are made quickly. Decision rule: Is it true or false?	*Group decision making* Only senior management makes decisions. Decisions are made slowly. Decision rule: Is it good or bad?
5. Implementation	*Slow* Managed from the top Responsibility of one person	*Fast* Involves participation of all levels Responsibility of group

ceive the same notice of delay, they might simply accept that the project would be delayed. Situation-accepting managers believe that they neither can nor should alter every situation that confronts them. Problem-solving managers believe that they both can and should change situations to their own benefit. Situation-accepting managers generally believe that fate or God's will intervene in the production process (external attribution), whereas problem-solving managers are more likely to believe that they are the prime or only influence on the same process (internal attribution). Consequently, while viewing exactly the same situation, an American manager might identify a problem long before his Indonesian or Malaysian counterpart would choose to recognize it as such. Comparative research has demonstrated that managers' perceptions of situations and their definitions of problems vary across cultures.

Information Search

After recognizing that a problem exists, where does the manager gather information to solve it? The noted psychoanalyst Carl Jung suggested two primary modes of gathering information (i.e., of perceiving): <u>sensing and intuition</u>. Sensers primarily use their five senses to gather information and facts about a situation; intuitive people more frequently use ideas from the past and future for their data gathering. Sensers rely on facts and are more inductive; intuitive people rely more heavily on images and are more deductive. Cervantes, the prototypical intuitive, captures the thinking pattern of intuitive people:

> When life itself seems lunatic, who knows where madness lies? Perhaps to be too practical is madness. To surrender dreams—this may be madness. To seek treasure where there is only trash. Too much sanity may be madness. And the maddest of all, to see life as it is and not as it should be.[2]

Cultures vary in the extent to which one or the other style of data gathering (perceiving) dominates. For example, during the 1973 war in the Middle East, the Americans, as typical sensers, assessed the situation pessimistically for the Israelis because 100 million Arabs were at war with less than 8 million Israelis. The Americans based their perception of the situation on fact-oriented, empirical evidence. The Israelis, who are typically more intuitive, based their predictions on their image of the future—the existence of a free Jewish state—and therefore were optimistic. Moreover, the Israelis felt that the number of Arabs and Israelis was relevant in determining *how* they would fight the war but was irrelevant in influencing their belief about *if* they would win. In a similar contrast of perceptual styles, many English Canadians—typically sensers—agonized over Quebec's diminishing economic base and consequently predicted the ousting of the Parti Quebecois government. Many French Canadians, more typically basing their observations on intuition, continue to reiterate their vision of a culturally and linguistically French province. These French Canadians, while recognizing the economic consequences, consider it less relevant in assessing the validity of their overall goal.

Constructing Alternatives

What types of alternatives do we construct? Are they predominantly new ideas or ideas that have been tried in the past? Are they ideas that demand large or moderate amounts of change? Based on a culture's underlying values, the types of alternatives will vary. For example, more future-oriented cultures, such as California, tend to generate more new alternatives. More conservative, past-oriented cultures, such as England, tend to search for historical patterns on which to base alternatives. Californians, when attempting to minimize urban congestion, would be more likely to consider monorails and "flying cars"; the British are more likely to consider improved traffic control mechansims. Both societies consider both types of alternatives; but, in each, one type is preferred. Similarly, Mutiso's observation (57:35) that, for some Africans, "being educated (is) equivalent to rejecting the ways of ancestors" underscores the contrasting orientations of present and past (see pages 30–32, time dimension).

Similarly, some cultures believe that adults can change, whereas other cultures believe that adults basically remain unchangeable (see pages 22–24, definition of the individual dimension). Cultures that believe in change stress alternatives that include learning and on-the-job training; those believing in permanence stress initial selection. Today a company's orientation toward change is often reflected in its approach to high technology: "Can we train our present employees to learn to use robots (change possible), or must we hire new employees who are already robotics experts (change impossible)?" Given Americans' strong belief in employees' and managers' ability to change, it is not surprising that the American Society for Training and Development has over 50,000 members.

Choice

Who makes the decisions for a company? Are decisions made quickly or slowly? Are information and alternatives discussed sequentially or holistically? Based on a culture's view of the relationships among people (see chapter 1), either individuals or groups will hold primary decision-making responsibility. In North American business, individuals usually make decisions. The slang phrase "the buck stops here" reflects the belief that ultimately a single person assumes responsibility for a particular decision. In Japan groups make decisions; most Japanese would find it inconceivable for an individual to make a decision prior to consulting his or her immediate colleagues and gaining their agreement (18;38;39;62;78).

At what level are decisions made? In more hierarchical cultures (see Hofstede's power distance dimension, pages 50–52), only very senior level managers make decisions. Lower level personnel hold responsibility for implementing decisions. For example, most lower level Indian employees would wonder about the competence of a superior who consulted them on routine decisions. The majority of Indian managers prefer an autocratic style, and up to 85 percent of their surveyed subordinates believe they work better under supervision (36). By contrast, most lower level Swedish employees expect to make most of their own decisions about day-to-day operations. Thus, it is not surprising that the Swedes, not the Indians, experimented with some of the first autonomous work groups at Volvo's Kalmar plant (21). There, management gave groups of employees total responsibility for producing cars. The group, not senior management, took responsibility for allocating and scheduling tasks and allocating rewards among workers. Management could only delegate this amount of discretion to the shop floor in a low power distance country.

Are decisions made slowly or quickly? American businesspeople pride themselves in being quick decision makers. In the United States being called "decisive" is a compliment. By contrast, most other cultures downplay time urgency—some cultures even increase a decision's value based on the length of time spent in making it. When managers from quick-paced cultures such as the United States attempt to conduct business with people from more slowly paced cultures such as Egypt, the mismatched timing causes problems. The Americans typically become frustrated at the Egyptians' slow, deliberate pace and begin to believe that their Middle Eastern counterparts lack interest in doing business. The Egyptians, on the other hand, in observing the Americans' "overly hasty race" to make decisions typically conclude that the Americans' unwillingness to take more time reflects the lack of importance they place on the business relationship and the particular deal being negotiated. Time (as discussed in chapter 1) is a crucial dimension in understanding business behavior cross-culturally.

How much risk is too much? As described by Hofstede in chapter 2, cultures vary in their uncertainty avoidance (29). Managers in some cultures take more risks than those in other cultures. The extent to which managers feel willing to experiment, to try previously untried alternatives, depends on their aversion to risk.

In what order do businesspeople discuss alternatives? When do they eliminate alternatives? When is the one, chosen alternative selected? As will be discussed in chapter 7, some holistic cultures, such as Japan (77) and China, discuss all alternatives before making any decisions; ✕ other sequence-oriented cultures, such as the United States, Germany, and Canada, tend to discuss alternatives in a preplanned sequence, ✗ making incremental decisions as they go along.

The overall process of decision making can be described in Jungian terms, with some people acting primarily as "thinkers" and others primarily as "feelers." Thinkers generally process data and make decisions by questioning whether an alternative is correct or incorrect, true or false. Feelers, while equally logical, question whether an alternative is good or bad. Thinkers orient themselves around a belief in absolute truth, whereas feelers orient themselves around a model of "fit": is there a good or bad fit between this alternative and what we are trying to accomplish. In selecting a new manager, the thinker might stress the individual's expertise and track record. The feeler might stress the candidate's ability to fit in with the other members of the organization. Both are equally logical and valid systems for decision making, but each leads to very different choices.

Implementation

If decisions are to have any value, they must be implemented. Again, depending on the culture, implementation can be quick or slow, innovative or disruptive, managed from the top or involving participation from all levels within the organization, managed by an individual or a group. Some of the most difficult international business decisions involve ethical considerations. In a survey of *Harvard Business Review* readers, almost half agreed that "the American business executive tends not to apply the great ethical laws immediately to work. He is preoccupied chiefly with gain." Only 5 percent listed social responsibility as a factor influencing ethical standards. Half of the respondents attributed unethical practices to superiors who were interested in results no matter how they were attained (11). International business decisions are often even more difficult to make than domestic decisions because the very basis of what is "right" and "wrong" is culturally determined.

The following excerpt presents four business decisions demanding ethical considerations. As you read each, observe the criteria you would use at each stage of the decision-making process: problem recognition, information search, constructing alternatives, choice, and implementation. To what extent are your criteria culturally determined? Under what conditions would you be willing to modify your perspective and decision?

Ethical Decision Making

In each of the following situations, first decide what you would do and why. Note what information you would use to investigate the question, what alternatives you would consider, and what criteria you would use to make the decision. After making your own decision, meet with a group of your colleagues — preferably including people from other cultures — and make a group decision. Again assess the type of information you considered, the range of alternatives you generated, the criteria you used to decide, and your implementation plan. Next, develop a contrasting culture decision; that is, make the opposite decision based on assumptions of a culture that is very different from your own. Finally, following the suggestions in chapter 4 for creating synergistic solutions, develop a decision and implementation plan that both you and a member of the "contrasting culture" could accept and support. The situations are not easy. Each is based on a true situation in which at least one manager believed unethical behavior was involved.

Case 1: Sales Representative in the Middle East

You are the sales representative for your construction company in the Middle East. Your company has bid on a substantial project that it wants *very much* to get. Yesterday the cousin of the minister who will award the contract suggested that he might be of help. You are reasonably sure that with his help the chances of getting the contract would increase. For his assistance the minister expects $20,000. You would have to pay this in addition to the standard fees to your agent. If you do not make this payment to the minister, you are certain that he will go to your competition (who has won the last three contracts), and they *will* make the payment (and probably get this contract, too).

Your company has no code of conduct yet, although a committee was formed some time ago to consider one. The government of your country recently passed a Business Practices Act. The pertinent paragraph is somewhat vague but implies that this kind of payment would probably be a violation of the act. The person to whom you report,

---

and those above him, do not want to become involved. The decision is yours to make.

Case 2: Hazardous Materials in West Africa

For one year now you have been international vice president of a multinational firm that produces and markets chemicals. The minister of agriculture in a small developing country in West Africa has requested a series of large shipments over the next five years of a special insecticide that only your firm prepares. The minister believes that this chemical is the only one that will rid one of his crops of a new infestation that threatens to destroy it. You know, however, that one other insecticide would probably be equally effective; it is produced in another country and has never been allowed in your own country.

Your insecticide, MIM, is highly toxic. After years of debate, your government has just passed a law forbidding its use in your country. There is evidence that dangerous amounts are easily ingested by humans through residue on vegetables, through animals that eat the crops, and through the water supply. After careful thought, you tell the minister about this evidence. He still insists on using it, arguing that it is necessary and it will be used "intelligently." You are quite sure that, ten years from now, it will begin to damage the health of some of his people.

Both the president and the executive vice president of your firm feel strongly that the order should be filled. They question the government's position, and they are very concerned about the large inventory of MIM on hand and the serious financial setback its prohibition will cause the company. They have made it clear, however, that the decision is up to you.

Note: The company has a code of conduct and your government has a Business Practices Act, but neither covers hazardous materials.

Case 3: The Southeast Asian Advertising Campaign

You are the new marketing manager for a very large, profitable international firm that manufactures automobile tires. Your advertising agency has just presented for your approval elaborate plans for introducing a new tire into the Southeast Asian market. The promotional material clearly implies that your product is better than all local products. In fact, it is better than some, but not as good as others. This material tries to attract potential buyers by explaining that for six months your product will be sold at a "reduced price." Actually, the price is reduced from a hypothetical amount that was established only so it could be "reduced." The ad claims that the tire has been tested under the "most adverse" conditions. In reality, it has not been tested in the prolonged heat and humidity of the tropics. Finally, your company assures potential buyers that, riding on your tires, they will be safer in their car than ever before. The truth is, however, that they would be equally safe on a competitor's tire that has been available for two years.

You know your product is good. You also know the proposed advertising is deceptive. Your superiors have never been concerned about such practices, believing they must present your products as distinctive in order to achieve and maintain a competitive edge. They are counting on a very favorable reception for this tire in Southeast Asia. They are counting on you to see that it gets this reception.

Whether you go with the proposed advertising or not is up to you. Your company has a code of conduct and your government has a Business Practices Act, but neither covers advertising practices.

Case 4: Cultural Conflict in the Middle East

You were quite upset last week when you read a strong editorial in the *New York Times*, written by a prominent journalist, that was highly critical of your company, especially its major project in a conservative Moslem country.

As the international vice president, you are responsible for this project, which is the building and running of a large steel plant. Based on the figures, this plant makes a lot of sense, both for your company and for the government of the country that approved the project. But as the journalist pointed out, it is to be built in a rural area and will have a very disruptive effect upon the values and customs of the people in the whole region. There will be many consequences. The young people from the other towns will move to work at the plant, thereby breaking up families and eliminating their primary source of financial and personal security. Working the second or third shift will further interfere with family responsibilities, as well as religious observances. Working year round will certainly mean that many people will be unable to return home to help with the harvest. As the young people will be paid more and more, they will gain more influence, thereby overturning century-old patterns of authority. And, of course, the Westerners who will be brought in will probably not live up to the local moral standards and will not show due respect for local women.

The journalist ended up charging your company with "cultural imperialism" and claiming that your plant, if actually built and put into operation, would contribute to the disruption of the traditional values and relationships that have provided stability for the country through many generations.

You had known there would be some social changes, but you did not realize how profound they could be. You have now examined other evidence and discovered that a factory built several years ago by another foreign firm in a similar location is causing exactly these problems — and more. Widepread concern in the country over these problems is one reason for the increasing influence of traditionalists and nationalists in the country, who argue for getting rid of all foreign firms and their disruptive priorities and practices.

Your company has a code of conduct and your government has a Business Practices Act, but neither deals with the destruction of traditional values and relationships. You are on your own here. A lot is at stake for the company and for the people of the region into which you had planned to move. The decision is yours.[3]

SUMMARY

Effective styles of management vary among cultures. Whereas managers in all countries must lead, motivate, and make decisions, the ways in which they approach these managerial behaviors is, in part, determined by their own cultural background and that of the work force. Far from learning only one way to lead, motivate, and decide, managers working across cultures must be flexible enough to adapt to each particular situation and each particular country. In moving from domestic to international management, leaders must develop a wider range of thinking patterns and behaviors along with the ability to select the pattern best suited to the particular situation. Effective international managers must be chameleons capable of acting in many ways, not experts rigidly adhering to one approach.

Most organizational behavior theories have been developed in the United States by Americans. The questions they raise — "How can I lead most effectively? How should I motivate the workforce? How can I make the best decisions?" — are universal, but the solutions are culturally specific. Rather than being applicable worldwide, many theoretical models are only effective within an American or North American context. International managers must decide to use autocratic or democratic styles of leadership, individual- or group-oriented motivation schemes, long-term or short-term criterion for decision making. Their decisions, to be most effective and most appropriate, must depend on the particular industry, organization, individuals, and culture involved. Far from being useless, theoretical models guide the questions we ask.

Only observation and analysis of the particular culture and situation involved can guide our answers.

QUESTIONS FOR REFLECTION

1. Publicly elected officials often display the leadership values and behaviors of a culture. Select two prominent world leaders and describe their behavior in cultural terms.

2. Imagine that you have just been selected to be an expatriate manager in a country in which your company has decided to open a new factory. Neither you nor your company has ever worked in this country before. What would you do to motivate the workers from the foreign country to join your company and to work hard. (Note: Select a specific foreign country before describing your motivation plan.)

3. Your company has just formed a strategic alliance with a company from another part of the world. You have been made the manager of a transition team including people from Singapore, Switzerland, Mexico, and Canada. Many decisions about the merger must be made right away. What could you do as manager to see that the decision-making process is as effective as possible?

4. What are your own assumptions about motivation? Why do you think people work? List your own motivation assumptions and then analyze them from a cross-cultural perspective. In what ways are your assumptions similar to those of most of the people from your country?

NOTES

1. While Maslow's hierarchy has been questioned within the United States, it has become one of the accepted bases for explaining and understanding behavior within organizations; generalizing from this United States–based acceptance to worldwide applicability is questioned in this chapter.

2. Quotation is from the play *Man of La Mancha* (as found in Otis L. Guernsey, Jr., New York: Dodd, Mead, 1966, p. 214), which is based on the book *Don Quixote* by Miguel Cervantes.

3. George W. Renwick and Robert T. Moran, "Basic Responsibility and International Business Ethics (BRIBE)," American Graduate School of International Management, January 1982.

REFERENCES

REFERENCES

1. Allen, D. B.; Miller, E. L.; and Nath, R. "North America," in R. Nath ed., *Comparative Management*. (Cambridge, Mass.: Ballinger, 1988), pp. 23–54.

2. Badawy, M. K. "Managerial Attitudes and Need Orientations of Mideastern Executives: An Empirical Cross-Cultural Analysis," *Academy of Management Proceedings*, vol. 39 (1979), pp. 293–297.

3. Badawy, M. K. "Styles of Mideastern Managers," *California Management Review*, vol. XXII, no. 3 (Spring 1980), pp. 51–59.

4. Bass, B. M. *Leadership and Performance Beyond Expectations* (New York: The Free Press, 1985).

5. Bass, B. M., and Stogdill, R. M. *The Handbook of Leadership*, 3d ed. (New York: The Free Press, 1989).

6. Bennis, W. *Why Leaders Can't Lead: The Unconscious Conspiracy Continues*. (San Francisco: Jossey-Bass, 1989).

7. Bennis, W., and Nanus, B. *Leaders*. (New York: Harper and Row, 1985).

8. Blake, R. R., and Mouton, J. S. "Motivating Human Productivity in the People's Republic of China," *Group and Organization Studies*, vol. 4, no. 2 (June 1979), pp. 159–169.

9. Blake, R. R., and Mouton, J. S. *The Managerial Grid*. (Houston, Tex.: Gulf Publishing, 1964).

10. Boyacigiller, N., and Adler, N. J. "The Parochial Dinosaur: The Organizational Sciences in a Global Context." Working Paper, San José State University, 1990.

11. Brenner, S. N., and Molander, E. A. "Is the Ethics of Business Changing?" *Harvard Business Review* (January–February, 1977), pp. 70–71.

12. Buera, A., and Glueck, W. "Need Satisfaction of Libyan Managers," *Management International Review*, vol. 19, no. 1 (1979), pp. 113–123.

13. Conger, J. A. *The Charismatic Leader: Behind the Mystique of Exceptional Leadership*. (San Francisco: Jossey-Bass, 1989).

14. Conger, J. A., and Kanungo, R. N., eds. *Charismatic Leadership*. (San Francisco: Jossey-Bass, 1988).

15. Crabbs, R. A. "Work Motivation in the Culturally Complex Panama Canal Company," *Academy of Management Proceedings* (1973), pp. 119–126.

16. Dewey, J. *How We Think* (Boston: D.C. Heath, 1933).

17. Driver, M. J. "Individual Decision Making and Creativity," in S. Kerr, ed., *Organizational Behavior* (Columbus, Ohio: Grid Publishing, 1979), pp. 59–91.

173

18. Drucker, P. F. "What We Can Learn from Japanese Management," *Harvard Business Review* (March–April 1971), pp. 110–122.

19. Foy, N., and Gadon, H. "Worker Participation Contrasts in Three Countries," *Harvard Business Review* (May–June 1976), pp. 71–84.

20. Gardner, J. W. *John W. Gardner on Leadership.* (New York: The Free Press, 1989.)

21. Gyllenhammer, P. G. "How Volvo Adapts Work to People," *Harvard Business Review*, vol. 55, no. 4 (1977), pp. 102–113.

22. Haire, M., Ghiselli, E. E.; and Porter, L. W. "Cultural Patterns in the Role of the Manager," *Industrial Relations*, vol. 2, no. 2 (February 1963), pp. 95–117.

23. Hammer, W. C. "Motivation Theories and Work Applications," in S. Kerr, ed., *Organizational Behavior* (Columbus, Ohio: Grid Publishing, 1979), pp. 41–58.

24. Herzberg, F. "One More Time: How Do You Motivate Employees?" *Harvard Business Review* (January–February 1968), pp. 54–62.

25. Herzberg, F.; Mausner, B.; and Snyderman, B. *The Motivation to Work*, 2d ed. (New York: John Wiley and Sons, 1959).

26. Hessling, P., and Keenen, E. E. "Culture and Subculture in a Decision-Making Exercise," *Human Relations*, vol. 22 (1969), pp. 31–51.

27. Hines, G. H. "Achievement, Motivation, Occupations and Labor Turnover in New Zealand," *Journal of Applied Psychology*, vol. 58, no. 3 (1973), pp. 313–317.

28. Hines, G. H. "Cross-Cultural Differences in Two-Factor Theory," *Journal of Applied Psychology*, vol. 58, no. 5 (1973), pp. 375–377.

29. Hofstede, G. "Motivation, Leadership and Organization: Do American Theories Apply Abroad?" *Organizational Dynamics* (Summer 1980), pp. 42–63.

30. Howell, P.; Strauss, J.; and Sorensen, P. F. "Research Note: Cultural and Situational Determinants of Job Satisfaction among Management in Liberia," *Journal of Management Studies* (May 1975), pp. 225–227.

31. Hundal, P. S. "A Study of Entrepreneurial Motivation: Comparison of Fast- and Slow-Progressing Small Scale Industrial Entrepreneurs in Punjab, India," *Journal of Applied Psychology*, vol. 55, no. 4 (1971), pp. 317–323.

32. Iacocca, L., and Novak, W. *Iacocca.* (New York: Bantam Books, 1984.)

33. Illman, P. E. "Motivating the Overseas Work Force," in *Developing Overseas Managers and Managers Overseas* (New York: AMACOM, 1980), pp. 83–106.

34. Jaggi, B. "Need Importance of Indian Managers," *Management International Review*, vol. 19, no. 1 (1979), pp. 107–113.

35. Jain, C. H., and Kanungo, R. *Behavioral Issues in Management: The Canadian Context* (Toronto: McGraw-Hill Ryerson, 1977), pp. 85–99.

36. Kakar, S. "Authority Patterns and Subordinate Behavior in Indian Organizations," *Administrative Science Quarterly*, vol. 16, no. 3 (September 1971), pp. 298–308.

37. Kaufman, F. "Decision Making—Eastern and Western Style," *Business Horizons*, vol. 13, no. 6 (December 1970), pp. 81–86.

38. Kavic, B.; Rus, V.; and Tannenbaum, A. S. "Control, Participation, and Effectiveness in Four Yugoslavian Industrial Organizations," *Administrative Science Quarterly*, vol. 16, no. 1 (March 1971), pp. 74–86.

39. Keizan, W. "Decision Making by Socialist Managers in Complex Organizations," *International Studies of Management and Organization*, vol. 9, no. 4 (1979), pp. 63–77.

40. Kotter, J. *The Leadership Factor* (New York: The Free Press, 1988).

41. Laurent, A. "The Cultural Diversity of Western Conceptions of Management," *International Studies of Management and Organization*, vol. 13, no. 1–2 (1983), pp. 75–96.

42. Lawler, E. E., III. "Job Design and Employee Motivation," *Personnel Psychology*, vol. 22 (1969), pp. 426–435.

43. Lawler, E. E., III. *Pay and Organizational Effectiveness: A Psychological View* (New York: McGraw-Hill, 1971).

44. Reprinted by permission of the publishers from *Executive* by Harry Levinson, Cambridge, Mass.: Harvard University Press, Copyright © 1968, 1981 by the President and Fellows of Harvard College. (As cited in R. H. Mason and R. S. Spich, *Management: An International Perspective* (Homewood, Ill.: Irwin, 1987), pp. 190–191.)

45. Likert, R. *New Patterns of Management* (New York: McGraw-Hill, 1961).

46. Likert, R. *The Human Organization* (New York: McGraw-Hill, 1967).

47. McClelland, D. C. *The Achieving Society* (Princeton, N.J.: Van Nostrand, 1961).

48. McClelland, D. C., and Burnham, D. H. "Power Is the Great Motivator," *Harvard Business Review*, vol. 54, no. 1 (March–April 1976), pp. 100–110.

49. McClelland, D. C.; Atkinson, J. W.; Clark, R. A.; and Lowell, E. L. *The Achievement Motive* (New York: Appleton-Century-Crofts, 1953).

50. McGregor, D. *The Human Side of Enterprise* (New York: McGraw-Hill, 1960).

51. Maslow, A. H. "A Theory of Human Motivation," *Psychology Review* (July 1943), pp. 370–396.

52. Maslow, A. H. *Motivation and Personality* (New York: Harper & Row, 1954).

53. Maslow, A. H. *Toward a Psychology of Being* (Princeton, N.J.: Van Nostrand, 1962).

54. Matsui, T., and Terai, I. "A Cross-Cultural Study of the Validity of the Expectancy Theory of Work Motivation," *Journal of Applied Psychology*, vol. 60, no. 2 (1979), pp. 263–265.

55. Miller, J. J., and Kilpatrick, J. A. *Issues for Managers: An International Perspective* (Homewood, Ill.: Irwin, 1987).

56. Mitroff, I. I. *Business Not as Usual* (San Francisco: Jossey-Bass, 1987).

57. Mutiso, G.-C. M. *Socio-Political Thought in African Literature: Weusi* (New York: Barnes and Noble, 1974).

58. Nath, R., and Narayanan, V. K. "A Comparative Study of Managerial Support, Trust, Openness, Decision-Making, and Job Enrichment," *Academy of Management Proceedings*, vol. 40 (1980), pp. 48–52.

59. Oh, T. K. "Theory Y in the People's Republic of China," *California Management Review*, vol. 19, no. 2 (Winter 1976), pp. 77–84.

60. Ohmae, K. *Beyond National Borders* (Homewood, Ill.: Dow Jones–Irwin, 1987).

61. O'Reilly, C. A., and Roberts, K. H. "Job Satisfaction among Whites and Nonwhites," *Journal of Applied Psychology*, vol. 57, no. 3 (1973), pp. 295–299.

62. Pascale, R. T. "Communication and Decision Making across Cultures: Japanese and American Comparisons," *Administrative Science Quarterly*, vol. 23 (March 1978), pp. 91–110.

63. Pfeffer, J. *Organizations and Organization Theory.* (Boston: Pitman, 1982).

64. Reitz, H. J. "The Relative Importance of Five Categories of Needs among Industrial Workers in Eight Countries," *Academy of Management Proceedings* (1975), pp. 270–273.

65. Reitz, J., and Grof, G. *Similarities and Differences among Mexican Workers, in Attitudes to Worker Motivation* (Bloomington, Ind.: Indiana University, 1973).

66. Sampson, E. D. "Psychology and the American Ideal," *Journal of Personality and Social Psychology*, vol. 35, no. 11 (November 1977), pp. 767–782.

67. Schlesinger, A. M., Jr. *A Thousand Days* (Boston: Houghton Mifflin, 1965).

68. Shelton, A. J. "Behavior and Cultural Value in West African Stories," *Lit-*

erary Sources for the Study of Culture Contact, Africa, vol. 34 (1964), pp. 353–359.

69. Simon, H. A. *Administrative Behavior* (New York: The Free Press, 1957).

70. Simon, H. A. *The New Science of Management Decision* (New York: Harper & Row, 1960).

71. Sirota, D., and Greenwood, M. J. "Understanding Your Overseas Workforce," *Harvard Business Review*, vol. 14 (January–February 1971), pp. 53–60.

72. Staw, B. M. "Organizational Behavior: A Review and Reformulation of the Field's Outcome Variables," *Annual Review of Psychology*, vol. 35 (1984), pp. 627–666.

73. Staw, B. M. "Rationality and Justification in Organizational Life," in B. M. Staw and L. L. Cummings, eds., *Research in Organizational Behavior*, vol. 2. (Greenwich, Conn.: JAI Press, 1980), pp. 45–80.

74. Steers, R. M., and Porter, L. W., eds. *Motivation and Work Behavior* (New York: McGraw-Hill, 1975).

75. Stephens, D.; Kedia, B.; and Ezell, D. "Managerial Need Structures in U.S. and Peruvian Industries," *Management International Review*, vol. 19 (1979), pp. 27–39.

76. Stogdill, R. M. "Personal Factors Associated with Leadership: A Survey of the Literature," *Journal of Psychology*, vol. 25 (1948), pp. 37–71.

77. Takamiya, S. "Group Decision Making in Japanese Management," *International Studies of Management and Organization*, vol. 2, no. 2 (Summer 1972), pp. 183–196.

78. Theobald, R. "Management of Complex Systems: A Growing Societal Challenge," in F. Feather, ed., *Through the 80s: Thinking Globally, Acting Locally* (Washington, D.C.: World Future Society, 1980), pp. 42–51.

79. Triandis, H. C. "Dimensions of Cultural Variations as Parameters of Organizational Theories," *International Studies of Management and Organization*, vol. 12, no. 4 (1983), pp. 139–169.

80. Tscheulin, D. "Leader Behavior Measurement in German Industry," *Journal of Applied Psychology*, vol. 57 (1973), pp. 28–31.

81. Tzu, L. *The Way of Lao Tzu (tao-te ching): Translated with Introductory Essays, Comments and Notes by Wing-tsit Chan.* (Indianapolis, Ind.: Bobbs-Merrill, 1963). (As cited in "Lao Leader Behaviors," *Management International Review*, vol. 19 [1979], p. 214. Lao Tzu wrote in the 6th century B.C.)

82. Van Fleet, D., and Al-Tuhaih, S. "A Cross-Cultural Analysis of Perceived

Leader Behaviors," *Management International Review*, vol. 19 (April 1979), pp. 81–88.

83. Vardi, Y.; Shrom, A.; and Jacobson, D. "A Study of Leadership Beliefs of Israeli Managers," *Academy of Management Journal*, vol. 23, no. 2 (1980), pp. 367–374.

84. Vroom, V. H. *Work and Motivation* (New York: John Wiley and Sons, 1964).

85. Vroom, V. H., and Yetton, P. W. *Leadership and Decision Making* (Pittsburgh, Penn.: University of Pittsburgh Press, 1973).

86. Williams, L. K.; Whyte, W. F.; and Green, C. S. "Do Cultural Differences Affect Workers' Attitudes?" *Industrial Relations*, vol. 5 (1966), pp. 105–117.

CHAPTER 7

▼

Negotiating with Foreigners

▲

Let us not be blind to our differences—but let us also direct attention to our common interests and the means by which those differences can be resolved.

John Fitzgerald Kennedy (33)

Joint ventures, mergers and acquisitions, licensing and distribution agreements, and sales of products and services—crucial aspects of all such interorganizational relationships are face-to-face negotiations. As the proportion of foreign to domestic trade increases, so does the frequency of business negotiations between people from different countries and cultures. To successfully manage these negotiations, businesspeople need to know how to influence and communicate with members of cultures other than their own (2).

A growing literature exists documenting international negotiating styles. For example, there are descriptions of the negotiating behavior of the French (11;40), Russians (5), Canadians (1), Mexicans (14;51), Brazilians (19;20), Middle Eastern Arabs (38;56); Chinese (3;26;34;41;45;49) and the Japanese (18;23;47;48;52), along with a number of multicountry studies (4;7;24;25;53). Do Russians enter bargaining sessions with the same expectations and approaches as Arabs?

No. Are Arab negotiating styles similar to those of Americans? Again, no. Russians, Arabs, and Americans negotiate in very different ways. Russians, as shown in Table 7–1 (15;9), typically use an axiomatic approach to negotiating—they base their arguments on asserted ideals. Russians generally do not expect to develop a continuing relationship with their bargaining partners and therefore see little need for rela-

TABLE 7–1 National Styles of Persuasion

	North Americans	Arabs	Russians
Primary Negotiating Style and Process	Factual: Appeals made to logic	Affective: Appeals made to emotions	Axiomatic: Appeals made to ideals
Conflict: Opponent's Arguments Countered with . . .	Objective facts	Subjective feelings	Asserted ideals
Making Concessions	Small concessions made early to establish a relationship	Concessions made throughout as a part of the bargaining process	Few, if any, concessions made
Response to Opponent's Concessions	Usually reciprocate opponent's concessions	Almost always reciprocate opponent's concessions	Opponent's concessions viewed as weakness and almost never reciprocated
Relationship	Short term	Long term	No continuing relationship
Authority	Broad	Broad	Limited
Initial Position	Moderate	Extreme	Extreme
Deadline	Very important	Casual	Ignored

SOURCE: Reprinted with permission from *International Journal of Intercultural Relations*, vol. 1, E. S. Glenn; D. Witmeyer, and K. A. Stevenson, "Cultural Styles of Persuasion." Copyright © 1984, Pergamon Press, Ltd.

tionship building. As a negotiation progresses, Russians make few, if any, concessions and view their opponents' concessions as signs of weakness. Russians often start with extreme positions, ignore deadlines, and, due to their very limited authority, frequently check back with headquarters.

By contrast, Arabs typically use an affective approach to negotiating (15) — they counter their opponents' arguments with emotional appeals based on subjective feelings. Arabs generally want to build long-term relationships with their bargaining partners. Therefore, they are often willing to make concessions throughout the bargaining process and will almost always reciprocate their opponents' concessions. Most Arabs do not feel limited by time or authority; they frequently approach deadlines very casually and rarely lack the broad authority necessary to discuss and agree on all issues pertinent to the negotiation.

Americans differ from both the Russians and the Arabs. Americans typically use a factual approach to negotiating (15) — they attempt to counter their opponents' arguments with logical appeals based on objective facts. Americans will make small concessions early in the negotiation in an attempt to establish a relationship, and they generally expect their bargaining partners to do likewise. Americans, far from casual about time and authority, generally take deadlines very seriously and have very broad authority.

What happens when Russians begin negotiating with Arabs or Americans? Who persuades whom when styles of negotiating differ? Who wins when the processes of negotiating — the very rules of the game — are defined differently? How can I get what my company and I want from them? To succeed in the international environment, negotiators must face and solve these questions.

NEGOTIATING INTERNATIONALLY

Negotiation is a process in which one individual tries to persuade another individual to change his or her ideas or behavior (8:152); it often involves one person attempting to get another to sign a particular contract or make a particular decision. Negotiation is the process in which at least two partners with different needs and viewpoints try to reach an agreement on matters of mutual interest (8:152). A negotiation becomes cross-cultural when the parties involved belong to different cultures and therefore do not share the same ways of thinking, feeling, and behaving (8:152). All international negotiations are cross-cultural. Some domestic negotiations, in spanning two or more ethnic groups, are also cross-cultural. Therefore, a Singaporian businessperson negotiating a raw materials contract with a Brazilian; a United Nations official negotiating with ambassadors concerning the agenda for upcoming disarmament talks; Mexican executives involved in joint venture discussions with Swedes; and French- and Flemish-speaking Belgians determining national language legislation are all negotiating cross-culturally.

Negotiation is one of the single most important international business skills (11;12;30;55). International negotiations contain all of the complexity of domestic negotiations, with the added dimension of cultural diversity. According to Professor Perlmutter of the Wharton School of Business, international managers spend more than 50 percent of their time negotiating (39). As highlighted in Tables 7–1 and 7–2, styles of negotiating vary markedly across cultures. Countries vary on such key aspects as the amount and type of preparation for a negotiation, the relative emphasis on task versus interpersonal relationships, the use of general principles versus specific details, and the number of people present and the extent of their influence.

According to international negotiations experts David Berlew and

TABLE 7-2 Negotiation Styles from a Cross-Cultural Perspective

Japanese	*North American*	*Latin American*
Emotional sensitivity highly valued	Emotional sensitivity not highly valued	Emotional sensitivity valued
Hiding of emotions	Dealing straightforwardly or impersonally	Emotionally passionate
Subtle power plays; conciliation	Litigation; not as much conciliation	Great power plays; use of weakness
Loyalty to employer; employer taking care of employees	Lack of commitment to employer; breaking of ties by either if necessary	Loyalty to employer (who is often family)
Group decision-making by consensus	Teamwork provides input to a decision maker	Decisions come down from one individual

TABLE 7-2 *(Continued)*

Japanese	North American	Latin American
Face-saving crucial; decisions often made on basis of saving someone from embarrassment	Decisions made on a cost-benefit basis; face-saving does not always matter.	Face-saving crucial in decision making to preserve honor, dignity
Decisions makers openly influenced by special interests	Decision makers influenced by special interests but often not considered ethical	Execution of special interests of decision maker expected, condoned
Not argumentative; quiet when right	Argumentative when right or wrong, but impersonal	Argumentative when right or wrong; passionate
What is down in writing must be accurate, valid	Great importance given to documentation as evidential proof	Impatient with documentation, seen as obstacle to understanding general principles
Step-by-step approach to decision making	Methodically organized decision making	Impulsive, spontaneous decision making
Good of group is the ultimate aim	Profit motive or good of individual ultimate aim	What is good for group is good for the individual
Cultivate a good emotional social setting for decision making; get to know decision makers	Decision making impersonal; avoid involvements, conflict of interest	Personalism necessary for good decision making

SOURCE: Reprinted from Pierre Casse, *Training for the Multicultural Manager: A Practical and Cross-Cultural Approach to the Management of People*, Washington, D.C. Copyright 1982, Society for Intercultural Education, Training, and Research (SIETAR International). Used with permission.

Ellen Raider, negotiation is not always the best approach to doing business. Sometimes the best stragegy is "take it or leave it," other times bargaining and, on some occasions, negotiation—involving problem solving—is most appropriate (42:6.24). Negotiation, compared with bargaining and the take-it-or-leave-it approach, demands more time. Managers should negotiate when the value of the exchange and of the

183

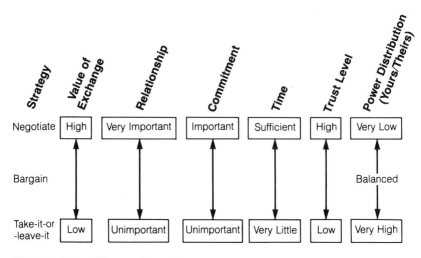

FIGURE 7-1 When to Negotiate
SOURCE: Adapted with permission from Ellen Raider, "Strategy Assessment," in *International Negotiations* (Plymouth, Mass.: Situation Management Systems, 1982), pp. 4–16.

relationship is important; as, for example, within the growing number of global alliances. As summarized in Figure 7–1, negotiation is generally the preferred strategy for creating win-win solutions in international situations. Businesspeople should, for example, consider selecting negotiation when any of the following conditions are apparent: their power position is low relative to their partner's; the trust level is high; available time is sufficient to explore both parties' multiple needs, resources, and options; or when commitment — not mere compliance — is important to ensure that the agreement is carried out. While focusing on negotiation, this chapter will use the terms *negotiator, bargaining partner,* and *opponent* interchangeably.

Cultural diversity makes effective communication more difficult. Because foreigners perceive, interpret, and evaluate the world differently, communicating needs and interests in ways foreigners will understand becomes more difficult, as does fully understanding their words and meanings. While communication becomes more difficult, creating mutually beneficial options can become easier. If negotiators can overcome communication problems, identifying win-win solutions — mutually beneficial solutions in which both parties gain — can become easier. For instance, based on their different perspectives, a seller from one culture may no longer want a particular business, whereas a buyer from another culture may find the business an especially interesting prospect. In negotiations between Americans and Japanese, American owners generally concern themselves more with the viability of an enterprise — with its predicted future cash flow. Japanese buyers, on the other hand, generally show more interest in the property and physical plant. A Japanese buyer may find an enterprise particularly valuable for one set of reasons, while the American owner may place it on the market for an entirely different set of reasons. As another example, Malaysians, with their high unemployment and low wage rates, may find producing labor intensive products a more attractive prospect than would Swiss manufacturers who face high wage rates and negligible unemployment. Differences, rather than similarities, form the basis of mutually beneficial solutions. The chances of substantial areas of difference, and therefore substantial areas for mutual gain, generally increase in multicultural situations.

In some cases negotiators go beyond mutually beneficial solutions to create synergistic agreements. While mutually beneficial solutions focus on comparative advantage — the exchange of items more highly valued by one party than the other — synergistic solutions use differences as a resource in creating new solutions that would have been impossible without those differences. Differences, the source of cross-cultural communication complexities and problems, ultimately become the primary resource in creating mutually beneficial, synergistic agreements (see chapter 4).

SUCCESSFUL NEGOTIATIONS: PEOPLE, SITUATION, AND PROCESS

Research has shown that each of the three areas on which the success of a negotiaion is based — individual characteristics, situational contingencies, and strategic and tactical processes — vary considerably across cultures (13;15;18). Although all three have been found to be important, negotiators have most control over the process — strategy and tactics. Negotiators can influence the success or failure of a negotiation most directly by managing the process. Each of the three areas will be discussed, cultural variations highlighted, and the most effective approaches recommended. Effective negotiators base their strategy and tactics on the characteristics of the situation and the people involved.

Although it would be easier for international managers if there were one best way to negotiate, no guaranteed formula for success exists.

Qualities of a Good Negotiator

What are the qualities of a good negotiator? According to John Graham's extensive research (18), the answer depends on whom you ask. As shown in Table 7–3, American managers believe that effective negotiators are highly rational. Brazilian managers, to the surprise of many Americans, hold almost identical perceptions and differ only in replacing integrity with competitiveness as one of the seven most important qualities. The Japanese differ quite markedly from Americans and Brazilians. They stress an interpersonal, rather than a rational, focus. Japanese differ from Americans in stressing both verbal expressiveness and listening ability, whereas Americans only emphasize verbal ability. In contrast to Americans, Brazilians, and Japanese, Chinese managers in Taiwan emphasize negotiators' rational skills and, to a lesser extent, their interpersonal skills. To the Chinese, a negotiator must be an interesting person and should show persistence and determination, the ability to win respect and confidence, preparation and planning skills, demonstrated product knowledge, good judgment, and intelligence.

The role that individual qualities play varies across cultures. According to Graham's research (18), favorable outcomes are influenced primarily by the negotiator's own characteristics in Brazil, the opponent's characteristics in the United States, the role in Japan (the buyer always does better), and a mixture of the negotiator's and opponent's characteristics in Taiwan. Specifically, Brazilian negotiators achieve higher profits when they are more deceptive and self-interested, have higher self-esteem, and when their opponents are more honest. American negotiators do better when their opponents are honest, not self-interested, introverted, not particularly interesting as people, and made to feel uncomfortable by the negotiator's actions. By contrast, in Japan buyers always do better than sellers. Both Japanese buyers and sellers can improve their positions by making their opponents feel more comfortable. In Taiwan, negotiators do better when they are deceptive and when their opponents are neither self-interested nor have particularly attractive personalities.

TABLE 7-3 Key Individual Characteristics of Negotiators

American Managers	Japanese Managers	Chinese Managers (Taiwan)	Brazilian Managers
Preparation & planning skill	Dedication to job	Persistence & determination	Preparation & planning skill
Thinking under pressure	Perceive & exploit power	Win respect & confidence	Thinking under pressure
Judgment & intelligence	Win respect & confidence	Preparation & planning skill	Judgment & intelligence
Verbal expressiveness	Integrity	Product knowledge	Verbal expressiveness
Product knowledge	Listening skill	Interesting	Product knowledge
Perceive & exploit power	Broad perspective	Judgment & intelligence	Perceive & exploit power
Integrity	Verbal expressiveness		Competitiveness

SOURCE: Professor John Graham, School of Business Administration, University of Southern California, 1983.

Buyer/Seller Relationship.   The hierarchical relationship between buyers and sellers is crucial in understanding the differences in negotiating styles across cultures (19). For example, as shown in Figure 7-2, Japanese buyers and sellers have a vertical, hierarchical relationship: buyers generally get most of what they ask for. However, sellers expect buyers to take care of them. When the Japanese explain this system to Americans, they frequently ask, "But won't the seller get taken?" The answer is "no," because, in Japan, management takes care of workers, government takes care of industry, and buyers take care of sellers. *Amae* —indulgent dependence— explains the buyer/seller relationship in Japan.

By contrast, buyers and sellers in the United States have a flatter, more equal, relationship. The American norm is not *amae*, but independent competition: "May the best person win." Buyers do not expect to take care of sellers, they expect to take care of themselves by getting the best deal possible for their company.

Problems arise when Japanese and American buyers and sellers negotiate with each other (23:28–29). From the American perspective, being a buyer in Japan is extremely beneficial. According to some Japanese, "Americans ask for the moon!" Many Japanese, in describing their initial bargaining sessions with Americans, say, "When we first went to the United States, we took a beating. As sellers, we gave the American buyers everything they wanted." But because they were working under a different set of expectations, the Americans did not then "take care of" the Japanese sellers. The Japanese thought the Americans took advantage of them, while the Americans believed they had merely driven a hard bargain.

In the reverse situation, American sellers, not trusting Japanese buyers to take care of them, act as equals. They thus fail to behave with appropriate deference; the Japanese, therefore, perceive them as arrogant. All too frequently, negotiations collapse as a result. Unfortunately, both sides tend to attribute the collapse to unacceptable product qualities and price, rather than to the actual cause—cross-cultural differences.

When negotiators bargain with people from many cultures, the most important individual characteristics are good listening skills, an orientation toward people, a willingness to use team assistance, high self-esteem, high aspirations, and an attractive personality, along with credibility and influence within the home organization (22). These individual characteristics, although significant, are not the most important factors determining negotiated outcomes. It is therefore unfortunate that many companies emphasize individual characteristics in

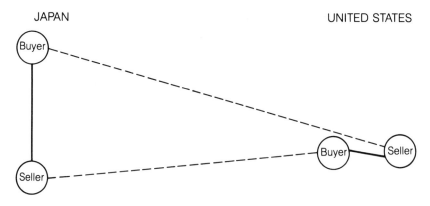

FIGURE 7–2 Buyer/Seller Relationship

selecting negotiating team members rather than training those selected to understand and more skillfully manage the negotiation process.

Negotiation Contingencies:
Characteristics of the Situation

Situations in which negotiators find themselves vary widely. Effective negotiators recognize and manage the impact of each situational factor on the bargaining process from both their own and their opponent's cultural perspective. In preparing for international negotiations, they attempt to imagine what the situation would look like through the eyes of the foreign team: What do they want? What is important to them? Who has power? What is at stake? What is our time frame? Where do they draw their personal and organizational bottom line? Situational contingencies influence success just as individual characteristics do, but they are rarely as critical to success as the strategy and tactics used.

Location. Should you meet at their office, your office, or at a neutral location? Negotiation wisdom generally advises teams to meet at their own or a neutral location. Meeting in a foreign country is disadvantageous to negotiators because it reduces access to information and increases travel-related stress and cost. Meeting at home allows a team to control the situation more easily. For example, a division of Caterpillar of California increased its control over negotiations by taking international clients out on their yacht. They gain the advantage of removing the client from phones, interruptions, and distractions while severely limiting their access to information.

Many negotiators select neutral locations. Business entertainment has become a common type of neutral location, used primarily to get to know and improve relations with members of the opposing team. Heavy users of business entertainment, the Japanese spend 1.9 percent of their GNP on it—even more than they spend on national defense (1.5 percent). Americans generally consider this high business entertainment cost absurd, but perhaps Americans' extraordinarily high legal expenses reflect the cost of insufficient relationship building.

In choosing neutral locations, business negotiators often select resorts located geographically halfway between the bargaining partners. For example, Asian and North American bargainers may select Hawaii for business meetings; both sides travel, both sides have reduced access to information, and consequently the incentive increases for both sides to conclude the negotiation as soon as possible. The cost of travel and hotels usually increases pressure to conclude a negotiation expeditiously, but not always. In one negotiation between an American and a Russian company, negotiators conducted the sessions at a resort in the south of France. The Russian bargainers made it clear that they did not want to end their "vacation" early by concluding the negotiation prematurely.

Physical Arrangements. In traditional American negotiations, the two teams face each other, often on opposite sides of the boardroom table. Unfortunately, this arrangement maximizes competition. Sitting at right angles, on the other hand, facilitates cooperation. If negotiators view the process as a collaborative search for mutually beneficial outcomes (win-win solutions), the physical arrangements should support cooperation, not competition. As an alternative to the boardroom table, negotiators from both teams may choose to sit on the same side of the table, "facing the problem" (14). In this way they compete with the problem, not with the people. The Japanese, in posting all information related to a negotiation on the walls, structure the environment so that all parties involved "face the problem" holistically.

Participants. Who should attend the formal negotiating sessions? Americans tend to want to "go it alone"—they consider extra team members an unnecessary expense. This strategy is ineffective in international negotiations, where more is better. Why? First, the physical presence of more people communicates greater power and importance—an essential nonverbal message. Second, as discussed earlier, communicating cross-culturally is complex and difficult. Having some team members primarily responsible for listening to conversations and observing nonverbal cues and other members primarily responsible for conducting substantive discussions is an extremely effective strategy.

The number of teams and audiences present at a negotiation varies. Should the press be present? Will public opinion make it easier or more difficult to develop mutually beneficial solutions? Should the union have direct representation? Should bargainers keep government agencies informed during the negotiation or only present them with the final agreement? The power that government, union, and public opinion have over business negotiators varies considerably across cultures. For example, negotiating with government officials from such open democracies as Australia, Canada, and New Zealand requires broader public debate than is generally necessary in the more tightly controlled governments of South Korea and Iran, or in communist countries such as North Korea, Cuba, and Albania. Effective international negotiators carefully manage access to the proceedings.

Time Limits.   The duration of a negotiation can vary markedly across cultures. Americans, being particularly impatient, often expect negotiations to take a minimum amount of time. During the Paris Peace Talks designed to negotiate an end to the Vietnam War, the American team arrived in Paris and made hotel reservations for a week. Their Vietnamese counterparts leased a château for a year. As the negotiations proceeded, the frustrated Americans were forced to continually renew their weekly reservations to accommodate the more measured pace of the Vietnamese.

Negotiators generally make more concessions as their deadline approaches. Americans' sense of urgency puts them at a disadvantage with respect to their less hurried bargaining partners. Negotiators from other countries recognize Americans' time consciousness, achievement orientation, and impatience. They know that Americans will make more concessions close to their deadline (time consciousness) in order to get a signed contract (achievement orientation). For example, one Brazilian company invited a group of Americans to Brazil to negotiate a contract the week before Christmas. The Brazilians, knowing that the Americans would want to return to the United States by Christmas, knew that they could push hard for concessions and an early agreement. The final agreement definitely favored the Brazilians.

Some negotiators attempt to discover their opponents' deadline and refuse to make major concessions until after that deadline has passed. The local team may determine their opponents' deadlines by checking hotel ×
reservations or politely offering to reconfirm return airline tickets. Effective international negotiators determine the best alternative to *not* meeting their deadline. If they find the best alternative acceptable, they may choose a less hurried pace than they had planned or than they typically use at home.

Status Differences.   The United States prides itself on its egalitarian, informal approach to life, in which titles do not seem particularly important and ceremonies are often considered a waste of time. American team members minimize status differences during negotiations: their

191

use of first names promotes equality and informality. Unfortunately, this approach, while succeeding at putting Americans at ease, makes many foreigners uncomfortable. Most countries are more hierarchical and more formal than the United States, and most foreigners feel more comfortable in formal situations with explicit status differences. The Japanese, for example, must know the other person's company and position before being able to select the grammatically correct form of address. For this reason, the Japanese always exchange business cards — *meishi* — before a conversation begins. In Germany, negotiators would almost never address colleagues on their own team, let alone those from the opposing team, by first name. Such informality would severely insult their sense of propriety and hierarchy.

Age, like title, connotes seniority and demands respect in most countries of the world. Sending a young, albeit brilliant, North American expert to Indonesia to lead a negotiating team is more likely to insult senior Indonesian officials than facilitate a successful exchange of technical information. In almost all cases, North Americans need to increase formality in dress, vocabulary, behavior, and style when working abroad.

NEGOTIATION PROCESS

Process is the single most important factor in predicting the success or failure of a negotiation. An effective process includes managing the negotiation's overall strategy or approach, its stages, and the specific tactics used. As with other aspects of negotiating, process varies markedly across cultures (25;31;44;50;55). An effective strategy reflects the situational characteristics and personal backgrounds of the negotiators involved. It balances the position, procedure, timing, and roles of the negotiating partners.

Negotiation Strategy:
A Culturally Synergistic Approach

In their excellent book entitled *Getting to Yes*, based on the work of the Harvard International Negotiation Project, Fisher and Ury (14) propose a principled approach to negotiating. As shown in Table 7–4, this approach involves four steps:

1. Separating the people from the problem

2. Focusing on interests, not on positions

3. Insisting on objective criteria (and never yielding to pressure)

4. Inventing options for mutual gain

Does this principled approach become easier or harder when negotiating internationally?

Let us analyze the principled approach from a cross-cultural perspective. Cultural differences make communication more difficult. Steps 1, 2, and 3 therefore become more difficult: understanding opponents, their interests, and their assessment criteria becomes more complex and fraught with cross-cultural communication pitfalls. By contrast, step 4 can become easier. Inventing options for mutual gain requires recognizing and using differences. The fewer the identical items sought by both bargaining partners, the greater the chances of simultaneously satisfying both teams' needs. If cross-cultural differences are recognized, clearly communicated, and understood (steps 1, 2, and 3), they can become the very basis of constructing win-win solutions. For example, Western European countries that import Indonesian batiks exchange an economically developed market for a labor intensive good. The Europeans could not afford to make the batiks in Europe, while the Indonesians could not command the price in stable currencies within their own country. This culturally synergistic approach, which uses cultural differences as a resource rather than a hindrance to organizational functioning, allows international negotiators to maximize the benefits to all parties. Each of the steps in the principled approach will be discussed as it relates to the four stages of the negotiating process.

Stages of a Negotiation

To prepare for an initial meeting, effective negotiators analyze the situation in terms of their own and their opponents' needs, goals, and underlying cultural values, determine the limits to their authority, assess power positions and relationships, identify facts to be confirmed, set an agenda, establish overall and alternative concession strategies, and make team assignments. They also determine their best alternative to a negotiated solution (14) — that is, the most favorable outcome in the event that they fail to reach agreement. This "best alternative to a

TABLE 7-4 Three Approaches to Each Stage of an International Negotiation

Traditional Approach (Competitive)	Principled Approach (Collaborative/ Individual)	Synergistic Approach (Collaborative/Cultural)
Preparation Define economic issues.	*Preparation* Define interests.	*Preparation* Cross-cultural training Define interests.
Relationship Building Assess counterpart.	*Relationship Building* Separate the people from the problem.	*Relationship Building* Separate the people from the problem. Adjust to their style and pace.
Information Exchange Exchange task-related information. Clarify positions.	*Information Exchange* Exchange task- and participant-related information. Clarify interests.	*Information Exchange* Exchange task- and participant-related information. Clarify interests. Clarify customary approaches.
Persuasion	*Inventing Options for Mutual Gain*	*Inventing Options for Mutual Gain Appropriate to Both Cultures*
Concessions	*Choice of Best Option* Insist on using objective criteria; never yield to pressure.	*Choice of Best Option* Insist on using criteria appropriate to both cultures.
Agreement	*Agreement*	*Agreement* Translate and back-translate agreement; if necessary, renegotiate.

NOTE: The traditional approach is based on John L. Graham and Roy A. Herberger, Jr., "Negotiators Abroad — Don't Shoot from the Hip," *Harvard Business Review*, vol. 61, no. 4 (July–August 1983), pp. 160–168. The principled approach is based on Roger Fisher and William Ury, *Getting to Yes*. (Boston: Houghton Mifflin Company and Penguin Books, 1981). The synergistic approach is based on Nancy J. Adler (see chapter 4). The table is adapted from the work of George Renwick (unpublished).

negotiated solution," unlike the conventional "bottom line," protects negotiators "from accepting terms that are too unfavorable and from rejecting terms it would be in . . . [their] interest to accept (14:104)."

Planning.   The Huthwaite Research Group conducted a study in the United Kingdom on the behavior of successful negotiators (42). The researchers interviewed and observed 48 successful negotiators in a total of 102 negotiations. Negotiators were not considered successful unless they were rated as effective by both sides, had a track record of significant success, and had a low incidence of implementation failure. As highlighted in Table 7–5, successful negotiators' planning behavior differed in the following ways from that of their less skilled colleagues (42):

1. *Planning time.* Both skilled and average negotiators use about the same amount of time for planning. Evidently "it is not the amount of planning time that makes the difference, but how the time is used" (42).

2. *Exploration of options.* Skilled negotiators consider twice as wide a range of action options and outcomes as do their less skilled colleagues. The greater the number of options, the greater the chances for success.

3. *Common ground.* Although all negotiators focus more on areas of conflict than of agreement, skilled negotiators spend over three times as much attention on common ground.

4. *Long terms versus short term.* All negotiators spend the vast majority of their time on short-term issues. However, skilled negotiators spend more than twice as much time on long-term issues.

5. *Setting limits.* Average negotiators set single point objectives, such as requesting $7 per unit. Skilled negotiators set range objectives, such as requesting $5 to $10 per unit. Setting ranges gives skilled negotiators more bargaining flexibility.

6. *Sequence versus issue planning.* Average negotiators use sequence planning. They plan to discuss point A, then point B, then point C, and so on. Skilled negotiators, by contrast, use issue planning—they discuss each issue independently. There is no predetermined sequence or order of issues.

Following the preparation, formal negotiations proceed roughly through four stages (17;22):

1. Interpersonal relationship building (learning about the people)
2. Exchanging task-related information (learning about the economic, legal, technical, and logistical issues)
3. Persuading
4. Making concessions and agreements

TABLE 7-5 How Successful Negotiators Plan

Planning Behavior	Skilled Negotiators	Average Negotiators
Overall time spent planning	No significant difference	
Number of options and outcomes considered per issue	5.1	2.6
Percentage of comments about areas of anticipated common ground	38%	11%
Percentage of comments about long-term considerations of issues	8.5%	4%
Planned order	Issues	Sequences
Average use of sequences during planning per session	2.1	4.9
Setting limits	Range	Fixed-point

SOURCE: Neil Rackham, "The Behavior of Successful Negotiators" (Reston, Va.: Huthwaite Research Group, 1976), as reported in Ellen Raider International, Inc. (Brooklyn, N.Y.), and Situation Management Systems, Inc. (Plymouth, Mass.), *International Negotiations: A Training Program for Corporate Executives and Diplomats* (1982).

Countries vary in the emphasis placed on each phase and the style used to approach it. As shown in Table 7-4, effective bargainers can approach each stage of the negotiation through principled strategies: to build interpersonal relationships, principled negotiators separate the people from the problem; to exchange task-related information, principled negotiators focus on interests, not on positions; to effectively persuade the other team, principled negotiators invent options for mutual gain, rather than relying on preconceived positions and high pressure "dirty tricks"; and to make appropriate concessions and reach agreement, principled negotiators insist on using objective decision criteria.

Interpersonal Relationship Building.   The first phase of the face-to-face meeting involves getting to know the other people and helping them to feel comfortable. During relationship building, parties develop respect and trust for members of the opposing team. In every negotiation, there is a relationship (you and them) and the substance (what you and they want). "Non-task sounding" begins the relationship building process of discovering general areas of similarity and difference in both the relationship and the substance. Similarities become the basis for personal relationships and trust; differences, the basis for mutual exchange. The strategy of separating the people from the problem implies that negotiators can reject their partners' suggestions without rejecting the people themselves, that they can disagree with their opponents' analysis without labeling them negatively, and that they can enjoy and trust their opponents as individuals while rejecting their proposals.

Being particularly task- and efficiency-oriented, Americans usually see little need to "waste time" on getting to know people in non-task-related conversations. Americans want to "get down to business"—to discussing and agreeing on task-related issues—almost immediately, often after only five to ten minutes. The United States' legal system also supports a task-oriented approach. Americans base their transactions on written contracts. Businesspeople in the United States trust the legal system to enforce written agreements (contracts) once they have been signed by all parties involved. Americans consequently focus on signing contracts rather than developing meaningful relationships with members of the opposing team. But this legal system is not replicated in every country. Many areas of the world do not have strong and consistently dependable legal systems to enforce contracts. Enforcement mechanisms are personal: people keep commitments to people, not to contracts. People honor contracts if they like and respect the people with whom they are doing business. They emphasize the relationship, not the written agreement.

Americans need to increase their emphasis on building relationships with bargaining partners. They need to discuss topics other than business, including the arts, history, culture, and current economic condition of the countries involved. Effective negotiators must view luncheon, dinner, reception, ceremony, and tour invitations as times for interpersonal relationship building, and therefore as key to the negotiating process. When American negotiators, often frustrated by the seemingly endless formalities, ceremonies, and "small talk," ask how long they must wait before beginning to "do business," the answer is simple: wait until your opponents bring up business (and they will). Realize that the work of conducting a successful negotiation has already begun, even if business has yet to be mentioned.

Exchanging Task-Related Information. The substance of a negotiation is in interests: your and theirs. Negotiators should therefore focus on presenting their situation and needs and on understanding the opponents' situation and needs. Presenting interests—a situation and needs—is *not* the same as stating a position. A position articulates only one solution for a particular situation from one party's perspective (usually the solution prepared prior to the negotiation). Stating positions limits the ways in which your interests (and by implication, your opponents' interests) can be met. For example, if, based on an analysis of personal needs (housing, clothing, food, transportation, health care, and entertainment), I tell my employer that I must have a minimum foreign service salary of $85,000 (a position) and she refuses to go above $60,000, we are at an impasse. My opponent (i.e., employer) finds my one solution to my needs — $85,000 — unacceptable. If, on the other hand, I present my situation and needs, my employer may offer me $60,000 plus company paid medical insurance, company-owned housing, and use of the company car. Would this offer meet my needs? Perhaps. Would it meet my initial position? No. Focusing on interests rather than positions allows both sides to draw on the widest possible range of mutually agreeable solutions.

Cross-cultural miscommunication causes numerous problems. For example, the Iranians' misinterpretation of a bargaining offer presented in English made the Iranian hostage crisis more difficult to resolve:

> In Persian, the word *compromise* apparently lacks the positive meaning it has in English (a "midway solution both sides can live with") and has only a negative meaning ("her virtue was compromised" or "our integrity was compromised"). Similarly, the word *mediator* in Persian suggests "meddler," someone who is barging in uninvited. In early 1980, United Nations Secretary General Waldheim flew to Iran to deal with the hostage question. His efforts were seriously set back when Iranian national radio and television broadcast in Persian a remark he reportedly made on his arrival in Tehran: "I have come as a mediator to work out a compromise." Within an hour of the broadcast, his car was being stoned by angry Iranians(14:34).

A clear understanding of foreign opponents' interests is difficult. There may be verbal and nonverbal barriers. Misperception, misinterpretation, and misevaluation pervade cross-cultural situations. To begin to understand, effective negotiators try to see the situation from both their own and the other party's perspective. Many negotiators use role reversal: they prepare for the negotiation as if they were their opponent. This role reversal exercise forces them to see the situation and issues from their opponents' point of view.

Persuading. In principled, synergistic negotiations, bargainers emphasize creating mutually beneficial options, whereas more traditional negotiators often emphasize persuading the other party to accept a particular option. For international negotiators, creating mutually beneficial options is particularly important. (Some of the more common methods of persuasion used domestically and internationally will be reviewed later under negotiating tactics.)

In a successful negotiation both parties' interests and needs are recognized and satisfied, and both parties win. Effective synergistic negotiators view their opponents' problem—their interests and needs—as a part of their own problem. Mutually beneficial options derive from (1) understanding both parties' real interests, values, and needs, (2) identifying areas of similarity and difference, and (3) creating new options based primarily on the differences between the two parties. Identifying interests more highly valued by one party than the other and using those differences as a resource underlies the creation of mutually beneficial options.

In cross-cultural negotiations, the possibilities for inventing mutually beneficial options exceed those in unicultural situations because of the inherent differences among the two parties. For example, if a company tells its employees that they cannot all take their vacations at the same time, management will probably have a problem in selecting who will have time off during the holiday season. If all employees are Christian, most will want a vacation Christmas week. If some employees are Christian and others Jewish, some will be happiest with a vacation Christmas week and others with the week of Hanukkah (which rarely coincides with Christmas week). Cross-cultural differences, when recognized, facilitate mutually beneficial solutions that are impossible when all employees share similar cultural and religious backgrounds.

Making Concessions and Agreement. In this fourth stage, principled negotiations insist on using objective criteria in deciding how to make concessions and agree, rather than resorting to a series of dirty tricks. Although numerous high-pressure tactics exist, such tactics diminish relationships and the possibility of developing synergistic solutions. (Specific tactics to avoid will be discussed later.)

Concessions, large or small, can be made at any time during a negotiation. Although the research is not definitive, it appears that negotiators who make early concessions put themselves in a disadvantageous position in comparison with those making fewer concessions primarily at the end of the bargaining session (43). Americans negotiate sequentially: they discuss and attempt to agree on one issue at a time.

piecemeal US

Throughout the bargaining process, Americans make many small concessions, which they expect their opponents to reciprocate; then they finalize the list of concessions into an overall agreement. In some ways making small concessions reflects Americans' task-oriented form of relationship building. Negotiators from many other cultures, unlike Americans, discuss all issues prior to making any concessions. These negotiators view concessions as relative and make them only as they reach a final agreement. This holistic approach to negotiating is particularly evident in Asia. Similiar to many Asians, most Russian negotiators make very few, if any, concessions during a negotiation and rarely reciprocate their opponents' concessions. Unlike many of their colleagues, Russian negotiators generally view concessions as signs of weakness, not as gestures of goodwill, flexibility, or trust. For example, in the seven rounds of postwar negotiations between the Soviet and United States governments, the United States made 82 percent of its concessions in the first round, considerably more than did the Russians (29). Mikhail Gorbachev's style in implementing political change in the Soviet Union highlights the Russian approach to negotiation.

None of the approaches to concessions has been proven to succeed more consistently than any of the others when negotiating internationally. Effective international negotiators respect their own and their partners' domestic styles and adjust accordingly. The following story highlights some of the differences in whom Malaysians and Americans select to negotiate and how negotiators from these two very different cultures perform.

Contrasting Styles: Malays Negotiating with Americans

Americans' patterns of negotiation differ depending on the context. Government officials working out a treaty, for example, negotiate somewhat differently from business executives "hammering out" a contract. The pattern portrayed here is more akin to that of the business executive.

The American businessperson usually begins a series of negotiating sessions in a cordial manner, but he is intent upon "getting things under way." He is very clear as to what he and his company wants, when it is wanted, and how he will go about getting it; he has planned his strategy carefully. And he has done what he could to "psych out" his counterpart with whom he will be negotiating.

From the outset, the American negotiator urges everyone to "dispense with the formalities" and get on with the business at hand. As soon as possible he expresses his determination, saying something like, "O.K., let's get down to brass tacks."

The American usually states his position (at least his first position) early and definitively. He plans before long to "really get down to the nitty gritty." He wants to "zero in" on the knotty problems and get to the point where "the rubber meets the road" (the point, that is, where "the action" begins). Once the negotiations are "really rolling," the American usually deals directly with obstacles as they come up, tries to clear them away in quick order, and becomes impatient and frustrated if he cannot.

Most of what the American wants to convey, of course, he puts into words: spoken words—often many of them.

His approach, therefore, is highly verbal and quite visible—and thoroughly planned. He has outlined his alternatives ahead of time and prepared his counterproposals, contingencies, back-up positions, bluffs, guarantees, and tests of compliance; all carefully calculated, and including, of course, lots of numbers. Toward the end, he sees that some bail-out provisions are included, but he usually doesn't worry too much about them; making and meeting business commitments "on schedule" is what his life is all about—he is not too concerned about getting out of the contract. If he has to get out, then he has to, and he will find a way when the time comes.

The American experiences real satisfaction when all the problems have been "worked out," especially if he has been able to get provisions very favorable to his company—and to his own reputation as a "tough negotiator." He rests securely when everything is "down in black and white" and the contract is initialed or signed.

Afterwards, the American enjoys himself; he relaxes "over some drinks" and carries on some "small talk" and "jokes around" with his team and their counterparts.

Malay patterns of negotiation, as might be expected, differ considerably. . . . When they are buying something, Malays bargain with the merchant; and when they are working, they socialize with their boss and co-workers. Their purpose is to develop some sense of relationship with the other person. The relationship then provides the basis, or context, for the exchange. Malays take the same patterns and preferences into their business negotiating sessions. When all is said and done, it is not the piece of paper they trust, it is the person—and their relationship with the person.

A Malay negotiator begins to develop the context for negotiations through the interaction routines appropriate to this and similar occasions. These routines are as complicated and subtle as customary American routines; they are cordial but quite formal. Like Americans using their own routines, Malays understand the Malay routines but are seldom consciously aware of them. Neither Malays nor Americans understand very clearly the routines of the other.

As the preliminary context is formed, it is important to the Malay that the proper forms of address be known beforehand and used, and that a variety of topics be talked about which are unrelated to the business to be transacted. This may continue for quite a while. A Malay negotiator wants his counterpart to participate comfortably, patiently, and with interest. As in other interaction, it is not the particular words spoken which are of most importance to the Malay; rather he listens primarily to the attitudes which the words convey — attitudes toward the Malay himself and toward the matter being negotiated. Attitudes are important to the relationship. At this point and throughout the negotiations, the Malay is concerned as much about the quality of the relationship as the quantity of the work accomplished. Motivation is more important to the Malay than momentum.

The Malay negotiator, as in other situations, is also aware of feelings — his own and those of his counterpart, and the effects of the exchanges upon both. He is also aware of, and concerned about, how he looks in the eyes of his team, how his counterpart looks in the eyes of the other team, and how both he and his counterpart will look after the negotiations in the eyes of their respective superiors.

The Malay is alert to style, both his own and that of his counterpart. Displaying manners is more important than scoring points. The way one negotiates is as important as what one negotiates. Grace and finesse show respect for the other and for the matter under consideration. Negotiating, like other interaction, is something of an art form. Balance and restraint are therefore essential.

The agenda which the Malay works through in the course of the negotiation is usually quite flexible. His strategy is usually rather simple. His positions are expressed in more general terms than the American's, but no less strongly held. His proposals are more offered than argued; they are offered to the other party rather than argued with him. Malays do not enjoy sparring. They deeply dislike combat.

In response to a strong assertion, the Malay negotiator usually expresses his respect directly by replying indirectly. The stronger the assertion and the more direct the demands, the more indirect the reply — at least the verbal reply.

The Malay and his team usually formulate their positions gradually and carefully. By the time they present their position, they usually have quite a lot of themselves invested in it. Direct rejection of the position, therefore, is sometimes felt to be a rejection of the person. Negotiating for the Malay is not quite the game that it is for some Americans.

If the Malay and his team have arrived at a position from which they and those whom they represent cannot move, they will not move. If this requires a concession from the counterpart, the Malays will not try to force the concession. If the counterpart sees that a concession from him is necessary, and makes it, the Malays, as gentlemen, recognize the move and respect the man who made it. A concession, therefore, is not usually considered by the Malay team to be a sign that they can press harder and extract further concessions. Instead, a concession by either side is considered as evidence of strength and a basis for subsequent reconciliation and cooperation.

What about getting out of a contract? Making and meeting business commitments is *not* what a Malay's life is all about. He has other, often prior, commitments. He therefore enters into contracts cautiously and prefers to have an exit provided.

In addition, Malays are less certain of their control over the future (even their control of their own country) than are Americans. Therefore, promising specific kinds of performance in the future by specific dates in a contract, especially in a long-term contract where the stakes are high, is often difficult for Malays. It is even more difficult, of course, if they are not certain whether they can trust the persons to whom they are making the commitment and from whom they are accepting commitments. Malays therefore give a great deal of thought to a contract and to the contracting party before signing it. And they are uneasy if provisions have not been made for a respectable withdrawal should future circumstances make their compliance impossible.[1]

NEGOTIATION TACTICS

Negotiation includes both verbal and nonverbal tactics. Whereas most Americans consider verbal tactics most important, many people from other countries do not. According to one study, words communicate only 7 percent of meaning, tone of voice communicates 38 percent, and facial expression 55 percent (37). Both verbal and nonverbal behavior cause problems. According to international negotiations experts David Berlew and Ellen Raider, "It's hard to read the writing on the wall if you don't know the language, much less where to find the wall."

(42:3.18) In the following section, we will review some of the most common verbal and nonverbal negotiating tactics. A series of "dirty tricks" are outlined, which, although common, do not particularly help in arriving at mutually beneficial agreements.

Verbal Tactics

Negotiators use many verbal tactics. Research (17) has shown that negotiators do better — their profits increase — as: (a) the number of questions asked increases; (b) the number of commitments made prior to the final agreement stage decreases; and (c) the amount of the initial request increases — that is, sellers ask for more and buyers offer less. Consequently, in most cultures, effective negotiators start by having high expectations and making high initial offers (or requests), proceed by asking a lot of questions, and refrain from making very many commitments until the final stage of the negotiation.

Initial Offers. The Chinese (36;41) and Russians (27) habitually use extreme initial offers and requests as their opening bargaining strategy. By contrast, Swedes initially request a price very close to the one they expect to get. Although they have not been evaluated internationally, research has shown that American domestic negotiators consistently reach higher and more satisfactory outcomes using extreme rather than moderate openers (43). Moreover, other research suggests that bargainers starting with extreme positions have a higher probability of reaching an agreement (34).

Why do extreme initial positions help? Although not thoroughly researched outside of the laboratory, some observers believe that an extreme position: (a) demonstrates to opponents that the bargainer will not be exploited (43), (b) allows the bargainer to gain more than expected, (c) prolongs the negotiating process and thus allows bargainers to gain more information about their opponents, (d) modifies opponents' beliefs about the bargainer's preferences, (e) allows more room to make subsequent concessions and thus exhibit cooperation, and (f) communicates the bargainer's willingness to play the game according to "usual" norms (54:727). Exceptions to the advantages of high initial offers also exist. For example, Japanese diplomats who make extreme opening offers in international negotiations often have them treated as phony by opponents (1). More importantly, extreme offers appear to discourage synergistic agreements. The following news report highlights the contrasting expectations of Americans and Japanese.[2]

Negotiating for Olympic Coverage

In 1984 the Olympic Committee in Los Angeles negotiated television broadcasting rights with various countries. From the American Broadcasting Company (ABC), the Olympic Committee received $225 million. From the Japanese, the Committee received $18.5 million. Why did the Japanese pay so much less?

The Japanese originally offered $6 million for the rights and the Olympic Committee countered with $90 million. The Committee's goal was $10 million. The Japanese argued that theirs was a smaller market than that of the United States. Moreover, the Japanese had only one Japanese television station bidding, whereas the Americans had the three major networks bidding up the price (ABC, CBS, and NBC). High expectations (for a low price), convincing arguments (smaller market), and little competition resulted in a final cost to the Japanese network that was twelve times lower than that of their American counterparts.

Range of Tactics. Some of the more common tactics used in negotiating include promises, threats, recommendations, warnings, rewards, punishments, normative appeals, commitments, self-disclosure, questions, and commands. Table 7-6 describes each briefly. The use and meaning of many of these tactics varies across cultures. As shown in Table 7-7, negotiators from Asia (Japanese), North America (Americans), and South America (Brazilians) use different verbal tactics in negotiating (20). For example, Brazilians say "no" nine times more frequently than do Americans, and almost fifteen times more frequently than do the Japanese. Similarly, Brazilians make more initial concessions than do Americans, who in turn make more than the Japanese (20).

The British Huthwaite study, documenting successful negotiators' behavior, analyzed the verbal behavior of skilled and average negotiators (42:6.6 to 6.13). As shown in Table 7-8, the most skillful British negotiators use fewer irritators, counterproposals, and defend/attack spirals, less argument dilution, and more behavioral labels, active lis-

TABLE 7-6 Verbal Negotiating Tactics

Tactic	Description	Example
Promise	I will do something you want me to do, if you do something I want you to do. (conditional, positive)	I will lower the price by $5 if you increase the order by 100 units.
Threat	I will do something you don't want me to do, if you do something I don't want you to do. (conditional, negative)	I'll walk out of the negotiation if you leak this story to the press.
Recommendation	If you do something I want you to do, a third party will do something you want. (third party positive)	If you lower your price, all of the teenagers will be able to buy your product.
Warning	If you do something I don't want you to do, a third party will do something you don't want. (third party negative)	If you don't settle, the press will spill this whole sordid story on the front page of every newspaper in the country.
Reward	I will give you something positive (something you want), now, on the spot. (unconditional, positive)	Let's make it easier on you tomorrow and meet closer to your office. I have really appreciated your willingness to meet at my building.
Punishment	I will give you something negative (something you don't want) now, on the spot. (unconditional, negative)	I refuse to listen to your screaming. I am leaving.
Normative Appeal	I appeal to a societal norm.	Everybody else buys our product for $5 per unit
Commitment	I will do something you want. (unconditional, positive)	I will deliver 100 units by June 15th.

TABLE 7-6 (Continued)

Tactic	Description	Example
Self-Disclosure	I tell you something about myself.	We have had to lay off 100 employees this month. We really need to sign a major contract by the end of the year.
Question	I ask you something about yourself.	Can you tell me more about your Brazilian operation?
Command	I order you to do something.	Lower your price. (or) We are going to talk about delivery now.

TABLE 7-7 Cross-Cultural Differences in Verbal Negotiating Behaviors

Behavior (Tactic)	Average number of times tactic was used in half hour bargaining sessions in:		
	Japan	*United States*	*Brazil*
Promise	7	8	3
Threat	4	4	2
Recommendation	7	4	5
Warning	2	1	1
Reward	1	2	2
Punishment	1	3	3
Normative Appeal	4	2	1
Commitment	15	13	8
Self-disclosure	34	36	39
Question	20	20	22
Command	8	6	14
"No"s (per 30 minutes)	5.7	9.0	83.4
Profit level of first offers (80 maximum)	61.5	57.3	75.2
Initial concessions	6.5	7.1	9.4

SOURCE: Based on John Graham, "The Influence of Culture on Business Negotiations," Table 1 and 3, *Journal of International Business Studies*, vol. XVI, no. 1 (Spring 1985), pp. 81–96.

TABLE 7-8 How Successful Negotiators Negotiate

Negotiating Behavior	Skilled Negotiators	Average Negotiators
Use of *irriators* per hour of face-to-face negotiating time	2.3	10.8
Frequency of *counterproposals* per hour of face-to-face negotiating time	1.7	3.1
Percent of negotiator's time classified as a *defense/attack spiral*	1.9%	6.3%
Percent of all negotiator's behavior immediately preceded by a *behavioral label*		
Disagreeing	0.4%	1.5%
All behavior except disagreeing	6.4%	1.2%
Active listening		
Testing for understanding	9.7%	4.1%
Summarizing	7.5%	4.2%
Questions, as a percent of all negotiating behavior	21.3%	9.6%
Feelings commentary, giving internal information as a percent of all negotiating behavior	12.1%	7.8%
Argument dilution, average number of reasons given by negotiator to back each argument or case that he or she advances	1.8	3.0

SOURCE: Neil Rackham, "The Behavior of Successful Negotiators" (Reston, Va.: Huthwaite Research Group, 1976), as reported in Ellen Raider International, Inc. (Brooklyn, N.Y.) and Situation Management Systems, Inc. (Plymouth, Mass.), *International Negotiations: A Training Program for Corporate Executives and Diplomats* (1982). Reprinted by permission.

tening, questions, and feeling commentaries. Each of these negotiating tactics is described briefly below (42):

1. Irritators are words that, while having negligible value in persuading opponents, cause annoyance. Irritators include such phrases as "generous offer," "fair price," and "reasonable arrangement." Average negotiators use over four times as many irritators as do skilled negotiators.

2. Counterproposals involve negotiators responding to their opponents' proposals by simply offering their own proposal. Average negotiators use counterproposals twice as frequently as skilled negotiators. Skilled negotiators clarify their understanding of opponents' suggestions before responding with their own proposals.

3. *Defend/attack spiral*. Negotiating, by definition, involves conflict. That conflict often leads to heated, value-laden accusations and defensive statements. Average negotiators frequently respond defensively and often attack, first gently and then harder and harder. Skilled negotiators, by contrast, rarely respond defensively. Although they also rarely attack, when they do so, they hit hard and without warning. Average negotiators attack more than three times as frequently as do skilled negotiators.

4. *Behavioral labeling* refers to describing what you plan to say before you say it. For example, "Can I ask a question?" and "Can I make a suggestion?" are behavioral labels for a question and a suggestion. Behavioral labels forewarn opponents. For all behavior except disagreement, skilled negotiators use labeling over five times as often as their colleagues. Average negotiators label disagreement three times as often as do skilled negotiators.

5. *Active listening* involves demonstrating to oneself and one's opponent that the previous statement has been understood. Active listening does not convey agreement or approval—it strictly reflects understanding. Skilled negotiators use two powerful active listening techniques — testing for understanding and summarizing — more than twice as often as their average colleagues.

6. *Questions* are a primary source of gathering information. Skilled negotiators use more than twice as many questions as do average negotiators.

7. *Feelings commentary* involves describing what a person feels about a situation. A negotiator might say, "I'm uncertain how to react to what you've just said. If the information you've given me is true, then I would like to accept it; yet I feel some doubts inside me about its accuracy. So part of me feels happy and part feels suspicious. Can you help me resolve this?" Skilled negotiators give almost twice as much feelings commentary as do average negotiators.

8. *Argument dilution*. Weak arguments generally dilute strong arguments. Skilled negotiators know that the fewer arguments, the better. Average negotiators use almost twice as many reasons to back each of their positions as do skilled negotiators.

In summary, the Huthwaite group found that skilled, British negotiators avoid irritators, counterproposals, defend/attack spirals, and argument dilution. They use behavioral labeling (except for disagreement), active listening, questions, and feelings commentaries. Unfortunately, this important study has not yet been replicated internationally.

Nonverbal Tactics

Nonverbal behavior refers to what negotiators do rather than what they say. It involves how they say their words, rather than the words themselves. Nonverbal behavior includes tone of voice, facial expressions, body distance, dress, gestures, timing, silences, and symbols. Nonverbal behavior is complex and multifaceted—it sends multiple messages, many of which are responded to subconsciously. Negotiators frequently respond more emotionally and powerfully to the nonverbal than the verbal message.

As with verbal behavior (language), nonverbal behavior varies markedly across cultures. As shown in Table 7–9, the extent to which Japanese, Americans, and Brazilians use silence, conversational overlaps, facial gazing, and touching during a negotiation varies considerably (20).

Silence. Japanese use the most silence, Americans a moderate amount, and Brazilians almost none at all. Americans often respond to silence by assuming that their bargaining partners disagree or have not accepted their offer. Moreover, they tend to argue and make concessions in response to silence. This response does not cause problems in negotiating with Brazilians, but it severely disadvantages Americans when

TABLE 7–9 Cross-Cultural Differences in Nonverbal Negotiating Behaviors

Behavior (Tactic)	Japanese	Americans	Brazilians
Silent periods (Number of periods greater than 10 seconds, per 30 minutes)	5.5	3.5	0
Conversational overlaps (Number per 10 minutes)	12.6	10.3	28.6
Facial gazing (Minutes of gazing per 10 minutes)	1.3	3.3	5.2
Touching (Not including handshaking, per 30 minutes)	0	0	4.7

SOURCE: Based on John Graham, "The Influence of Culture on Business Negotiations," *Journal of International Business Studies*, vol. XVI, no. 1 (Spring 1985), pp. 81–96.

they are dealing with Japanese. Whereas the Japanese silently consider the Americans' offer, the Americans interpret the silence as rejection and respond by making concessions (e.g., by lowering the price). Similar dynamics occur when non-native English speakers negotiate in English. As the non-native English speakers hesitate, to make certain that they have fully understood the meaning of the English words, the Americans assume that they are rejecting their position. Again, they tend to misinterpret the silence as rejection and to respond by making unnecessary concessions.

Conversational Overlaps. Conversational overlaps are the opposite of silent periods—they occur when more than one person speaks at the same time. As shown in Figure 7–3, Brazilian negotiators interrupt each other more than twice as often as either American or Japanese negotiators (20). Moreover, Brazilians frequently talk simultaneously. By contrast, when Japanese or American negotiators are interrupted, one or the other speaker generally stops talking—the conversational overlap is minimal. Since active listening increases negotiator effectiveness, ne-

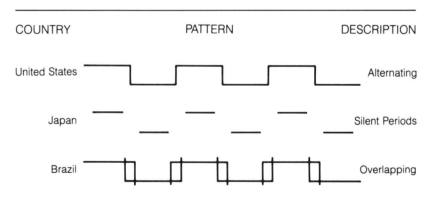

COUNTRY	PATTERN	DESCRIPTION
United States		Alternating
Japan		Silent Periods
Brazil		Overlapping

Negotiators in some cultures interrupt each other; in other cultures, they do not. A two-person negotiation is diagrammed for each of the three countries above. A line indicates that negotiator 1 or 2 is speaking. Blanks indicate that the negotiator is silent. Overlaps indicate that both negotiators are speaking at the same time.

FIGURE 7–3 Conversational Overlaps: Who Interrupts Whom
SOURCE: Based on John Graham, "The Influence of Culture on Business Negotiations," *Journal of International Business Studies*, vol. XVI, no. 1 (Spring 1985), pp. 81–96.

gotiators do best to avoid conversational overlaps. Moreover, cultures in which people do not talk while another person is talking interpret conversational overlaps as rude and disrespectful behavior.

Facial Gazing.   Facial gazing involves looking directly at one's partner's face. Eye contact is one of the most intense forms of facial gazing. The amount of eye contact and facial gazing often communicates the level of intimacy in a relationship—the more contact, the more intimacy. Confusion occurs when the appropriate amount of gazing for one culture communicates too much or too little intimacy for people from the other culture. In both cases foreign bargaining partners feel uncomfortable. Brazilians use four times as much facial gazing as Japanese, and one and one-half times as much as Americans (20).

Touching.   Whether negotiators touch each other during bargaining sessions depends on the cultures involved. Not including handshaking, Brazilian negotiators touch each other almost five times every half hour, whereas there is no physical contact between American or Japanese negotiators (20). Similar to facial gazing, touching communicates intimacy. A hug—a "double embrasso"—in Mexico communicates the development of a trusting relationship, whereas the same gesture offends Germans, for whom it communicates an inappropriately high level of intimacy.

Dirty Tricks

Neither all domestic nor all international negotiators search for mutually beneficial agreements. In attempting to gain the most for themselves, some negotiators resort to "dirty tricks"—tactics designed to pressure opponents into undesirable concessions and agreements. Negotiators can reduce the use of dirty tricks by (14) (a) not using them themselves; (b) recognizing them when their opponents use them, explicitly pointing them out, and negotiating about their use (i.e., establishing the "rules of the game"); (c) knowing what the cost is of walking out if the other party refuses to use principled negotiation (that is, knowing what the best alternative is to a negotiated solution); and (d) realizing that tactics that appear "dirty" to your team may be acceptable to people from another culture. Avoiding dirty tricks is more complex internationally than domestically. Effective negotiators must systematically question their interpretations of opponents' tactics rather than assuming that the tactics have the same intended meanings as they would at home. Table 7-10 outlines a series of common dirty tricks, including various types of deliberate deception, psychological warfare, and positional pressure tactics (14).

Reviewing the range of dirty tricks from a cross-cultural perspective reveals some of the possible misinterpretations international negotiators face. For example, Brazilians expect more deception among negotiators who do not know each other than do Americans. Many Brazilians are therefore more likely to use "phony facts" during the initial stages of an international negotiation than are some of their counterparts (20). The recommendation therefore is: "Unless you have good reason to trust someone, don't!" (14).

A negotiating team's discretion (the extent of their authority) varies across cultures. Russians and Eastern Europeans have very limited authority; they must check with their superiors if they want to deviate at all from the planned agenda. Americans, by contrast, generally have extensive authority; they expect to make the most important decisions at the bargaining table. When the other team has limited authority, experts recommend making all commitments tentative and conditional on the ability of the other party to accept and commit to their side of the deal (15). In cross-cultural encounters, negotiators must remember that the other party may not be using limited authority as a form of deliberate deception; they may simply come from a culture where authorities delegate very little discretion to individual team members.

Psychological warfare (tactics designed to make the other person feel uncomfortable) means different things in different cultures. For example, a common psychological trick involves too much touching or too little eye contact. As discussed earlier, both extremes make people uncomfortable; both make them want to get out of the situation quickly (and therefore conclude the negotiation as soon as possible). Problems arise in defining appropriate versus extreme amounts of touching and eye contact across cultures. Latins touch much more than Canadians, who in turn touch more than Swedes. Arabs maintain much greater eye contact than do Americans, who in turn use more than the Japanese. What appears to be a dirty trick from a domestic perspective may, in fact, express another culture's typical behavior. As with other potentially inappropriate tactics, negotiators must differentiate intended psychological warfare from unintended expressions of a culture's normal behavior patterns.

TABLE 7-10 What if They Use Dirty Tricks?

Tactic	Example (Ex) and Principled Response (R)
Deliberate Deception	
Phony Facts	R: Unless you have good reason to trust someone, don't.
Ambiguous Authority	R: "Alright. We'll treat it as a joint draft to which neither side is committed," or, "Good, you take it to your boss and I'll sleep on it. Then tomorrow either of us can suggest changes."
Dubious Intentions	R: Call the cards and build in a compliance system. Less than full disclosure is not the same as deception.
Psychological Warfare	Tactics designed to make you feel uncomfortable, so that you will have a subconscious desire to end the negotiation as soon as possible.
Stressful Situation	Ex: Room too hot or too cold, no private place to talk, their turf, too much touching, etc.
	R: Bring it up and change it.
Personal Attacks	Ex: Opponent comments on your clothes, your appearance ("Were you up all night?"), your status (by interrupting with other business, making you wait), your intelligence (making you repeat things, not listening), refusing to make eye contact.
	R: Recognizing it usually nullifies it. Bringing it up usually ends it.
Good Guy/Bad Guy Routine	Ex: "The price is $4,000 (bad guy)." "No, $3,800 (good guy)."
	R: "Why do you think $4,000 is reasonable, what is your principle?" Followed by a warning: "If $4,000, X will happen."
Positional Pressure Tactics	Bargaining tactics designed to structure a situation so that only one side can effectively make concessions.
Refuse to Negotiate	R: Ask why they refuse to negotiate. Will they be seen as weak? Suggest alternatives: negotiate through third parties, negotiate in private, send letters, etc.
Extreme Demands	Ex: Asking for $100,000 when it is only worth $25,000.
	R: Ask why it is a reasonable demand (price). Bring tactic to their attention.

TABLE 7-10 *(Continued)*

Tactic	Example (Ex) and Principled Response (R)	
Escalating Demands	Ex:	Making one concession and then adding new demands or reopening old demands.
	R:	Call the tactic to their attention and then take a break while you consider which issues you are willing to continue to negotiate on.
Lock-in Tactics	Ex:	Committing to a course of action, usually publicly. Paradoxically, you strengthen your bargaining position as you weaken your control over the situation.
	R:	Don't take lock-in seriously. Resist lock-in on principle: "I understand you are publicly committed to X, but my practice is never to yield to pressure."
Hardhearted Partner	Ex:	"I would agree, but my partner (i.e., boss) won't."
	R:	Get it in writing and/or negotiate directly with "hardhearted" partner.
Calculated Delay	Ex:	Waiting for the 11th hour. (Danger: If the 11th hour arrives, the other side may continue waiting.)
	R:	Make delaying tactic explicit and negotiate about it. Also create objective deadlines (such as starting to negotiate with another firm).
Take It or Leave It	R:	Ignore it. Or, explicitly recognize it, let them know what they have to lose if no agreement is reached, and look for a face saving way for them to back off.

SOURCE: Based on Roger Fisher and William Ury, *Getting to Yes* (New York: Penguin, 1981).

SUMMARY

"When in Rome, do as the Romans do?" No, when in Rome, or Beijing, or Osaka, act like an effective foreigner. Lucian Pye, in his excellent book, *Chinese Commercial Negotiating Style*, recommends that foreigners conducting business with the Chinese (41:xii):

(a) practice patience; (b) accept prolonged periods of no movement; (c) control against exaggerated expectations, and discount Chinese rhetoric about future prospects; (d) expect that the Chinese will try to influence by shaming; (e) resist the temptation to believe that difficulties may have been caused by one's own mistakes; and (f) try to understand Chinese cultural traits, but never believe that a foreigner can practice them better than the Chinese.

Pye recommends recognizing and understanding the cultural differences, not trying to become a member of the other culture.

Negotiating styles clearly vary across cultures (2;28;46;47;48;49). Words and behavior that effectively persuade people at home fail to influence overseas bargaining partners. The cultural context of the negotiation significantly influences who should be a part of the negotiating team, where the negotiation should be conducted, and what approach — including strategy and tactics — negotiators should use. International negotiation requires acute observation skills and a more tentative approach to understanding meaning than its domestic counterpart. Not only does international negotiation imply "not jumping to conclusions," it rarely allows the negotiator to conclude the negotiation definitively.

In preparing for an international negotiation, team members should learn as much as possible about the foreign culture, its negotiating patterns, and especially its style of negotiating with outsiders (2), and then approach the actual bargaining sessions with as wide a range of options and alternatives — in behavior and substance — as possible. In initial meetings negotiators should emphasize developing a relationship with their bargaining partners (remember, let *them* bring up business). During the discussions negotiators should assume difference in negotiation style until similarity is proven. It is easier to move from an expectation of difference to an acceptance of similarity, than to recoup the losses from mistakes incurred in acting as if the foreigners are just like you, when in fact they are not. Effective negotiators have high expectations and make high initial offers (or requests), proceed by asking a lot of questions, and refrain from making very many commitments until the final stage of the negotiation. During the bargaining sessions, effective negotiators use fewer irritators, counterproposals, and defend/attack spirals, less argument dilution, and more behavioral labels, active listening, and feeling commentaries than do less skilled negotiators.

The most effective negotiators approach sessions searching for synergistic solutions — solutions in which both sides win. The art of negotiation lies in developing creative options and alternatives, not in using persuasive tactics that more often result in giving offense than in gaining agreement.

QUESTIONS FOR REFLECTION

1. Review the four stages of negotiation. Analyze your own negotiating style: which stages do you emphasize more and which less? In what ways could your natural style of negotiation—the style that you use at home with a domestic counterpart—cause problems when negotiating abroad?

2. Why is a synergistic negotiation style often most effective in negotiations involving managers from different cultures?

3. How would you prepare and what would you make certain to do at a first session with negotiators from Bombay? from Paris? from Stockholm? from Rio de Janeiro?

4. When foreign negotiators hear that someone is coming to negotiate with them from your country, what do they expect? What is the stereotype—the most commonly expected behavior—of negotiators from your country? How can you use that stereotype to your advantage? In what ways is the stereotype a disadvantage? In which ways can you overcome the disadvantages associated with the stereotype of negotiators from your culture?

NOTES

1. Adapted from George Renwick, *Malays and Americans: Definite Differences, Unique Opportunities* (Yarmouth, Me.: Intercultural Press, 1985), pp. 51–54.

2. Example provided by John Graham, Graduate School of Management, University of California, Irvine.

REFERENCES

1. Adler, N. J., and Graham, J. L. "Business Negotiations: Canadians Are Not Just Like Americans," *Canadian Journal of Administrative Sciences*, vol. 4, no. 3 (September 1987), pp. 211–238.

2. Adler, N. J., and Graham, J. L."Cross-Cultural Interaction: The International Comparison Fallacy," *Journal of International Business Studies*. vol. 20, no. 3 (Fall 1989), pp. 515–537.

3. Adler, N. J., and Graham, J. L. "Business Negotiations in The People's Republic of China." Working paper, University of California, Irvine, 1990.

4. Adler, N. J.; Schwartz, T; and Graham, J. L. "Business Negotiations in Canada (French and English Speakers), Mexico and the United States," *Journal of Business Research*, vol. 15, no. 4, (1987), pp 411–429.

5. Beliaev, E.; Mullen, T.; and Punnett, B. J. "Understanding the Cultural Environment: U.S.A.–U.S.S.R. Trade Negotiation," *California Management Review*, vol. 27, no. 2 (Winter 1985), pp. 100–112.

6. Blaker, M. *Japanese International Negotiating Style* (New York: Columbia University Press, 1977).

7. Campbell, N.; Graham, J. L.; Jolibert, A.; and Meissner, H. "Marketing Negotiations in France, Germany, the United Kingdom, and the United States," *Journal of Marketing*, vol. 52, no. 2 (April 1988), pp. 49–62.

8. Casse, P. *Training for the Cross-Cultural Mind*, 2d ed. (Washington, D.C.: Society for Intercultural Education, Training, and Research, 1981).

9. Cohen, H. *You Can Negotiate Anything* (Secaucus, N.J.: Lyle Stuart, 1980).

10. Dupont, C. *La Négociation: Conduite, Théorie, Applications* (Paris: Dalloz, 1982).

11. Fayweather, J., and Kapoor, A. *Strategy and Negotiation for the International Corporation* (Cambridge, Mass.: Ballinger, 1976), pp. 29–50.

12. Fayweather, J., and Kapoor, A. "Simulated International Business Negotiations," *Journal of International Business Studies*, vol. 3 (Spring 1972), pp. 19–31.

13. Fisher, G. *International Negotiations: A Cross-Cultural Perspective* (Chicago: Intercultural Press, 1980).

14. Fisher, R., and Ury, W. *Getting to Yes* (Boston: Houghton Mifflin, and New York: Penguin, 1981).

15. Glenn, E. S.; Witmeyer, D.; and Stevenson, K. A. "Cultural Styles of Persuasion," *International Journal of Intercultural Relations*, vol. 1, no. 3 (Fall 1977), pp. 52–66.

16. Graham, J. L. "A Hidden Cause of America's Trade Deficit with Japan," *Columbia Journal of World Business* (Fall 1981), pp. 5–15.

17. Graham, J. L. "An Exploratory Study of the Process of Marketing Negotiations Using a Cross-Cultural Perspective," in R. Scarcella, E. Andersen, and S. Krashen, eds., *Developing Communicative Competence in a Second Language* (Rowley, Mass.: Newbury House Publishers, 1989).

18. Graham, J. L. "Brazilian, Japanese, and American Business Negotiations," *Journal of International Business Studies*, vol. XIV, no. 1 (Spring–Summer 1983), pp. 47–61.

19. Graham, J. L. "Deference Given the Buyer: Variations across Twelve Cultures," in P. Lorange and F. Contractor eds., *Cooperative Strategies in International Business.* (Lexington, Mass.: Lexington Books, 1987).

20. Graham, J. L. "The Influence of Culture on the Process of Business Negotiations," *Journal of International Business Studies,* vol. XVI, no. 1 (Spring 1985), pp. 81–96.

21. Graham, J. L. "The Problem-Solving Approach to Interorganizational Negotiations: A Laboratory Test," *Journal of Business Research,* vol. 14 (1986), pp. 271–286.

22. Graham, J. L., and Herberger, R. A., Jr. "Negotiators Abroad — Don't Shoot from the Hip," *Harvard Business Review* (July–August 1983), pp. 160–168.

23. Graham, J. L., and Sano, Y. *Smart Bargaining: Doing Business with the Japanese* (Cambridge, Mass.: Ballinger, 1984).

24. Graham, J. L.; Kim, D. K.; Lin, C. Y.; and Robinson, M. "Buyer-Seller Negotiations around the Pacific Rim: Differences in Fundamental Exchange Process, *Journal of Consumer Research,* vol. 15 (June 1988), pp. 48–54.

25. Harnett, O. L., and Cummings, L. L. *Bargaining Behavior: An International Study* (Houston, Tex.: Dane Publications 1980).

26. Hofstede, G., and Bond, M. H. : "Confucius and Economic Growth: New Trends into Culture's Consequences," *Organizational Dynamics* vol. 16, no. 4, (1988), pp. 4–21.

27. Ikle, F. C. *How Nations Negotiate* (New York: Harper & Row, 1964), pp. 225–255.

28. Jastram, R. W. "The Nakado Negotiators," *California Management Review,* vol. XVII, no. 2 (Winter 1974), pp. 88–90.

29. Jensen, L. "Soviet-American Behavior in Disarmament Negotiations," in I. W. Zartman, ed., *The 50 Percent Solution* (New York: Anchor, 1976).

30. Kapoor, A. "MNC Negotiations: Characteristics and Planning Implications," *Columbia Journal of World Business* (Winter 1974), pp. 121–130.

31. Kapoor, A. "Negotiation Strategies in International Business-Government Relations: A Study in India," *Journal of International Business Studies,* vol. 1–2 (Summer 1970), pp. 21–42.

32. Kennedy, J. F. Address given at American University, Washington, D.C., June 10, 1963.

33. Kirkbride, P. S.; Tang, S. F. Y.; and Westwood, R. I. "Chinese Bargaining and Negotiating Behaviour: The Cultural Effects." Working paper, City Polytechnic of Hong Kong, 1988.

219

34. Komorita, S. S., and Brenner, A. R. "Bargaining and Concession-Making under Bilateral Monopoly," *Journal of Personality and Social Psychology*, vol. 9 (1968), pp. 15–20.

35. Krauthammer, C. "Deep Down, We're All Alike, Right? Wrong," *Time* (August 15, 1983), p. 30.

36. Lall, A. *How Communist China Negotiates* (New York: Columbia University Press, 1966).

37. Mehrabian, A., and Ferris, S. R. "Inference of Attitudes from Nonverbal Communication in Two Channels," *Journal of Consulting Psychology*, vol. 31, no. 3 (1967), pp. 248–252. Also see Albert Mehrabian. "Communicating without Words," *Psychology Today* (September 1968), p. 53.

38. Muna, F. A. *The Arab Mind* (New York: Scribners, 1973).

39. Perlmutter, H. "More than 50 percent of international managers' time is spent in negotiating—in interpersonal transaction time influencing other managers," statement made at Academy of Management Meetings, Dallas, Texas, August 1983, and at The Wharton School, University of Pennsylvania, 1984.

40. Plantey, A. *La Négociation Internationale: Principes et Méthodes* (Paris: Editions du Centre National de la Recherche Scientifique), 1980.

41. Pye, L. *Chinese Commercial Negotiating Style* (Cambridge, Mass.: Oelgeschlager, Gunn and Hain, Publishers, 1982).

42. Raider, E. *International Negotiations: A Training Program for Corporate Executives and Diplomats* (Brooklyn, N.Y.: Ellen Raider International, Inc.; and Plymouth, Mass.: Situation Management Systems, Inc., 1982); and Berlew, Dave; Moore, Alex; and Harrison, Roger. *Positive Negotiation Programs* (Plymouth, Mass.: Situation Management Systems, Inc., 1978, 1980, and 1983). Reprinted by permission.

43. Rubin, J. Z., and Brown, B. R. *The Social Psychology of Bargaining and Negotiation* (New York: Academic Press, 1976).

44. Sawyer, J., and Guetzkow, H. "Bargaining and Negotiation in International Relations," in H. C. Kelman, ed., *International Behavior: A Social-Psychological Analysis* (New York: Holt, Rinehart and Winston, 1965), pp. 464–520.

45. Tang, S. F. Y., and Kirkbride, P. S. "Developing Conflict Management Skills in Hong Kong: An Analysis of Some Cross-Cultural Implications," *Management Education and Development*, vol. 17, pt. 3 (1986), pp. 287–301.

46. Terasawa, Y. "The Japanese Perspective in International Business Negotiations." Paper presented at the Academy of Management Meetings, Dallas, Texas, August 16, 1983.

47. Tung, R. L. *Business Negotiations with the Japanese* (Lexington, Mass.: Lexington Books, 1984).

48. Tung, R. L. "How to Negotiate with the Japanese," *California Management Review*, vol. XXVI, no. 4 (Summer 1984), pp. 62–77.

49. Tung, R. L. "U.S.–China Trade Negotiations: Practices, Procedures and Outcomes," *Journal of International Business Studies*, vol. 13 (Fall 1982), pp. 25–38.

50. Van Zandt, H. F. "How to Negotiate in Japan," *Harvard Business Review* (November–December 1977), pp. 72–80.

51. Weiss, S. E. "The Long Path to the IBM–Mexico Agreement: An Analysis of the Microcomputer Investment Negotiations, 1983–1985." Working paper #89-13, Stern School of Business, New York University, New York, N.Y., 1989.

52. Weiss, S. E. "Creating the GM–Toyota Joint Venture: A Case in Complex Negotiation," *Columbia Journal of World Business*, vol. 22, no. 2 (1987), pp. 23–37.

53. Weiss, S. E., and Strip, W. G. "Negotiating with Foreign Business Persons." Working paper # 85–86, New York Unversity, New York, N.Y., 1985.

54. Weiss-Wik, S., "Enhancing Negotiators' Successfulness," *Journal of Conflict Resolution*, vol. 27, no. 4 (December 1983), pp. 706–739.

55. Wells, L. T. "Negotiating with Third World Governments," *Harvard Business Review* (January–February 1977), pp. 72–80.

56. Wright, P. "Doing Business in Islamic Markets," *Harvard Business Review*, vol. 59, no. 1 (January–February 1981), pp. 34ff.

PART III

▼

Managing
Global Managers

▲

CHAPTER 8

▼

Cross-Cultural Transitions: Expatriate Employee Entry and Reentry

▲

If a man does not keep pace with his companions, perhaps it is because he hears a different drummer. Let him step to the music which he hears, however measured or far away.

Henry David Thoreau, *Walden*

International employees go through a predictable series of stages in transferring from a domestic to an international assignment and back home again. As shown in Figure 8–1, organizations recruit potential employees either from within the company or as off-the-street hirees. The organization then chooses whether or not to select the candidate, and the recruit chooses whether or not to accept the assignment. Next, many organizations conduct an orientation to describe the foreign culture and project as well as the logistical requirements of moving. Oriented employees and their families then proceed overseas to accomplish the assignment. Employees come back to their home country and either

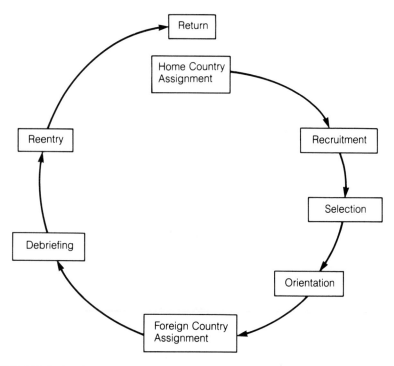

FIGURE 8-1 Expatriate International Career Cycle

return to a job within the same organization or leave the organization to find a job elsewhere. Very few organizations have reentry or debriefing sessions. The complete expatriate career cycle includes two major international transitions: cross-cultural entry and home country reentry. To be successful, organizations must understand and manage each phase of the expatriate international career cycle (2; 5; 6; 8; 12; 13; 19; 20; 21; 22; 23).

CROSS-CULTURAL ENTRY

Cross-cultural adjustment to a foreign country has been described as a U-shaped curve (7). In the initial phase, at the top of the curve, expatriates enjoy a great deal of excitement as they discover the new culture. Business travelers, as compared with expatriates, often have the luxury of remaining at this stage. As shown in Figure 8–2, this initial phase is followed by a period of disillusionment as the curve descends, during which it is no longer romantic to try to take a cab without knowing where to find the taxi stand; or to wait anxiously on Saturday for the arrival of a letter, only to discover that weekend mail delivery does not exist; or to try to converse intelligently with a severely limited vocabulary. The third phase, the bottom of the U-shaped curve, has been labeled *culture shock* — the frustration and confusion that result from being bombarded by uninterpretable cues. Following the culture shock phase, expatriates begin adapting to foreign ways as the curve rises: they generally begin to feel more positive, work more effectively, and live a more normal life. Neither the highs of the initial phase nor the lows of the culture shock phase usually mark this positive adjustment phase.

Culture Shock

Does everyone suffer from culture shock, or does it only afflict inexperienced travelers and people moving to very different countries? Surprisingly, many of the most effective international managers suffer the

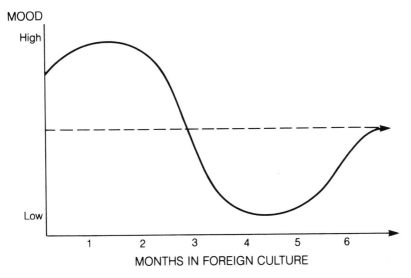

FIGURE 8–2 Culture Shock Cycle

most severe culture shock (16). By contrast, managers evaluated as not particularly effective by their colleagues described themselves as suffering little or no culture shock. Culture shock is not a disease, but rather the natural response to immersing oneself in a new environment. Economically and linguistically similar countries can cause culture shock as well as more dissimilar environments: the Quebec-based executive will experience culture shock arriving in France, as will the Australian transferring to Canada. Severe culture shock is often a positive sign that the expatriate is becoming involved in the new culture instead of remaining isolated in an expatriate ghetto. Expatriates therefore should view culture shock as a sign that they are doing something right, not wrong. The important question thus becomes how best to manage culture shock, not how to avoid it.

What exactly is culture shock? Culture shock is the expatriate's reaction to a new, unpredictable, and therefore uncertain environment. As discussed in chapter 3, culture shock results from a breakdown in the expatriate's selective perception and effective interpretation systems. Expatriates ask the questions, "To what should I pay attention?" and "What does it mean?" Millions of sights, sounds, smells, tastes, and feelings bombard expatriates, and they find it difficult to know which ones are meaningful and which ones are unimportant and therefore best screened out. Upon entering a foreign culture, they lack an interpretation system based on the new culture and therefore inappropriately and ineffectively use their home culture's interpretive system.

During the initial period in a new culture, expatriates find that other people's behavior does not seem to make sense, and—even more disconcerting—that their own behavior does not produce expected results. They find that the environment makes new demands for which they neither have ready-made answers nor the ability to develop new, culturally appropriate answers. For example, as a North American newly arrived in the Middle East describes:

> My third day in Israel, accompanied by a queasy stomach, I ventured forth into the corner market to buy something light and easy to digest. As yet unable to read Hebrew, I decided to pick up what looked like a small yogurt container that was sitting near the cheese. Not being one hundred percent sure it contained yogurt, I peered inside; to my delight, it held a thick white yogurt-looking substance. I purchased my "yogurt" and went home to eat—soap, liquid soap! How was I to know that soap came in packages resembling yogurt containers, or

that market items in Israel were not neatly divided into edible and inedible sections, as I remembered them in the United States. My now "clean" stomach became a bit more fragile and my confidence waned.

Stress.   Change causes stress, and expatriates face many changes in leaving their home country and organization and transferring to a new country and a new job. Separation from friends, family, children (perhaps for the first time), and parents (perhaps elderly or ill) increases stress. Upon arrival in the foreign country, different perceptions and conflicting values exacerbate the stress. Expatriates see situations that they neither understand nor believe to be ethically correct. For example, some North American expatriates become appalled by the poverty in many developing countries — especially in contrast to their own relatively luxurious international hotels and expatriate homes. Others feel very uncomfortable managing servants.

Stress-related culture shock may take many forms: embarrassment, disappointment, frustration, impatience, anxiety, identity confusion, anger, and physiological responses such as sleeplessness, stomachaches, headaches, and trembling hands. As one executive recalled, "There's some kind of traumatic reaction to it. It evidenced itself in my insomnia. There was something there . . . waking up at 4 A.M. every morning." Since culture shock is a sign that the expatriate is beginning to let go of the home culture and engage with the foreign culture, the appropriate response is *not* to try to eliminate the culture shock but rather to try to manage the stress it causes.

Expatriates have found many highly effective and creative stress management mechanisms for coping with culture shock. One method does not work any better than another; it depends on the particular individual and situation involved. Some people participate in regular physical exercise programs, some practice meditation and relaxation exercises, and others keep a journal ("Yell at the paper, not at the people!"). Many of the most effective international managers create "stability zones" (16). They spend most of their time totally immersed in the foreign culture, then briefly retreat into an environment — a stability zone — that closely recreates home. Examples of successful stability zones used by executives include checking into a home country hotel for the weekend, going to an international club and only talking with other compatriots, playing a musical instrument, listening to records, or watching video movies in one's native language. A North American expatriate manager in Brussels used a particularly creative stability zone: when she felt lonely and frustrated with the challenges of Brussels, she would get into her car and drive to new places in Belgium. She reduced stress by escaping into the culture—on her own terms and by herself.

On the job, managers can reduce the stress caused by culture shock by recognizing it and modifying their expectations and behavior accordingly. They can establish priorities and focus their limited energy on only the most important tasks; they can clearly define their responsibilities and educate the home office concerning the cultural and business difference between foreign and home country operations; and they can realize that they will not be as efficient or effective, especially initially, in the new job as they were in their prior job.

Many families and couples create stress management systems. For example, one family made a rule forbidding complaints during meals; they only allowed positive statements about the new culture. Another couple made a rule that there could be no complaints for the first twenty-four hours after the employee returned home from a business trip. The exact nature of the stability zone or stress management mechanism is less important than the fact that expatriates recognize the highly stressful nature of moving into a new culture and develop at least one mechanism that works for them.

Adjustment. After three to six months (depending on the individual and the assignment), most expatriates come up from their culture shock "low" and begin living a more normal life in the foreign country. Little by little, expatriates learn what is important and what is meaningful. They learn when "yes" means "yes," when it means "maybe," and when it means "no." They learn what to focus on and what to ignore. They learn to differentiate idiosyncratic behavior from behavior reflecting a cultural pattern. For example, one expatriate showed his confusion—his inability to differentiate idiosyncratic from culturally patterned behavior—by asking, "Is it that Budi is lazy while most people from this country work very hard to complete all of their assigned work [idiosyncratic behavior], or is it that most people from this country work slowly and only do half of their work [behavior reflecting a cultural pattern]?" Moreover, most expatriates begin to learn enough of the foreign language to make themselves understood in day-to-day conversations.

In addition to time (usually three to six months), the key to getting out of the culture shock "low" is problem solving. Successful expatriates recognize that the foreign environment makes many demands for which they must find or create solutions. In so doing, they realize that blaming others for their frustrations — host nationals, company, or spouse — is not useful. Ineffective approaches include:

1. Blaming the host nationals. "These foreigners [who, in fact, are the *natives*] are stupid; anyone who had any intelligence would never have laid out a city this way! Addresses seem to be scattered randomly down the streets."

2. Blaming the company. "Why didn't the company tell me that the street numbers in Tokyo would not be sequential! How do they expect me to find our clients, let alone make the sales? The least they could have done is given me a map and a guide."

3. Blaming one's spouse. "Here I've been traveling for the last two weeks, eating strange food, trying to get these foreigners to sign the biggest contract that the firm has ever gotten, and I come home to hear you complaining that the kids can't take a bath because the plumber doesn't speak English. Some help you are!"

While it is tempting to blame others, it is generally an unproductive stress management technique and never a good problem-solving approach.

The most successful expatriates constantly recognize that they may not fully understand the situation and that they must find ways to get reliable information and expertise. Their need for immediate decisions versus their lack of sufficient knowledge with which to make those decisions causes both the tenson experienced by successful international managers and the large number of inappropriate decisions made by less effective managers. Company-sponsored cross-cultural communication and management training programs can be highly effective in giving expatriates the skills to manage culture shock and work effectively in foreign countries.

Other expatriates and host nationals who have previously faced and dealt effectively with the same or similar situations can often best empathize with the newcomer's dilemmas.

An Italian colleague of mine described the horror of his first day in Philadelphia. He handed his secretary a stack of letters and manuscripts and told her to type them. Each day he expected her to present him with the finished work and each day he received nothing. Only at the end of a disappointing, frustrating, and unproductive week did an Italian friend of his explain that "In the United States, secretaries have more status than in Italy. You must *ask* them *if* they can do your typing, not *tell* them to do your typing. United States organizations are more egalitarian and less hierarchical than Italian firms." Sheepishly, my Italian colleague began to "ask"; slowly, he began to receive typed pages.

Host nationals, although often invaluable as cultural informants, can be somewhat inarticulate about their own culture. People do not consciously learn the dos and don'ts of their native culture. Rather, as children, they mimic the behavior of their parents and other adults. Eventually, with maturity, they can perform the behaviors, but they cannot explain them. For example, an American businessperson meeting with an Arab will not maintain sufficient eye contact. To the Arab, the American seems "shifty-eyed" and not to be trusted. If asked, the Arab will not be able to describe how often and how long appropriate eye contact should last. He can do it; he can't explain it. The frustrated American knows that he is doing something wrong but cannot find out how to behave correctly.

Whatever the source of information, patience and creativity remain essential. Effective international managers "know that they do not know." They recognize that they are in a difficult situation and that they will not act as effectively overseas as they did at home — especially in the initial stages. They recognize the need for good stress management techniques, including stability zones, that will not harm their relationship with colleagues, clients, or family. They also recognize that all members of the family experience culture shock in adjusting to the new country and that in many ways the transition affects the spouse more profoundly than the employee. Successful expatriates therefore view cross-cultural adjustment as a systems issue, not an individual problem. More will be said about this issue in the next chapter.

HOME COUNTRY REENTRY[1]

Cross-cultural reentry is the transition from the foreign country back into one's home country. It involves facing previously familiar surroundings after living in a foreign country for a significant period of time. Until recently, experts thought reentry was an easy process, but lately more companies see it as a major problem (14;15). According to Business International Corporation,

> Repatriating executives from overseas assignments is a top management challenge that goes far beyond the superficial problems and costs of physical relocation. . . . The assumption is that since these individuals are returning home . . . they should have no trouble adapting. . . . However, experience has shown that repatriation is anything but simple (4:65).

Twenty percent of the employees who complete overseas assignments want to leave their firm when they come home. According to the *Wall Street Journal's* report of a survey of thirty-four multinational companies, "Bosses might quickly become sensitive if they added up the cost to the company of unhappy workers" (24).

Reentry experiences frequently surprise returnees (3). When going overseas, employees generally expect new and unfamiliar situations, whereas they do not expect anything unfamiliar when returning home. Most returnees expect neither reentry shock nor trauma; they expect to slip back into their previous organizations, jobs, and lifestyles and to live easily and successfully again.

> I don't expect changes . . . Because it was only a short stay overseas, I expect to just slip right back into my old mold.
>
> I expect to have the same friends, the same activities, and the same family connections.
>
> I do not anticipate culture shock at reentry, . . . I don't expect much trauma.

Returnees come back neither to the world they left nor to the world they are expecting. While overseas, the employee has changed, the organization has changed, and the country has changed. Moreover, during the culture shock phase of adjusting to a foreign country, expatriates often idealize the home country, remembering only the good aspects of home — in essence, creating something to dream about.

> As I shivered in Quebec's −35° winter, I remembered Los Angeles' blue sky and sunshine, driving to the beach on a warm January morning . . . I didn't remember skies opaque with smog, freeways so clogged with cars that driving anywhere was impossible, nor did I remember my car being broken into while parked at the beach.

When returning home, employees face the real changes; the gap between the way it was and the way it is, and the gap between their idealized memories and reality. Most are surprised at their feelings and at the reality.

Returnees describe reentry as an even more difficult transition than the initial entry into the foreign country.

> Going home is a harder move. The foreign move has the excitement of being new . . . more confusing, but exciting. Reentry is frightening . . . I'll be happy to be home . . . I really wonder if I can adjust back.

Returnees describe stages similar to those of culture shock — first being in a very high mood, quickly plummeting to a low mood, and then

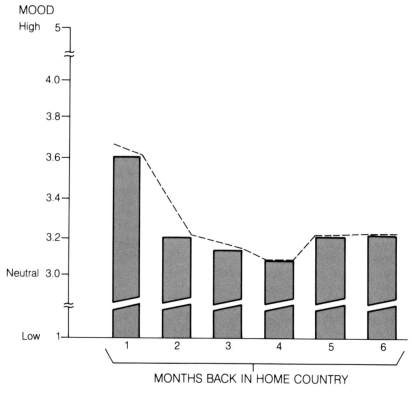

FIGURE 8-3 Reentry Adjustment Curve

slowly rising to their normal mood. As shown in Figure 8–3, the initial high mood is often very short, and described by such comments as:

> I was pleasantly surprised by neighbors. They really went overboard to welcome us back.
>
> It's cleaner . . . and just a reasonable number of people . . . fantastic! . . . freedom of mobility . . . quality of life is higher here and I notice it more.[2]

For most returnees the initial high mood lasts less than a month and many report it lasting only a few hours. The low period therefore begins earlier in reentry than in the entry transition. Returnees' lowest times usually occur during the second and third months back. As American managers returning from their assignments in Venezuela described,

> Some of my friends couldn't even imagine the foreign country . . . They asked me how it was, but they just wanted to hear "fine."
>
> In Venezuela, gettings things done was a hassle . . . and we said, "In the U.S.A. it would be so easy." When we came home, everything was delayed and frustrating. Here in the United States! The U.S.A. was a continual Venezuela story . . . and we had always said, "This will never happen at home" . . . HA!
>
> Calling friends, my sister, my mom . . . Everyone was so busy with their lives that they didn't have time to just talk. They cut me off . . . I understand, but . . .
>
> I came back with so many stories to share, but my friends and family couldn't understand them. It was as if my years overseas were unshareable.

By the sixth month at home, returnees generally accept their situations and report feeling "average" — neither much higher nor much lower than usual.

PROFESSIONAL REENTRY

Just as the new environment and lifestyle can cause problems when entering a foreign culture, so too can the professional transition back into the home organization cause problems. Professional reentry has often been more difficult than personal reentry, especially for returnees to companies that do not consider international experience critical to overall corporate success (17). Most managers from industrialized countries expect the international assignment to help their career; yet they return to discover that, at best, it has a neutral effect. Upon their return, companies traditionally promote fewer than half of their returnees (9:1;24). For many, especially in the short run, the career impact is negative. More than two-thirds of the returnees complain of suffering from the "out of sight, out of mind" syndrome (9:1;10). As various managers returning to North America have commented:

> My colleagues react indifferently to my international assignment . . . They view me as doing a job I did in the past; they don't see me as having gained anything while overseas.

> The organization has changed . . . work habits, norms, and procedures have changed, and I have lost touch with all that . . . I'm a beginner again!

> I had no specific reentry job to return to. I wanted to leave international and return to domestic. Working abroad magnifies problems while isolating effects. You deal with more problems, but the home office doesn't know the details of the good or bad effects. Managerially, I'm out of touch . . .

> I lost time. My career stopped when I left and started again when I returned.

Many employees complain that their reentry jobs bore them (11). Almost half of the repatriated executives surveyed by Korn/Ferry International found their reentry position less satisfying than their overseas position (9:4). Their overseas job offered more excitement and challenge, and they missed the greater responsibility, authority, status, decision-making autonomy, and variety of their overseas assignments. Returnees frequently feel disappointed, discouraged, and angry when they realize that their reentry jobs do not fit their expectations:

> I'm bored at work . . . I run upstairs to see what [another returning colleague] is doing. He says, "Nothing." Me, too.

> In a lot of ways the red tape and nonsense that we're experiencing now since we reentered are a lot worse. Maybe I didn't recognize these things before, or maybe I'd learned to live with them.

> While overseas, I realized that the home office doesn't do anything right . . . bosses call bosses to get anything done. I had to talk to seven

people to get one answer. It's a real bureaucracy. We have more chiefs than Indians.

In addition to facing reentry "invisibility" as well as diminished job responsibility and scope, returnees must also confront a major readjustment to the home country organizational culture. Whereas the foreign organization may have been very hierarchical and highly structured, risk averse, and individualistic, the home organization may have a very flat, matrixed structure, a high tolerance for uncertainty and ambiguity, and strongly emphasize group contributions over those of individuals. The transition from one organizational culture to another and from one set of organizational assumptions and behaviors to another can be difficult and stressful. Expatriates experience organizational culture shock at the same time as they are experiencing societal culture shock.

Effectiveness

Are returnees effective during their initial period back in the home organization? Yes, and no. As shown in Figures 8-4 and 8-5, returnees and their bosses do not agree on their perceptions of effectiveness. Returnees say they are initially *ineffective* and then become more effective. Bosses and colleagues, on the other hand, say returnees are initially *effective* and then become more effective. Bosses tend to compare returnees' reentry performance with their predeparture performance and do not realize that the expatriates have grown professionally while abroad and that they can handle more responsibilities than they could in the past. By contrast, returnees frequently compare their reentry performance with their work abroad and generally think they have accomplished relatively little in their first few months at home. Further complicating the reentry transition, bosses are often oblivious to the returnees' lower self-assessment and general dissatisfaction.

Xenophobic Response

As well as disagreeing on *how* effective returnees are, reenterers and their bosses also disagree on *who* is most effective. Returnees who think they are very effective are rarely seen as such by their bosses; similarly,

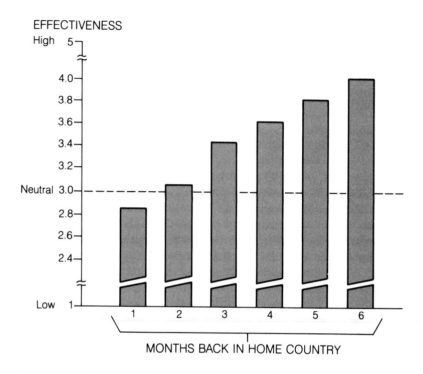

FIGURE 8-4 Returnee Assessed Effectiveness Curve

returnees who think they are ineffective are not always rated as such by their bosses. Home company bosses and colleagues frequently assess as most effective those returnees who appear "least foreign" — that is, who do not know or use foreign languages, do not have foreign friends, and were not born in a foreign country. Similarly, they often rank as most effective those returnees who do not explicitly use the skills and learnings from their foreign experience on the job back home. This *xenophobic response* — the bosses' fear and rejection of things foreign — severely handicaps organizations who want to gain from the experience of their overseas workforce.

By contrast, returnees' own assessments rank as most effective those colleagues who recognize and use their cross-cultural learnings to the greatest extent and who are least embedded in, or limited by, the home culture. Returnees who speak foreign languages, have foreign friends,

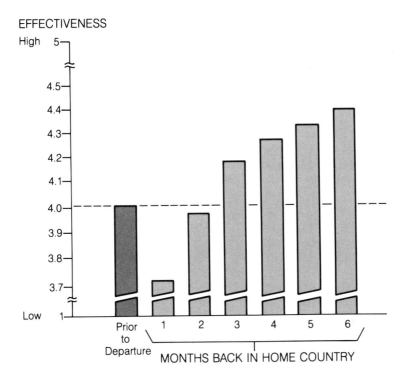

FIGURE 8-5 Boss and Colleague Assessed Effectiveness Curve

and know the foreign culture rank themselves more highly than do their less cross-culturally involved colleagues. Returnees whose bosses and colleagues give them greater job responsibility and more recognition also rank themselves as more effective than do other returnees.

What Do Managers Learn Abroad?

In reviewng their experiences abroad, returnees report that they improve their managerial skills more than their technical skills. As highlighted in the descriptions below, returnees report having enhanced many important professional skills, including those that are critical for managing in today's rapidly changing, highly competitive, global industries. Increased self-confidence and an improved self-image are the personal changes returnees most commonly recognize.

Skills Learned Abroad[3]

Managerial Skills, Not Technical Skills

Working abroad makes you more knowledgeable about the questions to ask, not the answers.

I learned how to work in two cultures . . . to compromise, not to be a dictator. It's very similar to two domestic cultures . . . like marketing and engineering.

I'm more open-minded . . . more able to deal with a wider range of people . . . because I ran into many other points of view.

Tolerance for Ambiguity

Because I only understood a fraction of what was really going on overseas, maybe 50 percent, I had to make decisions on a fraction of the necessary information. Now I can tolerate nonclosure and ambiguity better.

Things you never thought you'd put up with, you learn to put up with . . . I always thought I was right, until I went overseas.

Multiple Perspective

I learned what it feels like to be a foreigner . . . I could see things from their perspective.

I learned to anticipate . . . it's the role of a diplomat.

Ability to Work with and Manage Others

I increased my tolerance for other people. For the first time, I was the underdog, the minority.

I became a soft-headed screamer. I'm definitely better with others now.

I used to be more ruthless than I am now . . . I was the All-American manager. Now, I stop and realize the human impact more. I use others as resources. I do more communicating with others in the organization.

When recognized and used, these skills definietly *increase* the returnee's self-perceived contribution to the home organization. Unfortunately, if these same skills are associated with the foreign country, the boss's rating of the returnee's effectiveness generally *decreases*. This is not surprising, given that up until recently most organizations primarily transferred employees and managers in order to get a job done; rarely did they transfer people to develop either the organization or the expatriate's career. This narrow definition of the expatriate's role in the organization, combined with an inherent parochialism — "our home country's way of working is the best and only way to work"—severely diminishes the value of the returnees as recognized by the home organization.

Transition Strategies

The attitudes (or coping modes) that returnees use to fit back into their formerly familiar home country and home organization vary markedly. Some returnees become resocialized, some alienated, and others proactive.

Resocialized Returnees.   These returnees are the most common among corporate expatriates who work for organizations without a global orientation. As shown in Table 8–1, resocialized returnees neither recognize nor use their cross-culturally acquired skills and learnings. They try to fit back into the domestic corporate structure, to act like employees who have not been away. In treating the overseas experience as nontransferable, they negate the possibility of it improving their approach to home country work and life. Moreover, because home organization managers rarely appreciate returnees' potentially increased contribution, they often feel satisfied with resocialized returnees' fit-back-in strategy. The resocialized mode precludes both the individual and the organization gaining very much from the foreign experience. This lack of individual and organizational learning is particularly unfortunate today when firms need to continually learn just to compete.

Alienated Returnees.   These returnees are more common among employees who have had serial overseas careers than those who have had a single overseas assignment, more common among spouses than employees, and more common among volunteers (e.g., Peace Corps and Cana-

TABLE 8-1 Coping Modes: Approaches to the Reentry Transition

Home Country Orientation

Resocialized Returnees attempt to fit back in when they return to the home country. They do not recognize having learned skills that would be transferable to the home environment. In general they are not aware of changes in themselves or in their environment. They receive high effectiveness ratings from their bosses and from themselves and are quite satisfied with their reentry positions. Overall, resocialized returnees tend to remove themselves from the foreign experience. Similarly, while living overseas, most resocialized returnees *reject the foreign country*. Many live in expatriate ghettos separate from the host nationals; many are labeled by host nationals as "The Ugly Foreigner."

Proactive Returnees attempt to integrate their overseas and their home country experiences. They are highly aware of changes in themselves and their environment. They recognize and try to use the skills and learnings they acquired while overseas. While proactive returnees rate themselves as effective and as satisfied with their job, their bosses only rate them as moderately so. As expatriates, they also aim to effectively *integrate the home and foreign culture* ways of life; their approach is to attempt to adapt to living overseas.

Alienated Returnees often dissociate themselves from the home culture and home organization. Although they recognize that they have acquired skills and learnings while overseas, they see no way to use them within the home environment. Alienated returnees do not see themselves as particularly effective, nor, in general, do their bosses. They receive the least recognition of the three groups of returnees. Similarly, as expatriates, they also *reject the home culture*. Their approach to living overseas is to try to "go native," to assimilate into the foreign culture.

Foreign Country Orientation

dian University Student Overseas) than among corporate employees. While in the foreign country, alienated returnees tend to "go native"— they assimilate the values and lifestyle of the foreign culture. When they return, they evaluate the foreign culture as better than their own culture, believing that it offers a richer way of life. They reject their home culture, and in so doing frequently become personally isolated. Alienated returnees, in believing that they cannot fit back in or use their cross-culturally acquired skills and learnings in the home environment, often feel professionally unproductive and personally unsatisfied. Similar to resocialized reenterers, alienated reenterers contribute little to the home organization from their overseas experience. The home organization generally recognizes the loss through the alienated returnees' diminished productivity and ranks them as ineffective.

Proactive Reenterers. These reenterers neither reject their own nor the foreign culture. Rather, they combine aspects of both in creating a new way of life. Proactive reenterers usually feel optimistic and attempt to create the type of world in which they would like to live. They recognize and use their cross-culturally acquired skills and learnings to contribute within the work environment and to modify their personal lifestyle. Proactive returnees see themselves as more effective and more satisfied with their job than do users of any of the other coping modes. Proactive reenterers appear to have developed a highly sophisticated skill at perceiving their environment — whether foreign or home — and at describing their social and organizational situation rather than comparing and evaluating it. They are able to identify similarities and differences without needing to classify one as good and the other as bad. Proactive returnees are therefore able to create new, synergistic ways of perceiving and working within the home country environment based on their former home country experience and their experience abroad. This synergistic approach — the combining of home and foreign country ways of understanding how to work—allows returnees to work more effectively with their colleagues and clients, to make decisions based on a wider range of alternatives, and to act as leaders both in the realm of ideas as well as in the realm of actions. Proactive returnees' potential for contributing to the organization is great; however, the home organization must decide to use the returnees' potential contributions and not simply attempt to fit them back into the organization.

Managing Reentry

What makes some returnees more proactive than others? What causes some returnees to fit back in better than others? There are two primary differences between the three coping modes mentioned previously: communication and validation. *Communication* involves the extent to which expatriates receive information and recognize changes while abroad. Returnees who maintain close contact with the home organization while abroad become more proactive, effective, and satisfied in their reentry jobs. This communication includes news about new contracts and policies and changes in the political and economic environment, as well as news of a more personal nature. Returnees who do best are those who recognize positive and negative changes in themselves, their organization, and their community.

Validation involves the amount of recognition expatriates receive upon returning home. Returnees who receive more recognition from bosses and colleagues for both their foreign work and their potential future contributions do better than do less recognized returnees. Organizations that treat expatriates and returnees as if they were "out of sight, out mind," on vacation, or so far behind that they could not possibly be useful, diminish their proactivity. Although most organizations do not consciously choose to ignore returnees, many expatriates return when they complete the expatriate assignment and not necessarily when their company has an appropriate position available. Few companies have sophisticated international career path systems. One returnee, an engineer, explained that his company gave him a desk and a phone and told him to find himself a job within the organization. Another engineer was put in charge of designing reentry procedures for other expatriates, since "Clearly we don't know what to do with you or with the others who are coming back." External validation—recognizing and valuing the foreign and reentry experiences—is one of the most powerful management techniques for increasing returnees' satisfaction and effectiveness.

Returnees can facilitate their own reentry by using the same skills that they used successfully in adjusting to the foreign country. As summarized on page 240, returnees can attempt to describe the home organization, rather than comparing it with the foreign organization and evaluating it as good or bad. They can anticipate a higher level of ambiguity and attempt to tolerate it. They can attempt to remain open-minded, to see the value of new ideas and actions. Returnees can ask a lot of questions: by assuming that they "don't know," they can use their home country colleagues as "cultural informants" about the home organization. And perhaps most importantly, they can recognize the highly stressful nature of the reentry transition and manage it accordingly. Unfortunately, the very natural assumption of familiarity often blinds returnees to the reality of the reentry transition and strips them of the very skills that they so successfully developed overseas. Clearly, employees returning to global organizations that operate from an integrated, worldwide perspective find the reentry transition much easier than those who work for more domestically oriented companies.

UNDERUTILIZED INTERNATIONAL EMPLOYEE

The multinational business environment is highly competitive. Success is dependent on corporate excellence. To compete, companies must select the best people and use them appropriately. Unfortunately, organizations frequently fail to profit from their employees' foreign experience. To benefit fully from their investment, the organization and the returnees need to better understand the reentry transition. Both must identify job skills acquired or enhanced abroad and systematically find ways to productively integrate and use them. The home organization needs to understand the importance of staying in contact with expatriate staff members, planning for their return, and recognizing the value of their foreign experience. The attitudes of managers who stay at home must change, along with evaluation and reward schemes. Increasing effectiveness at each stage in the expatriate international career cycle is neither easy nor superficially accomplished, but rather takes a major commitment on the part of the organization to its employees. The following management recommendations are made:

1. *Selection.* Employees who are successful and satisfied prior to going abroad are usually successful and satisfied at reentry. Sending failures abroad will not bring home successes. The era of sending marginal employees abroad is over. Therefore, organizations should select effective rather than marginal employees for expatriate assignments. They should select employees whose careers will benefit from the foreign assignment and who in turn will enhance the organization.

2. *Predeparture Training.* Employees who adjust well abroad usually perform more effectively at reentry. Organizations should therefore provide predeparture training for employees and their families.

3. *Career Planning.* Many of the job-related problems during reentry are due to the narrow focus on the foreign assignment—rather than on the entire expatriate cycle—and the consequent lack of both career planning and emphasis on organizational learning. Prior to transferring employees abroad, management should discuss what will and what might happen to the expatriates once they return home. Can they expect a promotion, an equivalent assignment, or a lateral foreign transfer? Who will be responsible for finding them a reentry position—the returnee, a home country manager, or the international personnel manager? Many companies now make international career planning a part of the home country manager's job responsibility. Plans for international assignments should include the employee's career perspective as well as an organization development perspective, and not solely the demands of the foreign project. Companies should not send employees abroad until an explicit reentry process has been agreed to by both.

4. *Communication While Abroad.* Expatriate employees who recognize positive and negative changes in the organization work most effectively when returning home. Management should regularly inform expatriate employees regarding current organizational policies, projects, plans, and staffing changes. Head office managers should frequently visit expatriate managers and, if at all possible, bring them back home periodically.

5. *Reentry Job Responsibility.* The higher the job responsibility at reentry —within the returnee's capability—the more effective the returnee. Whenever possible, reentry jobs should be designed to use the returnee's country-specific knowledge as well as the broadest range of their skills (even if only to brief head office personnel who have continuing responsibilities in that area of the world). Managers who had extensive responsibility abroad should not be given low responsibility staff positions or temporary assignments.

6. *Using Skills Learned Abroad.* Because returnees often do not recognize or give value to the skills they have learned abroad, management and experienced expatriates should assist recent returnees in identifying their newly acquired and enhanced skills and in finding ways of using them within the home organization.

7. *Training for Home Country Managers.* Since managers who have not worked in foreign countries frequently discount the value of returnees' foreign experience, home country managers should be trained to recognize and develop ways of using cross-cultural skills. Because returnees

whose experience is recognized and valued by the organization become more effective and satisfied, and because a xenophobic response from home country managers is common, organizations should help their home country managers understand and explicitly value returnee's foreign experience.

8. Avoiding the "Similar Country" Trap. Because reentry from all parts of the world can be difficult, companies should be aware of the effects of reentry from similar countries (those using the same language and at the same level of economic development) as well as from dissimilar countries.

Debriefing and reentry training sessions can facilitate the transition back into the home organization as well as significantly increase home organization learning (12). In a debriefing session, management asks returnees to describe what they learned overseas. Together the returnees and home organization personnel attempt to integrate the new information and create synergistic approaches to the ongoing management of worldwide operations. In a reentry session, the focus is not on what was learned abroad, but rather on facilitating the transition back into the home organization. As a part of a reentry training session, experts describe the reentry transition process on both a social and a professional level and how the proactive approach can be used to manage their own transition. Then the home managers and returning expatriates attempt to develop synergistic ways of contributing to the organization. By including the managers in the debriefing and reentry sessions, the organization increases the international sophistication of all its personnel and significantly decreases organizational parochialism and xenophobia. Both the home-based and expatriate personnel learn to transcend their own experience and integrate their perceptions and understandings of the organization on a global level. As a result, both the returnees and the organization benefit.

In the past one may have wondered whether "effectiveness" meant simply fitting back in or contributing the maximum possible to the home organization. Is it most effective to use all available skills, including those acquired abroad, or strictly those most recognized within the home country organization? Although placing returnees back in their old jobs may have appeared to be a simple answer, companies usually found it an ineffective strategy for both the individual and the organization.

As personnel from the domestic organization become more multicultural and their clientele becomes more international, the need for cross-culturally skilled individuals increases. Meanwhile, both management and expatriates need to cultivate an understanding of the entry and reentry transitions and develop organizational strategies that benefit both parties. Companies can no longer afford to send any but their best people abroad. Neither the companies nor the individuals can afford to let the best fail.

SUMMARY

Transitions are a part of the international manager's career path. The expatriate manager is selected in the home organization, sent to the foreign country, and sent home again after the foreign assignment is completed. Transitions, whether entry or reentry, involve managing the stress involved in moving into an unfamiliar environment. In moving abroad, that stress is caused by culture shock. In moving home, it is caused by unmet expectations and a lack of validation. Returning expatriate employees need to think about what they have learned abroad and how that learning can be of benefit to the organization. They need to integrate their foreign perspective with their home country perspective in a proactive way to create a successful international career. Organizations need to focus on what they can learn from expatriate and returned-employees.

QUESTIONS FOR REFLECTION

1. Of the skills learned on a foreign assignment, which are the most valuable to returning managers? How can the organization best use the returnee's skills?

2. How might home companies best help expatriate managers to cope with the reentry transition? What should the home country managers themselves do to make the transition as easy as possible?

3. Given today's increased global competition, what are some of the main reasons that companies should be sending managers abroad?

4. If you were offered an expatriate assignment today to work for three years in an area of the world that is completely new to you, why would you want to go? Why would you reject going?

5. What is cultural shock? If you have experienced cultural shock, describe what it felt like? What would you recommend to minimize the impact of cultural shock on expatriate managers?

NOTES

1. The research and quotations on reentry, unless otherwise cited, are based on Nancy J. Adler, "Reentry: A Study of the Dynamic Coping Processes Used by Repatriated Employees to Enhance Effectiveness in the Organization and Personal Learning during the Transition Back into the Home Country," dissertation at the Graduate School of Management, University of California at Los Angeles (UCLA), Spring 1980. The research is summarized in Nancy J. Adler, "Reentry: Managing Cross-Cultural Transitions," *Group and Organization Studies*, vol. 6, no. 3 (1981), pp. 341–356.

2. Note that the average for the first month is a high mood, not a *very* high mood. The reason for this is that the initial high often lasts only a few days and frequently only a few hours.

3. Nancy J. Adler, "Reentry: Managing Cross-Cultural Transition," *Group and Organization Studies*, vol. 6, no. 3 (1981), pp. 341–356.

REFERENCES

1. Adler, N. J. "Reentry: Managing Cross-Culture Transitions," *Group and Organization Studies*, vol. 6, no. 3 (1981), pp. 341–356. Copyright 1981. Reprinted by permission of Sage Publications, Inc.

2. Borg, M. *International Transfers of Managers in Multinational Corporations* (Uppsala, Sweden: Acta Universitatis Upsaliensis, Studia Oeconomiae Negotiorum, no. 27, 1988).

3. Brislin, R. W., and Van Buren, H. "Can They Go Home Again?" *International Educational and Cultural Exchange*, vol. I, no. 4 (Spring 1974), pp. 19–24.

4. Business International Corporation. "Successful Repatriation Demands Attention, Care, and a Dash of Ingenuity," *Business International*, vol. XXV, no. 9 (March 3, 1978), pp. 57–65.

5. Coyle, W. *On the Move. Minimising the Stress and Maximising the Benefits of Relocation* (Sydney, Australia: Hampden Press, 1988).

6. Dowling, P. J. "Human Resource Issues in International Business," *Syracuse Journal of International Law and Commerce*, vol. 13, no. 2 (1986), pp. 255–271.

7. Gullahorn, J. T., and Gullahorn, J. E. "An Extension of the U-Curve Hypothesis," *Journal of Social Sciences*, vol. 19, no. 3 (1963), pp. 33–47.

8. Harvey, M. G. "The Multinational Corporation's Expatriate Problem: An Application of Murphy's Law," *Business Horizons*, vol. 26, no. 1 (January–February 1983), pp. 71–78.

9. Hazzard, M. S. *Study of the Repatriation of the American International Executive* (New York: Korn/Ferry International, 1981).

10. Howard, C. "The Returning Overseas Executive: Culture Shock in Reverse," *Human Resources Management*, vol. 13, no. 2, (1974), pp. 22–26.

11. "How to Ease Reentry after Overseas Duty," *Business Week* (June 11, 1979), pp. 82–84.

12. Mendenhall, M. E., and Oddou, G. R. "Acculturation Profiles of Expatriate Managers: Implications for Cross-Cultural Training Programs," *Columbia Journal of World Business* (Winter 1986), pp. 73–79.

13. Mendenhall, M. E.; Dunbar, E.; and Oddou, G. R. "Expatriate Selection, Training and Career-Pathing: A Review and Critique," *Human Resource Management*, vol. 26, no. 3 (1987), pp. 331–345.

14. Murray, J. A. "International Personnel Repatriation: Cultural Shock in Reverse," *MSU Business Topic*, vol. 21, no. 2 (Summer 1973), pp. 59–66.

15. Noer, D. M. "Integrating Foreign Service Employees to Home Organization: The Godfather Approach," *Personnel Journal* (January 1974), pp. 45–51.

16. Ratiu, I. "Thinking Internationally: A Comparison of How International Executives Learn," *International Studies of Management and Organization*, vol. XIII, no. 1–2 (Spring-Summer 1983), pp. 139–150.

17. Smith, L. "The Hazards of Coming Home," *Dun's Review* (October 1975), pp. 71–73.

18. Theoret, R.; Adler, N. J.; Kealey, D.; and Hawes, F. *Reentry: A Guide to Returning Home* (Hull, Quebec: Canadian International Development Agency, 1979).

19. Torbiorn, I. *Living Abroad: Personal Adjustment and Personnel Policy in Overseas Setting* (New York: John Wiley and Sons, 1982).

20. Tung, R. L. "Career Issues in International Assignments," *The Academy of Management Executive*, vol. 2, no. 3 (1988), pp. 241–244.

21. Tung, R. L. "Expatriate Assignments: Enhancing Success and Minimizing Failure," *The Academy of Management Executive*, vol. 1, no. 2 (1987), pp. 117–126.

22. Tung, R. L. "Selection and Training Procedures of U.S., European, and Japanese Multinationals," *California Management Review*, vol. 25, no. 1 (1982), pp. 57–71.

23. Tung, R. L. *The New Expatriates: Managing Human Resources Abroad* (Cambridge, Mass.: Ballinger, 1988).

24. "Workers Sent Overseas Have Adjustment Problems, a New Study Shows," *Wall Street Journal* (June 19, 1984), p. 1, col. 5.

SELECTED READINGS ON SELECTION AND TRAINING

Acuff, F. L. "Awareness Levels of Employees Considering Overseas Relocation," *Personnel Journal* (November 1974), pp. 809–812.

Aitken, T. *The Multinational Man—The Role of the Manager Abroad* (London: George Allen & Unwin, 1973).

Almaney, A. "Intercultural Communication and the MNC Executive," *Columbia Journal of World Business*, (Winter 1974), p. 23.

Baker, J. C., and Ivancevich, J. M. "The Assignment of American Executives Abroad: Systematic, Haphazard, or Chaotic?" *California Management Review*, vol. XIII, no. 3 (1971), pp. 39–44.

Bass, B. M. "The American Advisor Abroad," *Journal of Applied Behavioral Science*, vol. 7, no. 3 (May–June 1971), pp. 285–307.

Bass, B. M. "Utility of Managerial Self-Planning on a Simulated Production Task with Replications in Twelve Countries," *Journal of Applied Psychology*, vol. 62, no. 4 (1977), pp. 506–509.

Borrman, W. A. "The Problem of Expatriate Personnel and Their Selection in International Enterprises," *Management International Review*, vol. 8, no. 4–5 (1968), p. 37.

Business International Research Report, "Selecting and Training International Managers" (New York: Business International Corporation, 1974).

Cleveland, H.; Mangone, G. J.; and Adams, J. *The Overseas Americans* (New York: McGraw-Hill, 1960).

Desatnick, R. L., and Bennett, M. L. *Human Resource Management in the Multinational Company* (New York: Nichols, 1977).

Edstrom, A., and Galbraith, J. R. "Transfer of Managers as a Coordination and Control Strategy in Multinational Organizations," *Administrative Science Quarterly*, vol. 22 (June 1977), pp. 248–263.

Eldin, H. K. "Suggested Criteria for Selecting Foreign Management Consultants in Developing Countries," *Management International Review* (1971), pp. 123–132.

Fiedler, F. E.; Mitchell, T.; and Triandis, H. C. "The Culture Assimilator: An Approach to Cross-Cultural Training," *Journal of Applied Psychology*, vol. 55, no. 2 (1971), pp. 95–102.

Franko, Lawrence G. "Who Manages Multinational Enterprises?" *Columbia Journal of World Business*, vol. 8, no. 2 (Summer 1973).

Harrari, E., and Zeira, Y. "Training Expatriates for Managerial Assignment in Japan," *California Management Review*, vol. 20, no. 4 (Summer 1978), pp. 56–62.

Harris, P. R., and Moran, R. T. *Managing Cultural Differences* (Houston: Gulf, 1979).

Hays, R. D. "Ascribed Behavioral Determinants of Success–Failure among U.S. Expatriate Managers," *Journal of International Business Studies*, vol. 2, no. 1 (Spring 1971), pp. 40–46.

Hays, R. D. "Expatriate Selection: Insuring Success and Avoiding Failure," *Journal of International Business Studies* (Spring 1974).

Heenan, D. A. "The Corporate Expatriate: Assignment to Ambiguity," *Columbia Journal of World Business* (May–June 1970), pp. 49–54.

Howard, C. G. "Model for the Design of a Selection Program for Multinational Executives," *Public Personnel Management* (March–April 1974), pp. 138–145.

Howard, C. G. "The Multinational Corporation: Impact on Motivation," *Personnel* (January–February 1972).

Howard, C. G. "Why Expatriates Fail Abroad," *Human Resource Management*, vol. II, no. 1 (Spring 1972), pp. 32–36.

Illman, P. E. *Developing Overseas Managers and Managers Overseas* (New York: AMACOM, 1979).

Ivancevich, J. M. "Selection of American Managers for Overseas Assignments," *Personnel Journal* (1969), pp. 190–193.

Ivancevich, J. M., and Baker, J. C. "A Comparative Study of the Satisfaction of Domestic United States Managers and Overseas United States Managers," *Academy of Management Journal* (March 1970), pp. 69–77.

Lanier, A. R. "Selecting and Preparing Personnel for Overseas Transfers," *Personnel Journal* (March 1979).

Maddox, R. C. "Solving the Overseas Personnel Problem," *Personnel Journal* (June 1975).

Maddox, R. C. "Problems and Trends in Assigning Managers Overseas," *Personnel* (January–February 1971), pp. 53–56.

Miller, E. L. "A Study of Expatriate American Managers' Perceptions of Managerial Traits and Capabilities of Their Subordinates and Superiors," *Academy of Management Proceedings* (1975), pp. 294–297.

Miller, E. L. "Managerial Qualifications of Personnel Occupying Overseas Management Positions as Perceived by American Expatriate Managers," *Journal of International Business Studies* (Spring–Summer 1977), pp. 57–68.

Miller, E. L. "The International Selection Decision: A Study of Some Dimensions of Managerial Behavior in the Selection Process," *Academy of Management Journal*, vol. 16, no. 2 (June 1973), pp. 239–252.

Miller, E. L. "The Job Satisfaction of Expatriate Americans," *Journal of International Business Studies*, vol. 6, no. 2 (Fall 1975), p. 65.

Miller, E. L. "The Overseas Assignment: How Managers Determine Who Is Selected," *Michigan Business Review* (May 1972), pp. 12–19.

Miller, E. L. "The Selection Decision for an International Assignment: A Study of the Decision Maker's Behavior," *Journal of International Business Studies* (Fall 1972), pp. 49–65.

Miller, E. L., and Cheng, J. L. C. "A Closer Look at the Decision to Accept an Overseas Position," *Management International Review*, vol. 18 (1978).

Miller, E.; Bhatt, B.; Hill, R.; and Catteaneo, J. "Attitudes of American and German Expatriate Managers in Europe and Latin America," *Academy of Management Proceedings*, vol. 40 (1980), pp. 53–57.

"Mitsui's Big Machine for Choosing and Grooming Its International Managers," *Business International* (July 18, 1975), pp. 228–229.

Nath, R. "Orientation to Another Society: Training for Intercultural Effectiveness," *Kultura*, vol. 17 (1972), pp. 155–170.

Perlmutter, H. V., and Heenan, D. A. "How Multinational Should Your Top Managers Be?" *Harvard Business Review*, vol. 52, no. 6 (1974), pp. 121–132.

Schnapper, M. "Multinational Training for Multinational Corporations," in M. K. Asante; E. Newmark; and C. A. Blake, eds., *Handbook of Intercultural Communication* (Beverly Hills, Calif.: Sage Publications, 1979).

Shabaz, W. O. "Cross-Cultural Orientation for Overseas Employees," *The Personnel Administrator* (May 1978).

Stoner, J. A.; Aram, J. D.; and Rubin, I. M. "Factors Associated with Effective Performance in Overseas Work Assignments," *Personnel Psychology*, vol. 25 (1972), pp. 303–319.

Teague, B. W. "International Management Selection and Development," *California Management Review*, vol. XII, no. 3 (Spring 1970), pp. 1–6.

Teague, B. W. *Selecting and Orienting Staff for Service Overseas* (New York: The Conference Board, Inc., 1976).

Thiagarajan, K. M. "Cross-Cultural Training for Overseas Management," *Management International Review*, vols. 4–5 (1971), pp. 69–85.

Triandis, H. C., and Vassiliou, V. "Interpersonal Influence and Employee Selection in Two Cultures," *Journal of Applied Psychology*, vol. 56, no. 2 (1972), pp. 140–145.

Tsurumi, Y. "Myths that Mislead U.S. Managers in Japan," *Harvard Business Review* (July–August 1971), pp. 118–128.

Tucker, M. F. *Screening and Selection for Overseas Assignments: Assessment and Recommendations to the U.S. Navy* (Denver, Colo.: Center for Research and Education, 1974).

Tucker, M. F., and Schiller, J. E. *Overview Summary for an Assessment of the Screening Problem for Overseas Assignment* (Denver, Colo.: Center for Research and Education, 1975).

Tung, R. L. "U. S. Multinationals: A Study of Their Selection and Training Procedures for Overseas Assignments," *Academy of Management Proceedings* (1979).

Voris, W. "Considerations in Staffing for Overseas Management Needs," *Personnel Journal* (June 1975).

Yun, C. K. "Role Conflicts of Expatriate Managers: A Construct," *Management International Review*, vol. 13, no. 6 (1973).

Zeira, Y. "Management Development in Ethnocentric Multinational Corporations," *California Management Review*, vol. 18, no. 4 (Summer 1976), pp. 34–42.

Zeira, Y. "Rotations of Expatriates in MNC's," *Management International Review*, vol. 16, no. 3 (August 1976), pp. 37–46.

Zeira, Y., and Harrari, E. "Genuine Multinational Staffing Policy: Expectations and Realities," *Academy of Management Journal*, vol. 20, no. 2 (1977).

Zeira, Y., and Harrari, E. "Training of Expatriates for Managerial Assignments in Japan," *California Management Review*, vol. 20, no. 4 (Summer 1978).

Zuga, F. L. *The Personnel Assessment Center: An Aid in the Selection of Personnel for Cross-Cultural Assignments* (Monterey, Calif.: Naval Post-Graduate School, 1975).

SELECTED READINGS
ON CORPORATE REENTRY

Adler, N. J. "Reentry: Managing Cross-Cultural Transitions," *Group and Organizational Studies*, vol. 6, no. 3 (1981), pp. 341–356.

Austin, C. N. *Cross-Cultural Reentry: An Annotated Bibliography* (Abilene, Tex.: Abilene Christian University Press, 1983).

Cagney, W. F. "Executive Reentry: The Problems of Repatriation," *Personnel Journal*, vol. 54, no. 9 (1975), pp. 487–488.

Clague, L., and Krupp, N. B. "International Personnel: The Repatriation Problem," *The Bridge* (Spring 1980), pp. 11–13, 37. Reprinted from *The Personnel Administrator* (April 1978).

Gray, A. "Repatriation at the Burr Hamilton Bank," *Business Horizons* (March–April 1982), pp. 13–14.

Harvey, M. G. "The Other Side of Foreign Assignments: Dealing with the Repatriation Dilemma," *Columbia Journal of World Business*, vol. 17, no. 1, (1982), pp. 53–59.

Howard, C. G. "How Best to Integrate Expatriate Managers in the Domestic Organization: Providing Career Planning for the Returning Employee," *The Personnel Administrator* (July 1982), pp. 27–33.

Howard, C. G. "Integrating Returning Expatriates into the Domestic Organization," *The Personnel Administrator* (January 1979), pp. 62–65.

Howard, C. G. "The Expatriate Manager and the Role of the MNC," *Personnel Journal*, vol. 59, no. 10, pp. 838–844.

Howard, C. G. "The Returning Overseas Executive: Culture Shock in Reverse," *Human Resources Management*, vol. 13, no. 2 (1974), pp. 22–26.

"How to Ease Reentry after Overseas Duty," *Business Week* (June 11, 1979), pp. 82–84.

Kendall, D. W. "Repatriation: An Ending and a Beginning," *Business Horizons* (November–December 1981), pp. 21–25.

Murray, J. A. "International Personnel Repatriation: Cultural Shock in Reverse," *MSU Business Topic* (Summer 1973), pp. 59–66.

Murray, J. A., and Smetanka, J. A. "Cultural Shock: The Japanese Executives in Canada," *The Bridge* (Summer 1978), pp. 27–29.

Noer, D. M. "Integrating Foreign Service Employees to Home Organization: The Godfather Approach," *Personnel Journal* (January 1974), pp. 45–51.

Noer, D. M. *Multinational People Management: A Guide for Organizations and Employees* (Washington, D.C.: The Bureau of National Affairs, 1975). (See Chapter 3.)

Smith, L. "The Hazards of Coming Home," *Dun's Review* (October 1975), pp. 71–73.

"Successful Repatriation Demands Attention, Care, and a Dash of Ingenuity," *Business International* (March 3, 1978), pp. 65–67.

Tucker, M. F., and Wight, A. A. "Culture Gap in International Personnel Programs," *The Bridge* (Winter 1981), pp. 11–13.

Werkman, S. L. "Coming Home: Adjustment of Americans to the United States after Living Abroad," in G. V. Coelho and P. I. Ahmed, eds., *Uprooting and Development: Dilemmas of Coping with Modernization* (New York: Plenum Press, 1980).

CHAPTER 9

▼

A Portable Life:
The Expatriate Spouse

▲

We shall not cease from explorations
And the end of all our exploring
Will be to arrive where we started
And know the place for the first time.

T. S. Eliot (13)

In an international move, the spouse has the most difficult role of any family member. While employees have the basic company and job structure that continues from the home to the foreign country, and children have the continuity and routine of school, spouses often must give up their friends and activities. More and more frequently today, spouses must also leave a job or career in order to follow their partners to the foreign country. Spouses lose both the structure and the continuity in their lives (8;20;22). The spouse's dissatisfaction, which often leads to early return, is the single most important reason for failure on a foreign assignment—nearly half of 300 surveyed companies have brought families home early due to the unwillingness or inability of the spouse to adapt. The average cost to the company of repatriating an executive and the family exceeds $100,000 (6).

The experience of an international employee differs quite markedly from that of his or her spouse. The spouse becomes more immersed in the culture than the employee, and the challenges for successful adjustment are both different and greater. This chapter focuses on the most common spouses: the wives of international managers. The reason is not that all spouses are wives, but that, to date, very few married women have been sent abroad and even fewer have been accompanied by a husband (2;4;15). This chapter looks at the expatriate experience through the eyes of wives who have been moved from country to country in order to follow their husbands' careers. What challenges does she face in moving abroad? How does she adapt to the foreign culture? How does she create a meaningful, "portable" life for herself — one that works in whatever situation she encounters? This chapter will discuss her expatriate cycle: her initial reaction to the foreign move, her arrival in the foreign country, her ways of creating a new lifestyle, and her return to the home country. This cycle takes place concurrently with the employee's international career cycle but may or may not be recognized by the couple or the organization.

One hundred and ninety-seven wives of managers sent abroad by American and Canadian multinational corporations and by a government agency (the Canadian International Development Agency) described their international experiences in interviews and on questionnaires (5). The women had been sent to Asia, Africa, Europe, and Latin America. Some had lived in urban centers and others in rural areas; some in economically developed countries and others in extremely poor regions; some in linguistically similar areas (e.g., English or French speaking) and some in areas in which the language was totally foreign. Their ages and family situations also varied. Although the diversity of their backgrounds and foreign situations is noteworthy, the challenges they faced in attempting to survive the transition and create meaningful portable lives abroad are amazingly similar.

MOVING ABROAD: PREMADE DECISIONS

Companies' involvement in foreign operations takes many forms, including exporting, licensing, joint ventures, subsidiary operations, and strategic alliances. Companies therefore transfer employees for a wide variety of reasons, including staffing, management development, and organization development (5;9;10;11;12;18;19;24). Companies make staffing transfers when they lack sufficient local personnel to fill a given position, often in economically underdeveloped areas of the world, which lack technological and managerial expertise. They design management development transfers to give managers foreign experience as well as to staff foreign positions. Organization development transfers remain the least common of the three transfer types. Companies design organization development transfers to allow managers from different countries to (a) learn thoroughly the organization's operation, procedures, and culture worldwide, (b) get to know each other personally and thus develop an effective communication network, (c) develop the high level of flexibility and adaptability necessary to succeed in the wide range of environments encompassed by the organization, and (d) increase the overall integration and coordination within the firm.

By contrast, a wife is sent abroad because the company transferred her husband (23). Many wives are unaware of the possibility that they might move to a foreign country. At times they initially react with surprise or shock.

Argentina

I just didn't have any idea. I was thoroughly settled in Toronto. We were going to live there the rest of our lives. Our family and friends were all around us and everything was very comfortable. . . . I just didn't have any idea of what was ahead of me. I looked it up on the map and I knew it was an awful long way from Toronto. I remembered a little bit in school about Argentina — that Buenos Aires was the capital. But beyond that, it was just like stepping into oblivion. I had no idea what to expect.

Can a wife turn down an expatriate transfer? Although the company and the employee usually believe that the wife has a role in the decision to move abroad, she rarely does in actuality. By the time the company identifies the employees they want to transfer and announces its decision, it has made a large investment in their acceptance. Subtle pressure discourages open discussion of the pros and cons of the move. An employee often feels he would disappoint the company if he did not accept; his wife feels she would disappoint her husband. An employee often feels he would hinder his career by saying no; his wife is reluctant to disagree. Concerns that they could discuss and resolve prior to departure are never mentioned. At a time when communication is critical, open communication is often absent.

Venezuela

Bill came home in November and asked me what I thought about moving overseas. I was silent. Then he told me about what a big promotion it would be and what it would mean for the rest of his career. I told him that I was delighted. The company told us about the things to take and the name of an international school. And we were made busy with the preparations. We left.

The Carpenter case presents the conflicting pressures and dilemmas faced by an American couple when offered the opportunity of a first expatriate assignment.

The Carpenter Case[1]

Tom and Jane Carpenter are a young couple living comfortably in a New England town in the United States.

They have three children, Mary 11, Jerry 6, and Ann 3.

Tom works in the headquarters of a manufacturing company as an executive in the engineering department. He has an excellent salary and up until now has been satisfied with his job. A quiet, handsome man about thirty-six years old, he is intelligent, sensitive, ambitious, and known as "a good family man." He has the respect of his colleagues and subordinates. The upper echelons of management regard him as a promising candidate for senior management in this company. Tom is considered a practical man, able to take the changes in life with a basic optimism and adaptability that appear to give him a maturity beyond his years. He likes the material wealth and comfort that his years of conscientious work have produced. He enjoys the status of his company which has an excellent name in its field, being considered one of the most progressive and future-minded of U.S. companies of this type.

If Tom is the practical member of the family, Jane is the "dreamer." She is a pretty, energetic woman of thirty, a good wife and mother and an active member of several committees and voluntary groups. She is strongly attached to both her family and her parents who are in their early sixties and live in a nearby town. She is sincerely interested in many good causes and always finds the time and energy to devote to them. While she is not a very practical woman by nature, her enthusiasm for her projects is admired by her many friends.

Tom and Jane married early and struggled together for several years until they were able to achieve the comfortable life they now have. Their marital life has been happy and more or less undisturbed, and through the struggle of their earlier years they were able to develop between themselves a rewarding relationship. Although they have traveled to several parts of the U.S. with and without the children, neither Tom nor Jane had traveled abroad until two years ago. At that time Tom, together with three other executives, was sent to Latin America to explore the possibilities of setting up four new plants in different countries in Latin America.

Both Tom and Jane have been feeling more and more relaxed in the past years, since many of their dreams have been realized. They have a good family, financial security, and many friends. They are especially proud of their new home, recently finished. Jane has worked hard to find the furniture and the internal decorations they wanted and now her dream house seems completed. They have both been so far generally satisfied with their children, who are well adjusted to their present environment. There have been certain problems with Mary, who is a very sensitive and shy girl, and with Jerry who has had some difficulties adapting in school. But these were very minor problems and they have not disturbed seriously the otherwise happy family life.

Despite this very satisfactory picture of family life, there have recently been more and more occasions when Tom and Jane have felt (each one without admitting it to the other) that something is "missing."

More and more, Tom thinks that his life has become a comfortable routine. The new tasks he is given have less "challenge" and "adventure." For a long while he has been satisfied that his career had a steady development through the years. The time of anxiety and uncertainty has passed, but also with it the time of excitement and the inner feeling of searching and moving. He has begun to feel that he needs a change and it was at that time that he was sent for four months to Latin America. Tom felt that this trip was one of the most interesting and rewarding events of his whole life. Being away for the first time from his family for such a long period, he missed them and he was disappointed because the wives were not allowed to accompany their husbands on that trip. But the prospects of building up their company in Latin America have been attractive and he found that he liked to travel, to meet new people, to become acquainted with different ways of living, to be more a part of the "world" and of events outside of their hometown. The three other executives who took the trip with him had about the same feelings as he had. Each seemed to be a little "weary" of being "a little fish" at headquarters. The possibility of being a pioneer in the Latin America division to be created was an exciting prospect. Tom somehow felt reluctant to communicate to Jane all his satisfaction and his thoughts about that trip, as well as the fact that he was hoping to be chosen from among the executives to be responsible for setting up the plants in Latin America.

In a different way, but with the same feeling of restlessness and discontent, there are times now that Jane feels that the pleasant, well-organized life she has is lacking the excitement of unpredictability. She divides her time between many activities, but finds herself at times dreaming about the world outside of her hometown. She wonders at times, like Tom, whether their life has not become too settled, an almost unaltered routine, but unlike Tom, she checks herself by asking the simple question that, after all, isn't this what life really is?

When Tom came home with the news that Mr. Abbott, the president of the company, had offered him the key position in the Latin America operation, she was pleased to hear of the high esteem his superiors had for Tom. Actually, Jane too had been wondering for some time what could be the result of Tom's trip to Latin America. Although she would have liked to have been able to go with him at that time, the idea that they would have had to leave the children for such a long time forced her to exclude absolutely the possibility of her going, even if the wives of the executives had been allowed to go with them. After that, she used to wonder at times whether the company would choose him, if the decision was made. At that time the idea of having to move to a new environment was not an unpleasant one.

Now that the offer was a firm one, with a high salary, cost of living expenses, opportunity for travel throughout Latin America, she began to have some fears. As Tom talked excitedly about the challenging tasks he would have, her fears seemed to increase. She began to feel more and more that they had little to gain from this experience as regards their family and their life. It was a big step forward in Tom's career, to be sure, but Jane felt that Tom would be successful wherever he was. On the present job, Tom and she shared so much time together, while in the new job, as she understood it, Tom would have to travel a great deal. She was very unhappy and ashamed about her fears as opposed to Tom's enthusiasm and obvious willingness to venture ahead.

One evening she tried to sit down by herself and figure out why this new job was not so attractive to her. There was some urgency for Tom to make up his mind within a week, and she felt the need to understand what this decision to move abroad meant for her and for her family.

She tried to be honest with herself. She naturally had fears about moving to a new environment which was strange and where people spoke another language. She knew that the climate was very different and she believed that the living conditions were likely to offer fewer comforts. She would be far from her friends and her parents. Their furniture would have to be stored, and their new house rented or sold, since it was not clear how many years Tom would need to get the four new plants going.

She felt she would be isolated because she did not think that they could have a close contact with the local people for a long time. Whatever she had heard so far about the personality of the Latin Americans made her fear that close friendships would be difficult to achieve, at least for some time, because she had the impression that they were rather temperamental and unstable. Although she admitted to herself that this impression was based on hearsay and fiction, she somehow could not avoid believing it. She had also heard that there was a great deal of anti-American feeling in the country where they would first live. Furthermore, she wondered whether the sanitary conditions would be dangerous to the health of the children. The company had little experience in Latin America, so it would be likely that they would have to find their own way and learn, probably by hard experience, how to get along in these countries. She realized that what disturbed her more than anything else was probably that Tom was going to travel a lot. Then she would probably have to face a great deal of the problems of their adaptation there alone, while up until this time they had always shared whatever problems they had to face and they supported each other in finding solutions. This also meant that Tom would see more places, meet more people, in general he would enjoy more, and probably get more satisfaction out of the whole experience than she and the children would. She was distressed to realize that she was already resentful toward him for that and angry because she could sense that, although he was discussing the problem with her, he had already made up his mind.

Jane kept these fears more or less to herself, but she did communicate to Tom her reluctance to go and gave as one of her main reasons her worry about the effect this move was going to have on the education of their children as well as on their health.

Tom sensed most of Jane's fears and he reacted to her expressed doubts by saying that he thought that the children could adapt after a while and that the experience would be a very good one for them. They could learn a new language and they could make new friends after a while. As for themselves, he had the best of memories from his own trip and he believed that they were both going to find this new experience an enriching and rewarding one. He did not underestimate the difficulties involved, but he expressed the belief that they were capable of overcoming them, while enjoying all the advantages that living abroad would offer them. Inwardly Tom was disappointed with Jane's negative reactions and the difficulties she seemed to be having. He had always believed her to be a woman of courage endowed with curiosity and interest for the world outside. In times of crisis previously in their life, she had always proved to be strong and supportive and she had always shown a spirit of adventure and willingness to go ahead. It was a painful surprise for him to realize that this spirit would operate only in the security of the familiar environment, while a more profound change seemed to appear to Jane as a great threat to herself and her family. He had hoped that she would back him in this decision which was so important to his career. Nevertheless, he maintained his confidence in her and he believed that she would change her mind in time. He called a Berlitz school nearby and made plans for both of them to take Spanish lessons.

When Jane's parents came to visit during this period of time, Jane told them of the company's offer to Tom. Her father, who had been ailing for some time, was visibly depressed by the news. Her mother said that this was going to be a great experience for them, "a chance of a lifetime," as she put it. Jane knew that her mother had always regretted not being able to travel abroad. Now she was thrilled that the children were given the opportunity and she promised to come and visit them in Latin America if Tom accepted the job.

Dinner with Mr. Abbott

A few days later, Tom's boss, Mr. Abbott, invited Tom and Jane for dinner, saying that he always talked over a new job abroad with both husband and wife, because he felt that it was very important to take into consideration how the wife felt. Jane had many fears about this dinner. First, she resented being "looked over" by Mr. Abbott who, until now, had not really spent much time with them socially. Second, she did not want to reveal her doubts to Tom's boss, who had a reputation for making quick judgments about people, often not very favorable.

This dinner turned out to be a very pleasant one. Mrs. Abbott helped to put everyone at ease throughout the dinner, talking about her pleasant experience abroad when Mr. Abbott was managing director of a subsidiary branch in Europe. Mrs. Abbott had enjoyed Paris and Rome, but she admitted that she knew little about life in cities like Buenos Aires and Rio.

Mr. Abbott finally turned to Jane and said: "Well, we are very glad you are taking the news of this new assignment for Tom so well. I know you realize what an opportunity this job will be for him. It is a real challenge for him, far greater than what he can get here, you know." Tom hurriedly answered for Jane, who was about to reply to Mr. Abbott: "Jane is really a born traveler. I know that she is looking forward to this. She has already found out how she can take lessons in Spanish." Mr. Abbott seemed pleased. He said: "That is really fine. You know, Tom, that ours is becoming an international company. There will be few opportunities for executives at headquarters whose overseas experience is limited. Our policy is to create a management team which could base its decisions on actual experience abroad. Of course, having the kind of wife who is willing to take the risk of going off to the jungle is quite an asset. You are a lucky man, Tom."

While Jane joined in the laughter, she was inwardly very angry. That night, she and Tom had a quarrel which continued for the next few days. Jane resented the fact that the whole discussion was conducted as though Tom had already accepted the job, as well as the fact that she was not given a chance to talk about Tom's work with Mr. Abbott. Tom insisted that Mr. Abbott was not the kind of man to whom one could reveal any doubts about a decision of the company. Discussing the problem the next day with the children confused Tom and Jane more, because the children's reaction was not clear. Mary was unwilling to go, Jerry and Ann seemed excited, but it was more because of the thrill they felt than because they really understood the issue. By now Jane was finding it difficult to sleep, and Tom said that a formal decision was required by next Monday.

They had a long weekend to think over the decision and give a final answer to Mr. Abbott on Monday.

CROSS-CULTURAL TRANSITIONS

Expatriates must not only go through a grueling physical move abroad, they must adjust to the foreign culture and create a meaningful life as well. Much attention is generally given to the logistics of the transfer itself: what should be packed, which shipper used, where to stay upon arrival, and so on. Less attention is given to the skills necessary for adjusting to the foreign country: good language training, a knowledge of the culture and its people, and an awareness of culturally based differences in values, attitudes, and behaviors. Least attention is paid to assisting the spouse in creating a meaningful portable life abroad. While not recognized as a potent issue by either the employee or the children, the structureless role of the spouse demands explicit attention: if she is to have a fulfilling life abroad, she must design it. First the transition itself and the initial adjustment issues confronting the spouse will be discussed, then the broader and more fundamental issue of creating a meaningful life abroad will be investigated.

It's Harder for the Spouse

As mentioned earlier, when a wife moves abroad, she comes into more direct contact with the "foreignness" of the new culture than her husband. The husband generally works in the most internationally sophisticated strata of society: he meets people who speak English and have met foreigners before. The wife meets much less sophisticated people. Whether in caring for the family's daily living needs or in arranging for servants to perform household tasks, she meets people who do not always speak English and have rarely met foreigners. Whereas an employee often has a secretary and colleagues to translate the language and explain the foreign customs, the wife must depend on her own skills and ingenuity. Whereas an employee works in an office filled with other expatriates to answer his questions and share his frustrations, the wife often finds herself isolated in her home world. She must confront the differences on her own.

Many wives feel unprepared for their move. They know little about the country, the culture, or the specific lcoation. Their expectations and the foreign reality have little in common. Upon arrival, they often react with surprise and excitement mixed with bewilderment and fear. Below, three expatriate wives describe their arrival in Africa:

> Well, my expectations were very, how would I say, very large. For me, Africa was . . . totally unknown . . . except that I could equate it with wild animals, missionaries, nice black people, and a very different way of life than in Canada. . . . I didn't question anything. I was very young, just married, and very happy to discover a new country. I could imagine that they had modern cities, that Conakry would be a modern city with all the amenities, asked no questions and just left.

Finally I arrived at . . . this hazy airport. . . . I got off the plane, and there were . . . all of these black faces which I wasn't really used to in such mass. So I said, "It's so good to be here and I am so looking forward to getting into the house." . . . [My husband] didn't know how to say it, but he said, "But we don't have a house." So I burst into tears. I guess it was just the whole stress of thinking that finally I was going to be in a house, and the jet lag, and just being in a completely different culture and a completely different color.

Well, it was very different from what I had imagined. My first shock was in Dakar, where we had to change planes . . . I was very surprised to see all the white people left aside while the black people boarded the plane. The white people were like second class citizens. I could understand that later on, when I realized that Guinea had only been independent for a year.

Culture Shock: The Initial Period Abroad

Culture shock, as described in chapter 8, is the reaction of expatriates to entering a new, unpredictable and therefore uncertain environment. During the first few months in a foreign culture, expatriates often find that other people's behavior does not make sense, and even more disconcerting, that their own behavior does not produce expected results. The wives, being in more direct contact with the foreign culture than the employees, describe some of their initial reactions as surprise, bewilderment, and disorientation:

Guinea

Well, then we went into our building, a very modern building. We were on the ninth floor, and the building had no elevators. So we had to walk the nine floors. And then we arrived in this beautiful, huge apartment, with three bathrooms and no water.

Argentina

Everything I was comfortable with in a North American suburban setting, like my shopping, and the schools, and my daily routine, just was drastically different in Argentina. Perhaps the thing that struck me the most was when I set out to do my grocery shopping (which is something that we take for granted with our big supermarkets here), I found myself in the biggest supermarket in Argentina, which was just a filthy little dump really, and as I looked around to fill my grocery cart, the only thing I recognized was a box of Quaker Oats. Everything was packaged differently, everything had Spanish names on it, and I couldn't tell salt from icing sugar.

Hong Kong

Before I went to Hong Kong, I'd read a lot of books. I expected the Chinese to be dignified and very courteous. The Cantonese in Hong Kong are the opposite of that. They are very noisy and . . . very pushy. In Argentina I expected the romantic Latin. Instead, I was annoyed at the "macho-ness" of the men. The reality . . . was disappointing.

Frustration.   The first few months in a foreign culture are rarely easy. The constant frustration of not understanding and not being able to get simple things done follows the initial surprise.

It's the constant minor frustrations . . . the phone never works, the electric power is variable, and, oh yes, filling the water bottles at 4 A.M., just to be sure that we'd have some water.

I had my new Electrolux vacuum cleaner and I tried to show the help how to use it. . . . The next thing I knew they were vacuuming the patio and the grass. They just had no concept of what this [vacuum] was.

We were not aware of the fact that everything seems to be done through a bribe. We were insulted when it was suggested. I think we just didn't understand the culture. So we waited from January until May before our furniture was sprung from customs.

Things can be very difficult . . . [say] you have to put on a dinner party: dinner parties are very important because there is not very much entertainment, so you have to make your own entertainment. You have ten people coming, and there is no electricity, and you have just put the roast in the oven. Right, what do you do? And it's pouring with rain outside so you can't make a barbecue. So you raid the cupboard and find a tin of ham, and you find some tomatoes, and then you find this and that, and you all have a good giggle. You know, really, there is not other way of doing it. You can't get depressed about these things.

I like it . . . but things don't work and its frustrating. I didn't expect things not to work in Europe. In a developing country, yes, but not in Europe.

While the newness of the environment in large part causes the difficulties, they are exacerbated by insufficient language competence, loneliness, boredom, and a sense of meaninglessness.

Foreign Language Illiteracy.   Whereas most employees have less immediate need for foreign language competence than do their wives, many organizations only offer language training to employees. They expect the wife to enroll in language courses if she so desires and often not at company expense. Consequently, many women never become fluent in the foreign language and therefore have little possibility of becoming fully comfortable living in the culture.

Italy

I think the most difficult thing when you arrive in a country is not being able to communicate. You feel very isolated because you don't speak the language. So everything becomes very difficult; all small details, everyday life is difficult because you don't know how to communicate.

Mexico

The only foreign language I learned is Spanish . . . and I didn't find it easy. I was embarrassed to speak in case I didn't have it right, and this became a big problem. . . . I would pretend I hadn't been there very long, even when I had been there several months. And I'd have the children speaking for me in the taxi because they could speak far better Spanish than I could.

Argentina

I think the thing that bothered me the most was just my inability to express myself in Spanish. It was a while before I was able to take lessons, and I never did become fluent in the language. I could get by in English in most situations, but it was a little disappointing to see my husband learning Spanish through the office and my children learning it in school and yet I just could never seem to find the time or the concentration to sit down and master this thing.

Loneliness.   The lack of intimate friendships causes a major part of the difficulty of the initial period abroad. Most wives leave their family and friends at home and experience a void upon arrival abroad. The loneliness expresses itself in a number of ways:

I spent more time alone than anywhere ever. . . . . It's hard to spend so much time alone.

We had a lot of acquaintances, few good friends. . . . You can't make friends until you've learned the language.

Loneliness is the biggest problem with all the moves. I can remember moving from Mexico to the United States very worried about what we would find there. Looking down at the little family that was in just a shack in Mexico City and envying them because they had the whole family there. And I thought, they are better off than I am.

. . . In Hong Kong, not long after we arrived, our daughters were going back to school, my husband was going back with them on a business trip, and I felt, well, this is ridiculous. I am the only one here, and the rest of the family is on the other side of the world.

. . . I think that every country and every move has its low point and then you start going up. . . . I think loneliness is probably the low point.

When you live abroad and you suffer loneliness, you have to . . . be your own best friend.

So I was very alone, very lonely, and my husband was not going through the same problem as I . . . And I felt more lonely because I couldn't share my problems with him. It was very difficult for . . . at least a year, a year and a half.

Boredom and Meaninglessness. Many of the wives describe themselves as having hours and hours on their hands with nothing to do. They describe themselves as living in gilded cages: they have nice homes and servants to do the work but they do not have a meaningful role to fulfill. They no longer feel needed to perform many of the duties that they had previously fulfilled for their families, and, in addition, most are barred from working or continuing careers outside of the home.

I was like a prisoner in my own apartment. I had nothing to do. I had no books with me, except for one or two and that's very quickly gone through. . . . I had absolutely nothing to do. So I started to write letters. That was my only contact with the outside world; and I don't like writing letters!

I felt useless. I was a fifth wheel. There was the maid to do the work and no children that needed my attention.

I was going to be a nurse, but I had to have a work permit . . . so I threw myself into the women's club . . . bridge and golf, empty activities, but they filled my time.

Time . . . trying to find things to do with my time. I spent time sewing and I *hate* to sew. . . . We got together to crochet and talk. Blah!

After the novelty wears off, you have to find something to do with your time. I worked in a hospital, cooked, gardened. . . . I want to work again.

Separation and a Lack of Support

The employee's frequent absence compounds the difficulties present in adjusting to the new environment. Having just started a new job, the employee often works long hours. Exacerbating the situation further, many foreign assignments include regional responsibilities and a great amount of travel. Whereas the wife has just given up her friends, activities, and in many cases a job or career to follow her husband and family abroad, the husband continues and increases his major involvement in the job, often to the near exclusion of his wife. Separation and lack of support cause numerous complaints:

> My husband wasn't there to help me. He did nothing on the move. He works and travels.
>
> My husband was always away; never available. The men are so busy and the women have nothing to do.
>
> Well, I expected him to travel a little, but I didn't expect it to be so long or so often.
>
> My husband, as well as most of the men in the company, was away probably two weeks out of four. We knew before we left that there was going to be a lot of traveling, but it didn't really make its impact until he was actually doing it.

As shown in Figure 9–1, the husband's work often leaves him least available during the first few months abroad, exactly when the wife needs him the most to help with the logistics of settling in and to provide companionship and support. Unfortunately, the pattern of absent husbands and isolated wives reinforces itself in a vicious cycle. As more problems build up at home, many employees have less desire to spend time at home. By their own admission, many employees spend more time in the office and traveling than is necessary or required by the job. As the wife's situation becomes more difficult, the husband, often feeling guilty at the realization that his career caused the situation in the first place, increasingly avoids home.

AVAILABILITY
& NEED

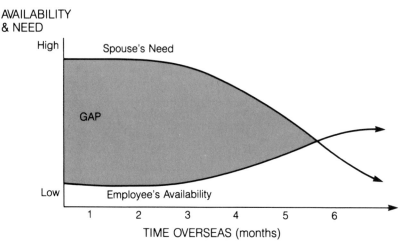

FIGURE 9-1 Availability Gap

CREATING A MEANINGFUL
PORTABLE LIFE

Following the initial period of adjustment, the wife faces the hardest task of all: creating a meaningful life abroad. She must identify what she wants to do and find a way to do it in the foreign country. For women who follow their husband from country to country, it becomes the search for a meaningful *portable* life.

> Being a transient, I tried to develop those things because . . . it is very difficult for me to have a career. And luckily, I am not particularly career-minded person. I want to take experiences and opportunities as they come. I want to learn different things, and I want to try different things. I mean, I only have one life. So a career and stepping up the ladder isn't important to me personally, it isn't. But it is important for me to take skills that are portable because, being a transient, you have to have something that you can grasp hold of, that you can take with you, that can be a certain continuity.

Creating a meaningful life abroad remains the most neglected aspect of the spouse's experience in the foreign country. People talk about the initial culture shock, learning a foreign language, and adjusting to the new culture. But adjustment is only half of the challenge; it brings a potentially negative situation to neutral, not to positive. Adjustment only brings the wife to the point where the foreign environment no longer constantly frustrates her; it does not provide motivation, direction, and a meaning to daily life overseas. Introspection and life planning remain necessary for the spouse to answer the questions, "What do I really want to do?" "What would I be happiest having accomplished during my years in this country?" "How can I continue doing the things that I find most important even while I am no longer living at home?"

The answers to these questions vary. One woman becomes an artist, another becomes a counselor to expatriate families, a third teaches English to immigrant children, a fourth does extensive volunteer work, and a fifth starts her own business. Many simultaneously remain very involved in raising a family. One French Canadian woman, who focused on learning the history, literature, and culture of the foreign country, described her growing sense of purpose.

> You start to understand the people around you. . . . They are different, but very often the difference is not so evident. But slowly, you go into knowing these differences, and it is a new world that opens up to you. . . . You discover the arts, and the folklore, and how the folklore is lived in the modern world. It is not so evident but there is always something that stays from these roots. You start to see all the small differences that you wouldn't notice if you were just a tourist for a month or so in the country. When you live there, slowly you get to know the people much more, the civilization, how they are and why they are like that, and then I think it is very enjoyable. You are gaining something, it is not just giving.

Today, more and more frequently, the questions center on identifying ways to continue a career while overseas.

RETURNING HOME

Expatriates often remember their home country as a more wonderful and perfect place than it actually is. As things get rough abroad and they experience culture shock and the difficulties in adjusting to a foreign culture, they dream of how easy and good life will be when they get back home. However, in reality, reentry often presents more difficulties than the initial foreign move. One woman, who had lived in a number of foreign countries, captured the difficulty and the disillusionment of returning home.

> Coming back was . . . the most difficult move of all. Why was it so difficult? Because . . . you change, the country changes, the people change. You are expecting . . . that you are coming back to your place and that you will feel good right away. . . . It is not true. You come back and you feel like a foreigner in your own country. . . . People deal with you as if . . . you are different. Even your way of speaking the language. So you feel cut off completely and it is your own country. The roots that you were not really consciously, but somehow, dreaming with. You know everybody needs some kind of roots and you come back to these roots and you don't feel well [sic] with them.

> [A British woman] I was in England recently. I was sitting in the train and I watched two English mums coming from the corner shop, standing and talking. And I said to my husband, "I know exactly what they are going to do, they are going to go home, have a little lunch, have a little sleep, and then they will watch a little bit of tele [television] and maybe do some ironing, then they will get dinner." It is a pity that I am not able to do that anymore. I'm wanting more from life. I am pleased that I have changed, that I have matured, that I have developed, but sometimes it would be easier if I had stayed content with that life. We don't feel we can go back to England. We have been gone too long. . . . They have changed and we have changed.

RECOMMENDATIONS

Expatriate wives have a range of suggestions for coping with cross-cultural transitions and creating a meaningful portable life abroad. The strongest recommendations include: know yourself and what you want out of life, and take responsibility for creating the type of life that you want to live. It is also important to treat the move as permanent, no matter how temporary. Persevere and be patient. Some recommendations focus on what the wives must do for themselves, others require the assistance of the organization and the husband. For example, wives must ask themselves what they really want out of the move; the company needs to include the spouse in a predeparture site visit and, if possible, in selecting a house; employees, to the extent possible, need to limit their travel during the first one to three months abroad. Most recommendations work best if all three — the organization, employee, and spouse — commit themselves to making the transition successful.

Many companies now interview the employee and spouse prior to an international move (14;16;17). They screen out couples with high probability of failure, including couples with excessive alcohol and drug use; indications of rigid and inflexible personalities or lifestyles; lack of communication among husband, wife, and children; and inappropriate or inadequate coping and stress management mechanisms. Research has shown that the worlds of work and family overlap (7; 21). Companies that screen couples recognize that the quality of home life will affect the employee's ability to perform at work, and similarly that the very nature of an expatriate assignment will strongly influence the family's daily life.

Although many organizations do an excellent job of handling the physical logistics of the move, few facilitate the spouse's creation of a meaningful life abroad. Companies usually leave it to the couple and, unfortunately, frequently to the wife alone, to identify those aspects of her life that she finds most important and to develop ways of incorporating them while abroad. This search, which is rarely an easy task, is best addressed explicitly by both members of the couple rather than left to chance. Creating a meaningful portable life is one of the areas in which much can be done to improve the expatriate assignment from the perspective of the spouse, the employee, and the company (21).

SUMMARY

The spouse's role is the most difficult of all family members'. The spouse must adjust to the foreign culture and create a meaningful life for herself in the foreign country. Her adjustment is made more difficult by her interaction with the least internationally sophisticated strata of society. Her ability to lead a meaningful life is challenged by the lack of structure in her foreign life and compounded by all of the activities, friends, and oftentimes a job or career that she has had to leave behind in the home country. Successful management of the transition abroad and the creation of a meaningful life in the foreign country demand the involvement of the expatriate employee, the company, and the spouse.

QUESTIONS FOR REFLECTION

1. What can multinational organizations do to help spouses adapt to the foreign environment and have a meaningful life while abroad?
2. If you were asked to move abroad as an expatriate spouse, why would you want to go? Why would you not want to go? What could you do to increase

the chances of success on the foreign assignment? What could your spouse do to increase the chances of your success? What could the company do to increase your chances of success?

3. As an international manager, you have just been offered a very interesting foreign assignment in Nigeria. As you drive home, you consider how to discuss the topic with your spouse. What are some of the approaches you could take, and what are their pros and cons?

4. Both men and women face very difficult challenges when they are transferred abroad in the spouse role. What are some of the challenges that would be particularly difficult for a male spouse (a man married to a female expatriate manager)? If you were the vice president of human resources for a major multinational organization and were sending a female expatriate manager abroad for the first time, what would you do to prepare the male spouse for his role?

NOTES

1. Copyright © by Foulie Psalidas-Perlmutter, Ph.D.

* The material in this chapter has been presented as a videotape program, *A Portable Life*, which presents the role of the spouse from the perspectives of four wives of international executives working for Alcan Aluminium Ltd. (see reference 1 in References). *A Portable Life* is available from McGill University, Instructional Communication Centre, 550 Sherbrooke Street West, Suite 400 Montreal, Quebec, Canada H3A 2K6 (telephone: 514-398-7200).

REFERENCES

1. Adler, N. J. *Managing International Transitions* (Montreal: Alcan Aluminum Limited, 1980).

2. Adler, N. J. "Pacific Basin Managers; A Gaijin, Not a Woman," *Human Resource Management*, vol. 26, no. 2 (Summer 1987), pp. 169–192.

3. Adler, N. J. "Reentry: A Study of the Dynamic Coping Processes Used by Repatriated Employees to Enhance Effectiveness in the Organization and Personal Learning during the Transition Back into the Home Country," Ph.D. dissertation, University of California, Los Angeles, June 1980.

4. Adler, N. J. "Women in International Management: Where Are They?" *California Mangement Review*, vol. XXVI, no. 4 (June 1984), pp. 122–132.

5. Adler, N. J., and Ghadar, F. "International Strategy from the Perspective of People and Culture: The North American Context," in A. M. Rugman, ed., *Research in Global Strategic Management: International Business Research for the Twenty-First Century: Canada's New Research Agenda*, vol. 1 (Greenwich, Conn.: JAI Press, 1990), pp. 179–205.

6. Baker, J. C. "An Analysis of How the U.S. Multinational Company Considers the Wives of American Expatriate Managers," *Academy of Management Proceedings*, vol. 35 (1975), pp. 258–260.

7. Culbert, S., and Renshaw, J. "Coping with the Stresses of Travels as an Opportunity for Improving the Quality of Work and Family Life," *Family Process*, vol. 11, no. 3 (September 1972), pp. 321–337.

8. D'Orazio, N. "Foreign Executives' Wives in Tokyo," *Institute of Comparative Culture Business Series*, Bulletin no. 82, Sophia University, Tokyo, 1981.

9. Edstrom, A., and Galbraith, J. R. "Alternative Policies for International Transfer of Managers," *Management International Review*, vol. 17, no. 2 (1977), pp. 11–22.

10. Edstrom, A., and Galbraith, J. R. "International Transfer of Managers: Some Important Policy Considerations," *Columbia Journal of World Business*, vol. 11 (Summer 1976), pp. 100–112.

11. Edstrom, A., and Galbraith, J. "Transfer of Managers as Coordination and Control Strategy in Multinational Organizations," *Administrative Science Quarterly*, vol. 22 (June 1977), pp. 248–263.

12. Edstrom, A., and Lorange, P. "Matching Strategy and Human Resources in Multinational Corporations," *Journal of International Business Studies*, vol. 15 (Fall 1984), pp. 125–137.

13. Eliot, T. S. *Four Quartets* (New York: Harcourt Brace Jovanovich, 1968).

14. "Gauging a Family's Suitability for a Stint Overseas," *Business Week* (April 16, 1979), pp. 127–130.

15. Jelinek, M., and Adler, N. J. "Women: World Class Managers for Global Competition," *Academy of Management Executive*, vol. 2, no. 1 (1988), pp. 11–19.

16. Karras, E. J., and McMillan, R. F. "Interviewing for a Cultural Match," *Personnel Journal* (April 1971), p. 276.

17. Labovitz, G. "Managing the Personal Side of the Personnel Move Aboard," *Advanced Management Journal*, vol. 42, no. 3 (Summer 1977), pp. 26–39.

18. Ondrack, D. A. "International Transfers of Managers in North American and European MNEs," *Journal of International Business Studies*, vol. 16 (Fall 1985), pp. 1–19.

19. Pazy, A., and Zeira, Y. "Training of Parent-Country Professionals in Host

Country Organizations," *Academy of Management Review*, vol. 8, no. 2 (1983), pp. 262–272.

20. Priestoff, N. "The Gaijin Executive's Wife," *The Conference Board Record*, vol. 13, no. 5 (May 1976), pp. 51–64.

21. Renshaw, J. R. "An Exploration of the Dynamics of the Overlapping Worlds of Work and Family," *Family Process*, vol. 15, no. 1 (March 1976), pp. 143–165.

22. Thompson, A. "Australian Expatriate Wives and Business Success in South-East Asia," *Euro-Asia Business Review*, vol 5, no. 2 (April 1986), pp. 14–18.

23. Wederspahn, G. M. "The Overseas Wife: Excess Baggage," *The Bridge*, vol. 5, no. 4 (Winter 1980), p. 16.

24. Zeira, Y., and Harrari, E. "Genuine Multinational Staffing Policy: Expectations and Realities," *Academy of Management Journal*, vol. 20, no. 2 (1979), pp. 327–333.

CHAPTER 10

▼

International Careers

▲

Ideally, it seems . . . [a global manager] should have the stamina of an Olympic runner, the mental agility of an Einstein, the conversational skill of a professor of languages, the detachment of a judge, the tact of a diplomat, and the perseverance of an Egyptian pyramid builder. [And] that's not all. If they are going to measure up to the demands of living and working in a foreign country, they should also have a feeling for the culture; their moral judgement should not be too rigid; they should be able to merge with the local environment with chameleon-like ease; and they should show no signs of prejudice.

Thomas Aitken (29)

As globalization evolves from a buzzword to a pervasive reality, demand increases for executives sophisticated in managing the complexities of international business. Corporate and government managers need to be able to think globally. They need to be able to work domestically on international projects and abroad on business travel and expatriate assignments. Global business is becoming so important that organizations cannot afford to consider candidates for executive positions unless they have had international experience.

According to Colby Chandler (14), the CEO of Eastman Kodak Company, "These days there is not a discussion or a decision that does not have an international dimension. We would have to be blind not to see how critically important international experience is." The *Wall Street Journal* (11) claims that "intensifying international competition will make the home-grown chief executive obsolete." Duane Kullberg, Arthur Andersen and Company's former Chief Executive Partner, agrees that future CEOs "will be . . . [people] with experience outside the borders of the U.S. . . . If you go back 20 years, you could be pretty insular and stll survive. Today, that's not possible" (11).

WHAT IT TAKES TO REACH THE TOP

North American companies compete with British, French, German, Scandinavian, and Japanese companies, among others, for global executives to manage their foreign subsidiaries (see 21). Yet what it takes to reach the top of a company differs from one country to the next; companies view managerial success through cultural blinders (see 12; 13;19). For example, American managers view ambition and drive as the most important characteristic for success; French managers must be labeled as having high potential (19); German managers, more than others, believe that creativity is essential for career success (19); and their British colleagues see creating the right image and getting noticed for what they do as essential (19).

Similarly, whereas Swiss and German companies respect technical creativity and competence, French and British companies often see managers with such qualities as "mere technicians" (12). Likewise, American companies highly value entrepreneurs, while their British and French counterparts see entrepreneurial behavior as highly disruptive (12). In a smiliar manner, just over half of Dutch managers (57%) see "skills in interpersonal relations and communication" as a critical determinant of career success, whereas almost ninety percent (89%) of their British colleagues do so (13).

International management expert André Laurent (19) describes German, British, and French managers' careers as follows (12:10):

> German managers, more than others, believe that creativity is essential for career success. In their mind, successful managers must have the right individual characteristics. German managers' outlook is ra-

tional: they view the organization as a coordinated network of individuals who make appropriate decisions based on their professional competence and knowledge.

British managers hold a more interpersonal and subjective view of the organizational world. According to them, the ability to create the right image and to get noticed for what they do is essential for career success. British managers view organizations primarily as a network of relationships between individuals who get things done by influencing each other using communication and negotiation.

French managers look at organizations as an authority network where the power to organize and control members stems from their position in the hierarchy. French managers focus on the organization as a pyramid of differentiated levels of power to be acquired or dealt with. They perceive the ability to manage power relationships effectively and to "work the system" as critical to their career success.

As companies integrate their global operations, the multiple national realities send conflicting messages to success-oriented managers. Various affiliates operate differently and reward different behavior based on their unique cultural perspectives (13). Regardless of what the head office desires or designs, there is no single best way to perform or to achieve global career success (13).

Expatriate assignments have been a key part of many international managers' careers. Traditionally, North American managers have been attracted to foreign work by the financial rewards, responsibility, challenge, and independence as well as the unique lifestyle. Yet during the 1970s, a weakened U.S. dollar, inflation, and additional taxes made financial packages less attractive to Americans. By the 1980s, dual-career marriages added complications to transfer decisions as well as exacerbating the financial situation; expatriate salary increases rarely made up for the reduction of a two-income family to a single salary. Stories of prior expatriates whose careers had been sidetracked while abroad made many managers hesitant to follow an international career path (4;15;17;20;22).

Yet today, it is no secret that business faces an environment radically different from that of even a few years ago, the result of increasingly global competition. That new global environment demands more, not fewer, internationally skilled managers. Rather than sidetracking a manager's career, international experience is rapidly becoming the only route to the top. According to the *New York Times* (14), slowly but surely, hands-on international experience is moving out of the "nice but not necessary" category and into the "must have" slot for those on the corporate fast track. Given the increasing demand and potentially diminishing interest in international assignments, what can we predict for the next decade? Will multinational corporations remain able to attract sufficient numbers of young managers? Are today's MBAs interested in international work? What do they see as the advantages and disadvantages of overseas assignments?

This chapter reports on a study addressing these questions.[1] As you read the chapter, ask yourself how prepared you are to work internationally? What are your strengths and weaknesses as a global manager?

WHO WERE THE EXPATRIATE MANAGERS?

Traditionally, who was the overseas executive? According to a study of 1161 expatriates in forty countries (15), the typical American international executive was about 31 years old when he first went abroad, stayed at least three years on each foreign assignment, and had three such assignments during his career. Expatriate executives were significantly younger than their domestic counterparts; with few exceptions, they were men. Twenty-one percent married foreign women. International executives came from a higher socioeconomic background than their domestic counterparts. Typically, expatriates rose rapidly in their career and stayed longer with one company: 41 percent worked for only one firm, 25 percent for only two firms, and 87 percent remained with the same firm after accepting their first foreign assignment. International executives were better educated than their domestic counterparts: 81 percent graduated from college as compared with 57 percent to 69 percent of domestic executives. International executives' education was less specialized than that of domestic executives, with more graduating in liberal arts and fewer in business and engineering. The majority did not view the foreign assignment as an end in itself but rather as a strategy for career development.

Today, the portrait of the international executive is changing. First, given the increasing importance of global business, more executives manage international projects and work with foreigners without ever leaving home. They work for foreign companies, buy from foreign suppliers, sell to worldwide clients, and, most significantly, create global strategies with colleagues from many different nations. Second, more fast-track managers are using expatriate assignments to gain the experience necessary to rise to the top of major, global corporations (7). Third, the percent of women seeking international assignments, although still small, is rising (6;8;18), with their overwhelming success beginning to break down the gender barrier (3).

Unlike their male counterparts, female expatriate managers are fairly junior within their organizations and careers. Their average age is under thirty (28.8 years). Nearly two-thirds are single, with very few having children. Female expatriates are very well educated and quite internationally experienced. Almost all hold graduate's degrees, with an MBA the most common. Over three-quarters have had extensive international interests and experience prior to their company sending them abroad. For example, more than three-quarters (77%) had traveled internationally and almost two-thirds had had an international focus in their studies prior to joining the company. The women generally speak two or three languages, with some speaking as many as six. In addition, most women selected for international assignments demonstrate excellent social skills (3).

TODAY'S INTERNATIONAL CAREERS

Why would today's young managers accept international assignments: for the job challenge, the adventure, the status? Why would young managers turn down foreign assignments? A survey was conducted to discover why the next generation's managers might accept or reject international assignments and careers.[2] Graduating MBA students from seven top schools in the United States, Canada, and Europe described their level of interest in international careers, their reasons for accepting or rejecting foreign assignments, and their assessment of international versus domestic opportunities.[3] Five schools had traditional MBA programs and two had international management programs — one in North America and one in Europe.[4]

Who Are the Future International Managers?

The backgrounds of the MBAs from the seven schools showed more similarity than difference.[5] Although 41 percent had an international focus in their MBA, few had extensive international work experience. Over

80 percent (84.2%) had traveled in foreign countries; few of their friends, however, were foreign nationals. As might be expected, MBAs at the international schools had more foreign experience than did those at domestic schools. Canadian MBAs had more international experience than did their American counterparts.

Do MBAs Want International Careers?

The future managers showed strong interest in pursuing the international aspects of their careers.[6] More than four out of five (84.2%) wanted an expatriate assignment at some time during their career. Just under half seriously considered pursuing an international career (46.9%), including accepting a series of foreign assignments (43.7%). More than a third of the future managers wanted to travel extensively for their job (38.1%). Yet, only one-third (33.1%) wanted a foreign assignment as their first job after graduation. Clearly, many MBAs show interest in international management, but fewer would like a foreign assignment "right now." Not surprisingly, students at the two international schools showed the most interest, followed by the Canadians, with Americans expressing least interest. Do you agree for your career?

How would you answer these questions in terms of your own career? Each question on the *Careers in International Management* questionnaire (see Figure 10–1) provides a way to assess your own interest in global management and an international career.

Why Future Managers Would Accept a Foreign Assignment

As shown in Table 10–1, the most frequently mentioned reason for accepting a foreign assignment is opportunity for cross-cultural and personal growth experiences. Over half the MBAs want to see other cultures, travel, learn new languages, and gain a greater understanding of another way of life; that is, they want to expand their horizons. The second reason is the job itself. Forty percent of MBAs see international jobs, as compared with available domestic jobs, as providing more interesting and challenging work, allowing for more autonomy, power, status, and responsibility, and as providing opportunities for more meaningful contributions to the company and society. The third reason is money. More than a quarter of the MBAs believe they would earn a

CAREERS IN INTERNATIONAL MANAGEMENT

Given the substantial increases in international trade and global operations over the last decade, it has become increasingly important for managers and corporations to understand the career aspirations of graduating MBAs. This questionnaire is designed to increase your understanding of your own career aspirations.

BACKGROUND: HOW PREPARED ARE YOU?

1. Counting your maternal language, which languages do you speak (relatively well)?

   _____

   _____

   _____

   _____

   _____

2. How many years have you studied outside of your country of citizenship (from grade 1 on)?

   _____ total number of years in _____
   country/countries

3. How many months outside your country of citizenship have you traveled, lived, or worked?

   _____

4. Did either of your parents travel internationally for their work?

   _____

5. How many of your friends are neither from your country of citizenship nor from the country in which you are currently living?

   a. _____ none   b. _____ a few   c. _____ about half

   d. _____ most e. _____ all

WHAT ARE YOUR CAREER PLANS?

The following section asks you a number of questions about your career plans. In the questions

   Home Country is your country of citizenship.

   An *International Assignment* is one in which the company sends an employee for a single assignment of a year or more to a foreign country.

FIGURE 10-1   Careers in International Management

An *International Career* is a series of foreign assignments in different foreign countries.

International Travel is a business trip to a foreign country without the employee moving there.

An *Expatriate* is an employee who is sent by the company to live and work in a foreign country.

How true is each of the following statements for you?

1. I am seriously considering pursuing an international career. _____

2. I would like my first job after my MBA to be in a foreign country. _____

3. If offered an equivalent position in my home country or in the foreign country of my choice, I would rather work at home. _____

4. While continuing to live in my home country, I would like to travel internationally more than 40% (approximately 20 weeks/year) of my time. _____

5. I would like to have an *International Assignment* at some time in my career. _____

6. I would like to follow an *International Career* in which I had a series of foreign assignments. _____

FIGURE 10–1 *(Continued)*

7. I had never thought
about taking an interna-
tional assignment until I
read this questionnaire.   _____

There are many reasons why people choose not to pursue an international career. Which of the following would discourage *you* from pursuing an international career or taking an international assignment?

8. I like living in my home
country.   _____

9. I do not want to learn
another language.   _____

10. I do not want to adjust
to another culture.   _____

11. My spouse would not
want to move to a for-
eign country.   _____

12. It is not good to move
children.   _____

13. I want my children to be
educated in my home
country.   _____

14. I do not want to live in:

a. Any foreign location   _____

b. North America   _____

c. Europe   _____

d. Latin or South
America   _____

e. Asia   _____

f. Africa   _____

FIGURE 10-1 (*Continued*)

287

g. the Middle East _____

h. my home country _____

i. other *(specify)* _____

15. International jobs involve too much travel. _____

16. If I live in a foreign country, my children will not gain a sense of national identity. _____

17. My spouse would not want to interrupt his or her career. _____

18. I will lose my sense of identity, my roots. _____

19. Foreign assignments put too much strain on a marriage. _____

20. When you are on a foreign assignment you become "invisible" to the company and tend to be forgotten for promotions. _____

21. It would be difficult to come back home after having lived and worked for a long time in a foreign country. _____

22. I do not want to be exposed to the political instability in some parts of the world. _____

23. I would be more socially isolated and lonely in a foreign country. _____

FIGURE 10-1 *(Continued)*

24. I would be exposed to
    more personal danger in
    a foreign country. _____

In comparing potential domestic and international careers, which do you think
could give you the greatest professional opportunities?

	Domestic Career	About Same	International Career
25. I could succeed faster in	_____	_____	_____
26. I could earn a higher salary in	_____	_____	_____
27. I could have greater status in	_____	_____	_____
28. I could be more recognized for my work in	_____	_____	_____
29. I could have a more interesting professional life in	_____	_____	_____
30. I could have a more satisfying personal life	_____	_____	_____

In comparing male and female MBA students, who do you think will have the
greater chance of being

	Males	Equal Chances	Females
31. Selected for an international assignment?	_____	_____	_____
32. Effective on an international assignment?	_____	_____	_____

FIGURE 10–1 (Continued)

	Males	Equal Chances	Females
33. Successful in advancing in an international career?	_____	_____	_____
34. Effective on domestic assignments?	_____	_____	_____
35. Successful in advancing in a domestic career?	_____	_____	_____
36. Socially isolated and lonely in a foreign country?	_____	_____	_____
37. Exposed to personal danger in a foreign country?	_____	_____	_____

IN YOUR OPINION

1. What are the main reasons that would lead *you* to accept an international assignment?

    a. _____

    b. _____

    c. _____

2. What are the main reasons why *you* would turn down an international assignment?

    a. _____

    b. _____

    c. _____

3. What, if any, are the blocks for women successfully pursuing international careers that include foreign assignments (which do *not* exist for men)?

    a. _____

    b. _____

    c. _____

FIGURE 10-1 (*Continued*)

higher salary and more fringe benefits in an international than in a domestic position.

The fourth reason for accepting a foreign assignment is career advancement. One MBA in five sees expatriate positions as increasing company-wide exposure and thus the potential for promotion. The fifth reason is a good location. Almost 16 percent expressed more willingness to accept a foreign assignment in a politically stable country with a good climate, good social and living conditions, few threats to personal safety, and with an English-speaking population. MBAs are most attracted to countries that are more similar to their own country and more economically developed. The sixth reason is the more satisfying life abroad. Eleven percent look forward to a change, less routine, more fun, more adventure, more excitement, more variety, more personal freedom, and a higher quality of life than they imagine having in their home country.

When the MBAs compare the advantages of international versus domestic careers, they see the primary benefits of an international assignment as greater challenge and responsibility, more interesting work, and better financial rewards. By contrast, they see domestic careers as leading to slightly greater status, a more satisfying personal life, more rapid career advancement, and greater recognition for their work than would an international career. MBAs at the international schools see more benefits from international careers than do either Canadians or Americans.[7]

Why Future Managers Would Reject a Foreign Assignment

The MBAs identified seven major reasons for turning down foreign assignments. As shown in Table 10–2, the most frequently mentioned reason is a bad location. More than half the MBAs would reject an assignment if the host country appeared too politically unstable, "uncivilized," dangerous, or hostile towards expatriates, or to have a high potential for war and public violence. The second reason is the job itself and potentially negative career impact. One-third of the MBAs would turn down an foreign assignment if the job appeared unchallenging or boring. Similarly, a third see foreign assignments as a bad long-term career strategy. They fear the higher risk of job failure abroad and the possible damage to their career caused by extended isolation from the company's

TABLE 10-1   Reasons MBAs Would Accept International Assignments
(1129 MBAs citing 1867 reasons)

Percent MBAs Citing Reason	Reason for Accepting International Assignment
52.2%	*Cross-Cultural Experience and Personal Growth* See other cultures Learn new languages Gain greater understanding of another way of life Personal growth: expand horizons, broaden background
40.2	*Job* More interesting and challenging More opportunities, responsibilities, chances for useful work More power, autonomy, status
27.7	*Money* Higher salary, more fringe benefits, more savings
20.7	*Career Advancement* Increased exposure Increased opportunities Future domestic promotion
15.9	*Good Location* Politically stable country Good climate Good social and living conditions Safe English speaking or similar to home country
10.9	*Satisfying Life* Greater personal freedom More fun, excitement, adventure More variety, less routine, a change Higher quality of life
3.5	*Spouse and Family* Good situation for the spouse (i.e., job) Good situation for family (education, health facilities) Spouse willing to go
2.6	*Short Term* *Other* No domestic jobs available Female managers respected by foreigners Personal business opportunities available in foreign country Single

Note: 1129 graduating MBAs cited 1867 reasons for accepting international assignments; the most frequently cited reasons are given here. Listed numbers are the percent of MBAs citing the particular reason.

TABLE 10-2 Reasons MBAs Would Reject International Assignments
(1129 MBAs citing 2308 reasons)

Percent MBAS Citing Reason	*Reason for Rejecting International Assignment*
58.5%	*Location* Politically unstable "Uncivilized" Dangerous Hostility toward expatriates Extreme poverty High potential for war or violence
34.6	*Job and Career* Boring, unchallenging, professionally uninteresting Not good long-term career strategy Higher risk of job failure Isolation from domestic company Displacement from company's hierarchy: forgotten at promotion time, "lost" at reentry
33.4	*Spouse and Family* Inadequate medical or educational facilities Children wrong age to move (especially teenagers) Problem of dual-career marriage Spouse unwilling to move Spouse unable to find position to further career
22.9	*Money* Salary and benefits package inadequate
19.4	*Unpleasant Life Abroad* Unwillingness to learn new language, adjust to new culture Isolation, loneliness, fear, uncertainty Restrictions on personal life: lack of physical and intellectual freedom, access to people
13.8	*Disruption to Home Country Life* Disruption to personal and social life Reneging on commitment to family, parents, friends
5.8	*Contract Too Long* *Other* Women not accepted as managers Existing good domestic position Opposition to company's international policies, product, or marketing strategy Too much travel

Note: 1129 graduating MBAs cited 2308 reasons for turning down international assignments; the most frequently cited reasons are given here. Listed numbers are the percent of MBAs citing the particular reason.

domestic headquarters. They fear being "lost" at reentry and forgotten at times of promotion.

The third reason, also mentioned by one-third of the MBAs, describes their concern about spouse and family. MBAs view dual-career marriages as a major problem, especially if the spouse cannot find a suitable position abroad. They also fear the increased marital strain as well as the potentially inadequate educational and medical facilities for children. The fourth reason is money. Nearly one-quarter of the MBAs would reject an assignment if the salary and benefits package inadequately compensated them for the disruption and additional problems caused by moving and living in a foreign country. MBAs cite the potentially unpleasant foreign lifestyle as their fifth reason. Nearly 20 percent reject introducing too much change into their life, learning a new language, adjusting to a new culture, or subjecting themselves to the isolation, loneliness, fear, and uncertainty associated with living abroad. Similarly, one MBA in seven rejects disrupting his or her current, enjoyable home country lifestyle. Other reasons mentioned by some of the MBAs include the contract being too long, fear that the foreigners would not accept female managers, the assignment requiring too much travel, or unacceptable home company policies toward the host country.

MBAs consistently rate international work as offering greater *job satisfaction;* domestic work as offering greater *organizational recognition* and a more *satisfying private life.* MBAs would accept foreign positions for the cross-cultural experience and opportunity for personal growth, the job itself, and the higher salary and financial benefits. They would reject foreign assignments due to the negative impact on spouse and family, the personal danger and inconvenience of living in a "bad" location, and the potentially detrimental effect on career advancement both while abroad and when returning home. MBAs' perceptions of the advantages and disadvantages of living and working abroad reflect those of many managers. Experienced expatriates frequently have described such advantages as increased personal growth opportunities and the inherently more interesting, challenging, and responsible work abroad, as well as traditionally generous salaries and benefit packages.

Today's MBAs show a greater awareness than their predecessors of the disadvantages of expatriate positions on their private lives and careers. Research has shown that the major cause of failure on foreign assignments, often leading to early return, is dissatisfaction of the spouse (23). Nearly half of 300 surveyed companies have brought families home early due to the spouse's inability to adapt (10). With the increasing prevalence of dual-career couples, the impact of foreign assignments on the spouse and family will increase, not decrease. MBAs appear well aware of these problems.

Potentially negative impacts of international assignments on employees' careers have also become more widely recognized. In the past most expatriates believed that foreign assignments would help their career; the majority returned to discover the opposite (4). Returning employees have all too frequently discovered that home country jobs were at substantially lower levels of responsibility and authority than were their expatriate positions or, more dramatically, that there were no jobs at all to return to (see chapter 8). Meanwhile, returnees found that domestic colleagues had been promoted while their own career had plateaued. Today's MBAs appear considerably more aware of the hazards of moving abroad and successfully returning home than were the managers of five, ten, and fifteen years ago. MBAs consequently are less likely to accept a foreign assignment that could jeopardize their career. Luckily, with increasing globablization and the parallel rise in importance of international experience and positions, the risks of derailing one's career by going abroad are diminishing just as young managers' interest is increasing.

Which Future Managers Show Most Interest in International Careers?

MBAs who express most and least interest in international careers differ in their background characteristics and attitudes towards working abroad. The most interested MBAs are slightly younger, more frequently single, and specializing in international management. They come from families in which at least one parent has traveled internationally for work. They are more likely to have lived abroad themselves and to speak more languages. Moreover, the most interested MBAs have less desire to live in their home country and less concern about living in a "bad" foreign location or encountering personal danger. They express a greater willingness to adapt to foreign cultures and to learn foreign languages, less fear of losing their national identity, and less concern about potentially negative consequences for their spouse and family. On only one dimension do the most international MBAs show more concern than their less interested colleagues: reentry. Most international MBAs show more concern about the potential personal and career problems they will face when returning home.

WOMEN IN INTERNATIONAL MANAGEMENT

Are men and women equally interested in international careers? Yes. Although fewer than 3 percent of the current, North American, expatriate managers are women (6), male and female MBA students express an equal willingness to accept international assignments and pursue international careers (5). In fact, women MBAs feel less strongly than do men about a number of the negative aspects of international assignments.

Although equally interested, both male and female MBAs believe that companies offer fewer opportunities for women than for men in international management; both believe that companies offer fewer opportunities for women in international than in domestic management. The MBAs are right. In a survey of 60 major North American multinationals, over half (54%) showed reluctance to select female managers for foreign assignments (2). The two primary concerns, expressed by three-quarters of the companies, are their belief that foreigners are prejudiced against female managers and that the difficulties faced by international, dual-career couples are insurmountable. Even with the barriers and hesistance, 72 percent of the companies believe that the number of women working internationally will increase in the coming decade (2).

Similar to the companies, over 80 percent of the MBAs believe that foreigners' prejudice against female managers poses the primary problem facing expatriate women (1;5). Over 70 percent label the home company's reluctance to select women for foreign assignments and the difficulties faced by international dual-career couples as the second and third most important barriers (5). Whereas MBAs correctly see companies' current selection processes as creating barriers, neither they nor the companies correctly understood foreigners' prejudice. A major study of North American women working as expatriate managers in countries around the world showed that the women are successful (3;8;18). As one female expatriate manager stated, "The most difficult job is getting sent, not succeeding once sent."

Women succeed because they are seen as foreigners who happen to be women, not as women who happen to be foreigners. Although the difference may appear subtle, the effect is huge. Countries such as Japan, Korea, and Saudi Arabia, which promote few of their own women into significant management positions, treat foreign women with the respect they accord male expatriate managers. As one woman who works successfully in Hong Kong explained, "It doesn't make any difference if you are blue, green, purple, or a frog, if you have the best product at the best price, the Chinese will buy." In essence, in global business pragmatism wins out over prejudice.

While more barriers may exist for women than for men, today's organizations clearly can select international managers from equally interested groups of male and female MBAs. When considering a woman for an international position, the organization would be wise (a) not to assume that she does not want to go — she probably does; (b) not to assume that foreigners are so prejudiced that such assignments would be bad for both the company and the woman's career; and (c) not to assume that dual-career issues are insoluable. Many North American female expatriates actually find it easier to balance the seemingly conflicting roles of professional, wife, and mother in the foreign environment, where they have the luxury of household help which they often do not have at home. Luckily, just at the time when the intensity of global competition demands that companies use nothing but their best managers, both the companies and the women are discovering that success is both possible and probable.

SUMMARY

Do MBAs want international careers? Yes, under certain conditions. Whereas most male and female MBAs see more advantages from domestic than international careers, 84 percent would like to have a foreign assignment at some time during their career. Are American MBAs equally interested in international management as their Canadian and European counterparts? No. From all perspectives, American MBAs express less interest in pursuing foreign assignments and international careers than do their Canadian and international counterparts. Recently, many government leaders have strongly criticized Americans' apparent parochialism (see chapter 1). Unfortunately, that same parochialism appears to exist within the ranks of some of today's graduating MBAs.

QUESTIONS FOR REFLECTION

1. For you personally, why would you want to accept a foreign assignment? Why would you reject a foreign assignment?

2. If you were the vice president of human resources for a major multinational organization and wanted to attract the very best managers to accept international assignments, what would you offer them?

3. What are some of the best ways to attract women to accept international assignments? What should the company and the woman do to make certain that the foreign assignment is a success?

4. Dual-career marriages have been considered a major problem in foreign transfers. How would you recruit a top manager for an international assignment if the manager's spouse also was a senior manager for another company?

5. What kinds of international experiences would you like to have in your career? When? Why?

NOTES

1. This chapter is based on the study reported in Nancy J. Adler "Do MBAs Want International Careers?" *International Journal of Intercultural Relations*, vol. 10, no. 3 (1986), pp. 277–300. The research was supported by a grant from the Social Sciences and Humanities Research Council of the Canadian Government. The author thanks Blossem Shaffer for her creative ideas and research assistance in conducting the study.

2. Ibid.

3. In the study MBA students rated the importance of various reasons for accepting or rejecting international assignments with respect to their own career plans.

4. The two Canadian MBA programs are McGill University in Montreal and the Universtiy of Western Ontario in London, Ontario. The three American MBA programs are The Tuck School at Darmouth, the University of California at Los Angeles (UCLA), and a large midwestern university that chose to remain anonymous. The international North American school is the American Graduate School of International Management in Phoenix, Arizona, and the European program is INSEAD (Institut Européen d'Administration des Affaires) in Fontainebleau, France.

5. The surveyed MBAs were young (average age 26.5 years), most were single (68%), approximately a third were women (32%), and most were studying

for their MBA in the country in which they were born, held citizenship, and had received their undergraduate education. The most common undergraduate degrees were business and economics (33.8%) and engineering (10.8%), while the most common MBA concentrations were finance (43.5%) and marketing (28.5%). While 38% had no work experience, the majority had worked for a short time (approximately two years) prior to entering the MBA program. Over a third (36.1%) had never lived abroad. Few of the MBAs' parents had worked internationally. See Table 1 in Adler (1).

6. See Table 2 in Adler (1).

7. See Table 3 in Adler (1).

REFERENCES

1. Adler, N. J. "Do MBAs Want International Careers?" *International Journal of Intercultural Relations*, vol. 10, no. 3, (1986), pp. 277–300.

2. Adler, N. J. "Expecting International Success: Female Managers Overseas," *Columbia Journal of World Business*, vol. 19, no. 3 (Fall 1984), pp. 79–85.

3. Adler, N. J. "Pacific Basin Managers: A Gaijin, Not a Woman," *Human Resource Management*, vol. 26, no. 2, (Summer 1987), pp. 169–192.

4. Adler, N. J. "Re-entry: Managing Cross-Cultural Transitions," *Group and Organization Studies*, vol. 6, no. 3, (September 1981), pp. 341–356.

5. Adler, N. J. "Women Do Not Want International Careers: And Other Myths About International Management," *Organizational Dynamics*, vol. 13, no. 2 (Autumn 1984), pp. 66–79.

6. Adler, N. J. "Women in International Management: Where Are They?" *California Management Review*, vol. 26, no. 4 (Summer 1984), pp. 78–89.

7. Adler, N. J., and Ghadar, F. "Globalization and Human Resource Management," in Alan M. Rugman, ed., *Research in Global Strategic Management: A Canadian Perspective*, vol. 1 (Greenwich, Conn.: JAI Press, 1989).

8. Adler, N. J., and Izraeli, D. N. *Women in Management Worldwide* (Armonk, N.Y.: M. E. Sharpe, 1988).

9. Aitken, T. "What It Takes to Work Abroad," in T. Aitken, *The Multinational Man: The Role of the Manager Abroad.* (New York: Halstead Press, 1973). The pronoun "he" has been changed in the quote to "they" to include male and female expatriates.

10. Baker, J. C. "An Analysis of How the U.S. Multinational Company Con-

siders the Wife of American Expatriate Managers," *Academy of Management Proceedings*, vol. 35 (1975), pp. 258–260.

11. Bennett, A. "Going Global: The Chief Executives in Year 2000 Will Be Experienced Abroad," *Wall Street Journal* (February 27, 1989), pp. A1, A9.

12. Derr, C. B. *Managing the New Careerists.* (San Francisco: Jossey-Bass, 1986).

13. Derr, C. B., and Laurent, A. "The Internal and External Careers: A Theoretical and Cross-Cultural Perspective." Working paper, University of Utah (USA) and INSEAD (France), 1987.

14. Deutsch, C. H. "Losing Innocence, Abroad," *The New York Times* (July 10, 1988), Business section, pp. 1, 26.

15. Gonzales, R. F., and Neghandi, A., R. *The United States Overseas Executive: His Orientations and Career Patterns.* (East Lansing: Graduate School of Business Administration, Michigan State University, 1967).

16. Heenan, D. "The Corporate Expatriate: Assignment to Ambiguity," *Columbia Journal of World Business*, vol. 5 (1970), pp. 49–54.

17. Howard, C. "The Returning Overseas Executive: Culture Shock in Reverse," *Human Resources Management*, vol. 13, no. 2 (Summer 1974), pp. 22–26.

18. Jelinek, M., and Adler, N. J. "Women: World Class Managers for Global Competition," *Academy of Management Executive*, vol. 2, no. 1 (1988), pp. 11–19.

19. Laurent, A. "The Cross-Cultural Puzzle of International Human Resource Management," *Human Resource Management*, vol. 25, no. 1 (Spring 1986), pp. 91–102. Copyright © 1986 John Wily & Sons, Inc. Reprinted by permission of John Wiley & Sons, Inc.

20. Murray, A. "International Personnel Repatriation: Cultural Shock in Reverse," *MSU Business Topics*, vol. 21, no. 2 (Summer 1973), pp. 59–66.

21. Perham, J. C. "The Boom in Executive Jobs," *Dun's Review*, vol. 110, no. 5 (November 1977), pp. 80–81.

22. Smith, L., "The Hazards of Coming Home," *Dun's Review* (October 1975), pp. 71–73.

23. Tung, R. L. "U.S. Multinationals: A Study of Their Selection and Training for Overseas Assignments," *Academy of Management Proceedings*, vol. 39 (1979), pp. 298–301.

▼

Epilogue

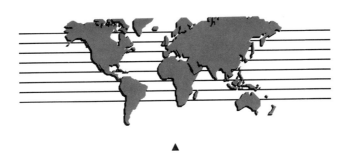

▲

Culture directs the organization of the psyche, which in turn has a profound effect upon the ways people look at things, behave politically, make decisions, order priorities, organize their lives, and last but not least, how they think. Self-awareness and cultural awareness are inseparable, . . . [people] must now go beyond culture, as the greatest separation feat of all, in order to free . . . [themselves] from this grip of unconscious culture.

Edward T. Hall[1]

The world has gotten smaller. International and global business has become more important. Managers worldwide are becoming more sophisticated. It is only as we recognize the extent to which we are culture bound that we can go beyond the limitations of our own necessarily narrow perspectives. It is only as we work internationally that we can recognize and benefit from a world economy. We have entered an era in which global organizations, corporations, and alliances determine our economic and social well-being. To the extent that organizations recognize individual cultural differences, they allow us to contribute based on our uniqueness. To the extent that they transcend national boundaries, they encourage a world, fraught with wars and animosities, to collaborate and to cooperate. If we fail to recognize cultural differences and choose to maintain staunchly ethnocentric domestic approaches, we condemn the world to divisiveness and its own demise.

In the past, multinational corporations have not been celebrated for their contribution to world peace or understanding. Perhaps it is only today, as we recognize the need for understanding and cooperation for our very survival, that the function of global corporations becomes apparent. Governments reflect national boundaries; transnational corporations go beyond national boundaries and national definitions. Corporations can use their transnational status, their creative public-private partnerships, and their ever-growing network of alliances in ways that benefit and enrich their worldwide constituencies or in ways that impoverish us all. The challenge is immense. The importance is without bound.

NOTE

1. Edward T. Hall, *Beyond Culture* (Garden City, N.Y.: Anchor Press, 1977). The word *man* has been changed to *people*.

Index

Achievement, 154
Administrative theory, 161
Africa
  baby food sales, 98
  community-oriented, 153
Aitken, Thomas, 279
Amae (indulgent dependence), 187
America. *See* United States
Americans
  CEOs, 12
  cultural norms, 97
  cultural orientation, 17, 20–21, 24
  defined, 34
  hierarchical structure, 42–43
  how others see us, 78
  individualism, 48–49
  initiative, 44
  management, 45–46
  masculinity dimension, 56
  misinterpretation, 75–76
  motivation, 30
  new product, 101–102
  office space, 33
  organization culture, 58–59
  parochialism, 11
  perception, 68–69
  personnel in Europe, 100
  personnel in Hong Kong, 25
  personnel in Iran, 112
  persuasion, 180–81
  power distance and uncertainty
    avoidance, 54
  problem definition, 110
  self-awareness, 24, 77
  values, 23, 79
Anglophones, 14, 17, 69, 72–73, 154,
  164
  See also Canadian
Arabs, persuasion, 180–81
Argentina
  individualism, 48–49
  masculinity dimension, 56
  power distance and uncertainty
    avoidance, 54
Asians, hierarchy concerns, 43
Association of Southeast Asian Nations
  (ASEAN), 50
Attitude
  defined, 17
  managerial, 40–42
  problems, 129
Attribution, 85
Australia
  individualism, 48–49
  masculinity dimension, 56
  power distance and uncertainty
    avoidance, 54

Austria
  individualism, 48–49
  masculinity dimension, 56
  misinterpretation, 75
  power distance and uncertainty
    avoidance, 53–56

Bahamas, 31
Bahrain, importance of time, 31
Balinese, reincarnation, 82
Bass, B., 80, 90
Behavior, 17
  culturally "bizarre," 67
  influence of culture, 16
  negotiators, successful, 196
  work, 39–56
Being-oriented culture, 28–30
Belgium (Belgians)
  individualism, 48–49
  masculinity dimension, 56
  power distance and uncertainty
    avoidance, 54
Berlew, David, 183, 203
Beyond National Borders, 148
Bible, 26
Blinders, subconscious, 75–77
Brazil
  individualism, 48–49
  masculinity dimension, 56
  power distance and uncertainty
    avoidance, 54
  view of Americans, 78
Bribery, 17
Brown, Lester, 120
Burger, P., 80, 90
Burke, W. Warner, 111

California, multiculturalism, 124
Canadian
  cultural differences, 96–98, 102,
    110–11
  economy, 5
  Free Trade Agreement, 4
  individualism, 27, 48–49
  Inuits, 22
  long term vs. short term, 32

  masculinity dimension, 56
  perception, of people, 22–23
  personnel in Philippines, 41
  power distance and uncertainty
    avoidance, 54
  stereotypes, 72–76
  See also Anglophones, Franco-
    phones
Cantonese, cross-cultural communication, 65
Careers
  international, 279, 283, 291–95
  managers, 283–84
  prejudice, 297
  questionnaire, 285–91
  reaching the top, 280–82
  women in management, 296–97
  See also Expatriate employee
Categories, 70–71
Caveat emptor (let the buyer beware),
  22
Chief Executive Officers (CEOs), 12
Child, John, 57, 61
Chile
  individualism, 48–49
  masculinity dimension, 56
  power distance and uncertainty
    avoidance, 54
China, People's Republic of
  Chairman Mao, 150
  harmony with nature, 24–26
  leadership in, 147
  management theories, 22, 151
  medical values, 18
  motivation, 151
  power distance, 51–52
*Chinese Commercial Negotiating
  Style*, 215
Collectivism, 26–28, 46–49, 60
Colombia
  individualism, 48–49
  masculinity dimension, 56
  power distance and uncertainty
    avoidance, 54
Commerce Department, U.S., 4, 49
Communication
  "bizarre" accident in Thailand, 67

cross-cultural, 64–67, 86–88
  effective, 64
  encoding, 64
  improving, techniques for, 84–85
  misevaluation, 82–83
  misinterpretation, 70–81
  misperception, 67–69
  model, 65
  problems, 131
Confucian tradition, 22
Converging meanings, 57, 84–85
Corporate evolution
  cross-cultural, 8
  international, 7–8
Criterion, self-reference, 83
Cross-cultural
  awareness, 77–78, 114
  communication, 64–67
  communication model, 65
  differences, 49–50, 59, 139
  employee entry–reentry, 225–29
  entry, 226–32
  international interaction, 123
  management, 10–13, 45, 98
  misevaluation, 82–83
  misinterpretation, 70–81
  misperception, 67–69
  negotiation, 179–217
  reentry, 232–45
  transitions, 225–49
Cultural
  behavior, influence on, 16
  blindness, 96–97, 102
  contingency, 108–109
  dimensions of difference, 46
  diversity, 17–18, 95–105, 139
  individualism/collectivism, 46–50
  invisible, 96
  managing diversity, 139
  national, 58–60, 96
  norms, 97, 110
  organizations, impact, 231
  orientations, 15–16
  shock, 227–29
  stress, 229
  synergy, 111
  values, 16, 79–80

Culture
  alternatives, 165
  basic steps, 162
  decision making, 138, 160
  ethics, 168–71
  implementation, 167
  information search, 164
  Occidental, 46
  organizational, 58–60, 96, 103,
    110, 116
  Oriental, differences, 46
  See also Groups

Decision making, 160–71
  basic steps, 162–63
  cultural contingencies, 163
  ethical, 168–71
  groups, 138
  individual, 173
Decoding, 64
Denmark (Danes)
  individualism, 48–50
  masculinity, 56
  uncertainty avoidance, 52–54
  working with Saudis, 82
Derr, C. B., 280–81
Dirty tricks, 212–15
  See also Negotiating
Diversity, cultural, 17–18, 96–97
  advantages, 99
  impact, 103, 106, 127
  importance of, 122
  managing groups, 139
  process losses, 128
Doing-oriented culture, 28–30
Domestic
  multiculturalism, 124–25
  organizations, 14
Driver, M., 162, 173
Dun & Bradstreet, 12, 36

Eddy, William, 109
Education Department, U.S., 76
Egypt, cultural synergy, 110–11
Eliot, T.S., 257

Employee
  debriefing and reentry training,
    247–48
  selection, 245–47
  underutilized internationally, 245–
    48
Employment, lifetime, 52
England
  miscommunication, 66
  proper guest channels, 51
  stereotypes, 71
English Canadians. *See* Anglophones
Equifinality, 108–109
Ethiopians, view of Americans, 79
Ethnocentrism, 8–9, 104, 108, 140,
  303
Europe
  communication, 101
  hierarchy, 42–43, 46
  multinational corporations, 58–59
  past-oriented, 30
European Economic Community, 4,
  100, 148
Expatriate employee
  adjustment, 230–32
  alienated returnees, 241–45
  future assignments, 291–95
  initial selection, 245–46
  reentry, 225–41, 243, 247–48
  resocialized returnees, 241
  skills learned overseas, 239–41
  spouse, 257–76
  transition strategies, 241–45
  validation, 244–45
  women in management, 296–97
  xenophobic response, 237–39
  See also Careers, International ca-
    reers
Expatriate spouse, 257–76
  boredom, 270–71
  culture shock, 267–70
  foreign language illiteracy, 269
  frustrations, 268
  loneliness, 269–70
  moving overseas, 258–65
  portable life, 272–73
  recommendations, 274–75

returning home, 273–74
separation, lack of support, 272
stress, 266–67
transitions, 265–66
See also Women
Expectancy theory, 157–60

Femininity/masculinity, 46, 53–57,
  60–61, 151
Feng Shui, 25
Filipinos. *See* Philippines
Finland
  individualism, 48–49
  masculinity dimension, 56
  power distance and uncertainty
    avoidance, 54
Fisher, R., 184, 215
Florida, multicultural, 125
Foreign assignments, 284–85
Foreign negotiating, 179
Foreign Trade Council, 4
Fortune, 12, 22, 115
France
  cross-cultural misperception, 67,
    69, 71
  cultural diversity, 98
  hierarchy, 42–46
  individualism, 48–49
  masculinity dimension, 56
  organization culture, 59
  power distance and uncertainty
    avoidance, 54
  view of Americans, 78
Francophones, 14, 17, 69, 74, 154,
  164
  See also Canadian
French Canadians. *See* Francophones
Freud, Sigmund, 161
Fuller, R. Buckminster, 105

Geographic dispersion, 14
Germany (West)
  cross-cultural misinterpretation, 73
  cultural diversity, 100
  hierarchy, 42–43
  individualism, 48–49

masculinity dimension, 56
organization culture, 57–58
personal relationships, 28
power distance and uncertainty
　avoidance, 54
view of Americans, 78
Getting to Yes, 192, 194, 215
Ghadar, F., 8
Ghana, personnel policies, 27
Ghiselli, E., 151
Global
　competition, 4
　enterprise, 3
　managers, 223
　organizations, 14
　strategy, 6–10
Globalization
　dimensions of, 5
　international careers, 279
　production, 120
Good versus evil, 23
Goodstein, Leonard, 111
Graham, John, 186–87, 207, 210–11
Great Britain
　hierarchy, 42–43
　individualism, 48–49
　masculinity dimension, 56
　power distance and uncertainty
　　avoidance, 54
　view of Americans, 78
　workers, 101
Greece
　individualism, 48–49
　lifetime employment, 52
　masculinity dimension, 56
　power distance and uncertainty
　　avoidance, 54
Greenwood, Michael J., 158–59
Group-oriented societies, 27
Groups
　communication problems, 131
　decision making, 138
　diversity, 126–34
　effectiveness, 132
　ethics, 168
　ideas, 133
　potential productivity, 132

stress, 131
types of, 127
work, stages, 137–39
See also Task groups
Groupthink, 133
Gyllenhammer, P., 166, 174

Haire, Mason, 151, 154
Hall, Edward, 39, 77, 302
Harris, P., 105
Harvard Business Review, 167, 194
Hawaii, multicultural, 125
Herzberg, F., two-factor theory, 156–57
Heterogeneity, 108–109
Hierarchy, 46, 51–53
Hindu, belief, 29
Hofstede, Geert, 46, 48–49, 53–54,
　58, 60–62, 151, 153, 155, 157,
　160, 166
Holland. *See* Netherlands
Homogeneity, 108–109
Hong Kong
　collective societies, 27
　cross-cultural communication, 65
　high job mobility, 52
　individualism, 48–49
　legislative council, 65
　lucky numbers, 65
　masculinity, 5
　power distance and uncertainty
　　avoidance, 54
Huthwaite Research Group, 195–96,
　205, 208–209

Iacocca, Lee, 149
Illman, P., 160, 174
Implementation, 114
India
　individualism, 48–49
　managers, 166
　masculinity dimension, 56
　power distance and uncertainty
　　avoidance, 54
　view of Americans, 77
Individualism, 26–28, 46–49, 60

Indonesia
  Association of Southeast Asian Nations (ASEAN), 50
  group-oriented society, 27
  hierarchy, 42–43
  managerial role, 44
  view of Americans, 79
Information search, 164
Internal and External Careers, 280–81, 300
International careers
  accepting, 292
  job satisfaction, 294
  management, 120
  organization recognition, 294–95
  questionnaire, 284–91
  reaching the top, 280–82
  rejecting, 293
  satisfying private life, 294–95
  See also Expatriate employee
International Negotiations, 184
International trade, 3–6
Interpretation, 70, 110, 112–14
Inuits, 22
  See also Canadian
Iran, cultural, 112
Ireland
  individualism, 48–49
  masculinity dimension, 56
  power distance and uncertainty avoidance, 54
Israel
  group orientation, 26
  individualism, 48–49
  masculinity dimension, 56
  power distance, 50, 54
Italians
  hierarchical structure, 44
  managers, 58

Japan
  collectivism, 47
  cultural diversity, 99
  cultural synergy, 110–14
  future-oriented, 30–32
  goals and achievements, 148
  group-oriented society, 26–27

harmony needs, 159
hierarchy, 42
high uncertainty avoidance, 52
individualism, 48–49
managerial role, 44
masculinity dimension, 54–56
miscommunication, 66
power distance and uncertainty avoidance, 54
Scottish experience in, 86–89
space, 17, 33
view of Americans, 78
Joss (Chinese luck), 158
Journal of International Business Studies, 207
Jung, Carl, 164

Kashmir, religious customs, 29
Kennedy, President John F., 148, 179
Kenya, view of Americans, 77
Kim, S., 36
Kluckhohn, F., 18, 20–21, 33–34, 36
Korea. *See* South Korea
Kovach, C., 135
Kroeber, A., 15, 37
Kuwait, communication, 75

Lane, H., 21, 37
Latin American
  behavior, 16
  values, 17
Laurent, André, 41–46, 58–60, 62, 151, 280
Leadership
  Chinese vision of, 147
  choice, 165
  culture conflict, 170–71
  decision making, 146, 160–72
  ethics, 168–71
  implementation, 167
  implications of, 149
  information search, 164
  management, 151
  motivation, 152–60
  theories, 146–52
Levinson, H., 149

Lifetime employment, 52
Likert, R., 151

Macro level issues, 57
Malaysia
   Association of Southeast Asian Nations (ASEAN), 50
   family-oriented, 30
   group-oriented, 27
Management
   cross-cultural, 10–13, 83
   cultural orientations, 20–21
   foreign assignments, 284–85
   global, 223
   reentry, 244–45
   role, 45
   skills, overseas, 239–41
   transition strategies, 241–45
Managerial attitudes, 40–45, 80–81
Managerial grid, 151
Masculinity/femininity dimension, 46, 53–57, 60–61
Maslow, A., 152–56
Materialism, 53
Maternity/paternity leave, 55
Mathews, J., 37
Mathews, L., 37
Maugham, William, 125
McClelland, D., three motives, 154–55
McGill International Symposium, 98
McGregor, Douglas, 40–41, 62
   "Theory X and Y," 150–51
Mexico, 53–54, 57, 68
   activity-orientation, 30
   individualism, 48–49
   uncertainty avoidance, 53–54
   view of Americans, 78
Micro level issues, 57
Middle East, 17, 32, 76
Misevaluation, 82–83
Misinterpretation
   cross-cultural, 70–82
   sources of, 75–82
Mitroff, Ian, 4, 6, 146
Monkey King, 32
   See also China, People's Republic of

Moran, R., 105
Morocco, stereotypes, 130
Motivation, 85, 155
   culture bound, 160
   dragon slayer campaign, 152
   Herzberg's two-factor theory, 156–57
   Maslow's theory, 152–54
   McClelland's three motives theory, 154–55
   Vroom's expectancy theory, 157–60
Mouton, Jane, 151
Multiculturalism
   Association of Southeast Asian Nations, (ASEAN), 127
   California, 124
   defined, 14
   environment, 60
   European Economic Community (EEC), 127
   Hawaii, 125
   managing workforce, 121
   misleading assumptions, 109
   New York City, 125
   teams, 120
   United Nations, 127
Multinational companies, 4–5, 12, 46, 58–60, 98
Mutiso, G., 153, 165

Negotiating
   approaches to, 194
   contrasting styles, 200–203
   cross-cultural, 179–85
   dirty tricks, 212–15
   nonverbal, 210–12
   Olympic coverage, 205
   personal qualities of, 185–89
   process, 192–203
   psychological warfare, 213
   situation of, 189–92
   stages of, 193–95
   strategy, 192
   successful, 185
   tactics, 203–217
   time, 184, 191
   verbal, 204–209

Nehru, Jawaharlal, 63–64
Netherlands
    hierarchy, 42–43
    individualism, 48–49
    masculinity dimension, 56
    personnel records, 100
    power distance and uncertainty
        avoidance, 54
Neutrality, 101
New Zealand
    individualism, 48–49
    masculinity dimension, 56
    power distance and uncertainty
        avoidance, 54
Norms in society, 17–18
North Americans. See Americans
Norway
    individualism, 48–49
    Japanese in, 66
    masculinity dimension, 56
    power distance and uncertainty
        avoidance, 54

Occidental cultures, 46
Oh, T., 150
Ohmae, Kenichi, 148
O'Reilly, C., 154
Organization
    culture, 58–60, 116, 231
    domestic, 14
    global, 14
    leadership, 147
    microcosm, 125
    pyramid, 53
    synergistic, 104, 110, 114
Oriental cultures, 46
Orientations
    cultural, 20–21, 28–30
    time, 30–32
    values, 19

Pakistan
    individualism, 48–49
    masculinity dimension, 56
    power distance and uncertainty
        avoidance, 54

Panama, Canal Zone study, 156
Parochialism, 11–13, 81–82, 88, 104,
    108–109
Pascal, Blaise, 3
Paternity/maternity leave, 55
Peace Corps, 241
Perception, 68–69
    culturally determined, 68
    dominance versus harmony, 25–26
    impact of perceptual filters, 70
    learned, 68
    selective, 68
    world, 25
Perlmutter, Howard, 182, 276
Personnel policies, 27
Persuasion, styles of, 180
Peru
    individualism, 48–49
    masculinity dimension, 54
    power distance and uncertainty
        avoidance, 54
Philippines
    group-oriented, 50
    individualism, 48–49
    managerial style, 41–42
    masculinity dimension, 56
    miscommunication, 113
    power distance, 50–51
    power distance and uncertainty
        avoidance, 54
Physical space, 33
Portable life
    cross-cultural transitions, 265–73
    moving overseas, 258–65
    returning home, 273–75
Porter, Lyman, 151–52, 174
Portugal
    individualism, 48–49
    masculinity dimension, 56
    power distance and uncertainty
        avoidance, 52, 54
Power distance, 46, 48, 50–51, 54, 60
Problems, group, 129–31
Problem solving, 110–17
Process losses, 128
    See also Groups
Productivity, group potential, 132

Projected similarity, 80–82
Proverbs, North American, 79–80
Psalidas, Foulie, 276
Psychological warfare, 213
  See also Negotiating
Puritans' orientation, 19
Pye, Lucian, 215–16
Pyramid organizations, 53

Questionnaire, foreign career, 284–91
  See also Careers

Rackham, Neil, 196
Raider, Ellen, 183–84, 196, 203, 208
Ratiu, Indrei, 73, 90
Reentry
  debriefing, 247–48
  entry and, 225–41
  home country, 232–35
  proactive, 243
  professional, 235–37
Renwick, George, 194
Rhinesmith, S., 18
Roberts, K., 154
Role reversal, 82, 84
Russians
  persuasion, 180–81
  See also Soviet

Saudis, working with Danes, 82
Scandinavian, masculinity dimension, 55
Schlesinger, Arthur, 148
Self-reference criterion, 83
Similarity, projected, 80–82
Simon, Congressman Paul, 11
Simon, H., 161, 177
Singapore
  individualism, 48–49
  masculinity dimension, 56
  power distance and uncertainty
    avoidance, 52, 54
Sirota, David, 158–59
Situation description, 110–13
Societies, group–oriented, 27

Society norm, 17–18
South Africa
  cultural differences, 96–98
  individualism, 48–49
  masculinity dimension, 56
  power distance and uncertainty
    avoidance, 54
South America, 11
South Korea
  miscategorization, 71
  new ideas, 101
Soviet, communication, 76
  See also Russians
Space, physical, 33
Spain, 100
  individualism, 48–49
  masculinity dimension, 56
  power distance and uncertainty
    avoidance, 54
Spouse, 257–76
  See also Women
Steers, R., 152, 176
Stereotypes, 69–74, 129
Stress, 229
Strodtbeck, F., 18, 20–21, 33–34, 36
Sweden
  autonomous work, 166
  business commitment, 55
  cultural diversity, 100–101
  doing-oriented, 29
  good vs. evil, 23
  hierarchy, 43–44
  individualism, 48–49
  masculinity dimension, 56
  power distance and uncertainty
    avoidance, 54
  uncertainty avoidance, 54–58
Switzerland
  cross-cultural misevaluation, 82–83
  cultural diversity, 99–100
  individualism, 48–49
  masculinity dimension, 56
  power distance and uncertainty
    avoidance, 54
Symington, Congressman James, 11
Synergy, cultural, 95–115

Tahiti, motivation, 155
See also Motivation
Taiwan
individualism, 48–49
masculinity dimension, 56
power distance and uncertainty
avoidance, 54
Task groups
bicultural, 127
diversity, 126, 139
equal power, 140
feedback, 140
goal, 140
homogeneous, 127
innovative, 136
productivity, 126
See also Groups
Taylor, Donald, 73, 89–91
Team
effectiveness, 134–39
See also Groups, Task groups
Thailand
cross-cultural communication, 67
mutual respect, 140
stages, 137
Theobold, Robert, 161
Theory X and Y, 40–41, 150–51
*Theory Y in the People's Republic of
China*, 176
Third World countries, 13
Thoreau, Henry, 225
Time, orientation, 30–32
Toffler, Alvin, 120
Transitions
entry, 226–32
reentry, home country, 232–35
reentry, professional, 235–45
strategies, 241–45
underutilized employee, 245–48
Trends and Issues, 111
Triandis, H., 147
Turkey
individualism, 48–49
masculinity dimension, 56
power distance and uncertainty
avoidance, 54
view of Americans, 77
Two-factor theory, 156–57

Uncertainty avoidance, 46, 52–54, 60
Understanding, 84–85
Underutilized employee, 245–48
United Kingdom, 100
United Nations, 29
United States
cross-cultural awareness, 77
cultural synergy, 108, 114
culture, 58–60
hierarchy, 42–43
individualism, 26–28, 47–50
managers, 22–23
masculinity dimension, 55–56
parochialism, 11–13
product development, 101
time, 30–32
uncertainty avoidance, 52–54
Utopian societies, 19

Values
cultural, 16
proverbs, 79–80
Venezuela
individualism, 48–49
masculinity dimension, 56
power distance and uncertainty
avoidance, 50, 54
Vietnamese Ministry of Education, 76
Vroom, V., 157–60

Way of Lao Tzu, The, 147
Wilson, Ian, 160
Women
boredom, 270–71
culture shock, 267–70
expatriate spouse, 257–76
management, 296–97
moving overseas, 258–65
recommendations, 274–75
returning home, 273–74
separation, lack of support, 272
stress, 266–67
transitions, 265–66
work behavior, 39–56
See also Expatriate spouse
Work problem description, 138

Yugoslavia
 individualism, 48–49
 management theories, 151
 masculinity dimension, 56
 perceptions, 23

power distance and uncertainty
 avoidance, 53–54
values orientation, 28

Ziller, R., 119